OCR
Succeed in
iTQ

Levels 1 and 2 for the QCF

Nicola Bowman

Ann Jones

HODDER
EDUCATION
AN HACHETTE UK COMPANY

Orders: please contact Bookpoint Ltd, 130 Milton Park, Abingdon, Oxon OX14 4SB. Telephone: +44 (0)1235 827720. Fax: +44 (0)1235 400454. Lines are open from 9.00am to 5.00pm, Monday to Saturday, with a 24-hour message-answering service. You can also order through our website www.hoddereducation.co.uk

If you have any comments to make about this, or any of our other titles, please send them to educationenquiries@hodder.co.uk

British Library Cataloguing in Publication Data
A catalogue record for this title is available from the British Library

ISBN: 978 0 340 969 74 8

First Edition Published 2009
Impression number   10 9 8 7 6 5 4 3 2 1
Year   2012 2011 2010 2009

Hachette UK's policy is to use papers that are natural, renewable and recyclable products and made fromwood grown in sustainable forests. The logging and manufacturing processes are expected to conform to the environmental regulations of the country of origin.

Cover photo pixland/punchstock
Typeset by Fakenham Photosetting Ltd, Fakenham, Norfolk
Printed in Italy for Hodder Education, an Hachette UK company, 338 Euston Road, London NW1 3BH

Contents

Acknowledgements   iv

1.   Improving Productivity Using IT   1

2.   Using the Internet   30

3.   Using Email   76

4.   Database Software   132

5.   Spreadsheet Software   193

6.   Presentation Software   249

7.   Word Processing Software   292

8.   IT Communication Fundamentals   345

Index   369

Acknowledgements

The authors and publishers would like to thank the following for use of photographs and illustrations in this book:

Figure 2.1 © Alex Slobodkin/iStockphoto.com; Figure 2.2 © Norman Chan/iStockphoto.com; Figure 2.10 © IAC Search & Media, Inc. 2009. All rights reserved. ASK.COM, ASK JEEVES, the ASK logo, the ASK JEEVES logo and other trade marks appearing on the Ask.com and Ask Jeeves websites are property of IAC Search & Media, Inc. and/or its licensors; Figure 2.16 © Alex Slobodkin/iStockphoto.com; Figure 2.17 © Norman Chan/iStockphoto.com; Figure 2.29 © IAC Search & Media, Inc. 2009. All rights reserved. ASK.COM, ASK JEEVES, the ASK logo, the ASK JEEVES logo and other trade marks appearing on the Ask.com and Ask Jeeves websites are property of IAC Search & Media, Inc. and/or its licensors; Figure 8.9 © IAC Search & Media, Inc. 2009. All rights reserved. ASK.COM, ASK JEEVES, the ASK logo, the ASK JEEVES logo and other trade marks appearing on the Ask.com and Ask Jeeves websites are property of IAC Search & Media, Inc. and/or its licensors.

Microsoft product screen shots reprinted with permission from Microsoft Corporation.

Every effort has been made to trace and acknowledge the ownership of copyright. The publishers will be glad to make suitable arrangements with copyright holders whom it has not been possible to contact.

Video demonstrations and recall text on Hodderplus (www.hodderplus.co.uk/itq)

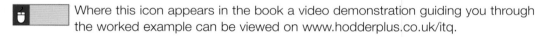 Where this icon appears in the book a video demonstration guiding you through the worked example can be viewed on www.hodderplus.co.uk/itq.

To carry out the tasks in the book you will need to download the files provided on the Hodderplus website (www.hodderplus.co.uk/itq). Copy these to your file area so that you can use them to complete the tasks.

To access the site you will need the following username and password:

Username: itq2009
Password: download

1

Improving Productivity Using IT

Level 1

This unit will develop your knowledge, understanding and skills relating to the use of IT. You will plan and review your use of commonly used IT tools and techniques when creating straightforward or routine work activities. After reviewing your work, you will be able to identify and use automated methods or alternative ways of working to improve work.

An example could be to set up a shortcut to automate a common task.

This unit contains two IT solutions that can be created using different software packages.

By working through the **Overview** and **Worked Examples** in this chapter, you will demonstrate the skills required for Improving Productivity Using IT Level 1:

ELEMENT The competent person will…	PERFORMANCE CRITERIA To demonstrate this competence they can…	KNOWLEDGE To demonstrate this competence they will also…
IPU: A1 Plan the use of appropriate IT systems and software to meet requirements	A1.3 **Plan how to carry out the task** using IT to achieve the required purpose and outcome A1.5 Select IT systems and software applications as appropriate for the purpose	A1.1 Identify the **purpose for using IT** A1.2 Identify the **methods, skills and resources** will be required to complete the task successfully A1.4 Identify **reasons for choosing particular IT systems and software applications** for the task A1.6 Identify any **legal or local guidelines or constraints** that may affect the task or activity
IPU: A2 Use IT systems and software efficiently to complete planned tasks	A2.2 Use automated routines that aid **efficient processing or presentation** A2.3 Complete planned tasks using IT	A2.1 Identify automated routines to **improve productivity**
IPU: A3 Review the selection and use of IT tools to make sure that tasks are successful	A3.1 **Review outcomes** to make sure they match requirements of the task and are fit for purpose	A3.2 Decide whether the IT tools selected were appropriate for the task and purpose A3.3 Identify the **strengths and weaknesses of the completed work** A3.4 Identify ways to make further **improvements to work**

Examples are provided as a demonstration of what to do. These demonstrations are based on the Microsoft Office® 2003 suite. Review the **Overview** in each section and then watch any demonstrations in the **Worked Example**.

Throughout the **Worked Example** sections, the demonstrations relate to a word processing solution. A **Mini Assignment** is included at the end of each chapter, which can be used for additional practice only and is based on a presentation scenario.

You will need to download the files provided on the Hodderplus website (www.hodderplus.co.uk/itq). Copy these to your file area so that you can use them during the exercises in this chapter.

A1 Plan the use of appropriate IT systems and software to meet requirements

In this section you will find out about the task that you will be required to complete. You will describe the purpose, plan how you will carry out the task, select the software and describe why you have chosen it.

A1.1   Identify the purpose for using IT

Before you start any task, you need to find out who the information is for and what the purpose of the task is. You need to know when it should be finished, what information to include and where it will be used, for example, on screen, posted or printed.

> **Worked Example A1.1**

You have been asked by the Administration Officer at the Porchester Zoo to produce a newsletter to customers. The newsletter is to advise customers of new animals that are available for adoption and developments that have occurred at the zoo over the last few months. In order to complete this task, you have been provided with the following files:

- news.doc (contains text that can be used in the newsletter)
- giraffe.jpg, tiger.jpg, elephant.jpg.

The newsletter is to be sent out today.

Write an introductory statement describing what the information is for, when it must be finished, what information needs to be included and where it will be used.

Suggested answer

Example: I have been asked by the Administration Officer to produce a newsletter today. This newsletter is about adoption of animals at the Porchester Zoo and I have been provided with a number of files that I need to review before starting this project.

A1.2   Identify the methods, skills and resources required to complete the task successfully

Now that you have been informed what the task will be, you now need to describe what methods, skills and resources you will need to complete it.

> **Worked Example A1.2**

When producing the newsletter, you will need to include a number of resources.

a   List the computer resources that are required to complete this task.
b   List the software you think would be appropriate for this task.

c   Identify why you have chosen this software.
d   What methods will you use to complete the task?
e   What skills will be required to complete the task?

Suggested answer

Example: When producing the newsletter I will need to have access to a computer and a printer. As I was to produce a newsletter I decided that word processing software would be the best option and I decided that Microsoft Office® Word® would be the most appropriate as it would allow me to produce a document in a newsletter style. I could add images and format the text and could use a template. I will read through the files I have been provided with and then decide what information to include. I will have to be competent at using Microsoft Word® to produce a professional newsletter. This will include setting page layout, inputting/importing any text, importing any images, laying out the paragraphs and using appropriate numbering. I will also use appropriate headers and footers. I will need to use a wide range of Level 1 skills for word processing to complete the task.

A1.3   Plan how to carry out the task using IT to achieve the required purpose and outcome

Now you are ready to plan how you will carry out the tasks. A plan is crucial when considering any kind of project. The plan will allow you to make decisions about the structure and layout of the solution, the style and format of the solution and a description of automated features to be used.

A plan shows you what you hope to achieve and it lists the steps that you will take to complete the solution. A table or a flowchart is a good way to present this information.

> **Worked Example A1.3**

Create a plan to produce the newsletter.

Suggested answer

Example: The following is a plan of how the newsletter could be produced and uses a flowchart approach.

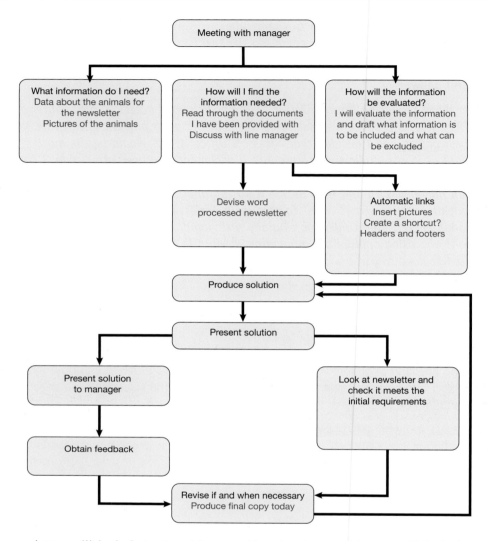

The newsletter will include text and images. The structure and layout will include:

- at least two pages
- details of where graphics will be included
- the company logo
- appropriate styles.

Company house style is to use Verdana 11 so this will be used for the body text. Any subheadings will be emboldened.

A1.4   Identify reasons for choosing particular IT systems and software applications for the task

A1.5   Select IT systems and software applications as appropriate for the purpose

You need to describe why you have chosen the software application that you have chosen and why this is appropriate and fit for purpose. For example, why is Microsoft Word® more appropriate when producing a newsletter than Microsoft Publisher®, and why not use a database? Think about how you would complete this task if you did not have access to a computer. What benefits are there of using IT over manual methods for preparing, processing and presenting the information? What are the limitations? How will this meet needs, quality and accuracy?

1   Describe why you have selected the IT system and software applications you have and discuss why these are appropriate to purpose.

Suggested answer

Example: I decided to use my laptop instead of my PC as I have Microsoft Office® 2003 on this and I am more familiar with this IT system. I have decided to use Microsoft Word® as this is a professional word processing package and it will allow me to use various tools and techniques to produce the newsletter. I could use Microsoft Publisher® but I feel I have not used this software very often and would need lots of practice before I could commence on the newsletter.

The benefits of using IT are that I can save the information regularly and come back to it later. I can make changes to the newsletter more easily by using a computer than by hand and it is quicker and more accurate. Editing is easier with a computer than by hand and I can use the spell check tool to check my work. The limitations of using IT are that the computer may crash, if I don't save my work properly it could be lost and the file could become corrupt. I will therefore make sure that I save the file regularly and keep backup copies as I work through my document. I will also need to consider health and safety and make sure that I work safely at my workstation so this will mean that I will take regular breaks, ensure that my workstation, is set up correctly and that my seat provides me with the appropriate support.

A1.6   Identify any legal or local guidelines or constraints that may affect the task or activity

When completing the solution, you need to ensure that you comply with any data protection, copyright, software licensing, organisational house style or branding guidelines.

The newsletter will include company data that may be subject to data protection and therefore this data will be kept secure and not be disclosed to unauthorised users. Computers should be locked with a password so that other people cannot see the data. The files are copyright of the author and publishers. However, this should not cause a problem when completing this task.

The organisational house style and branding guidelines are to use the Verdana 11 font and to include the company logo on the right-hand side of each document.

1   List the legal aspects that you will need to consider when completing this IT solution.

Suggested answer

Example: I will need to consider health and safety, data protection, copyright and organisational house style when completing this task. I will make sure I take regular breaks. I will ensure that my computer is locked if I take a break. I will ensure that I use the information so that it does not breach copyright legislation and I will use the organisational guidelines I have been provided with.

A2: Use IT systems and software efficiently to complete planned tasks

A2.1   Identify automated routines to improve productivity

Shortcuts allow you to improve efficiency and work more effectively. There are a number of shortcuts available in Microsoft Word®.

SHORTCUTS	Shortcuts are already displayed on your toolbars, but not all shortcuts that are available are displayed.
	You may find using the drop-down menus to close files time-consuming. There are different options available:
	File → Close
	Click on the 'x' in the top right of the window for the document
	or you can add the File Close icon to your toolbar.
	Other shortcut options are to record everyday text and assign to keyboard letters. Then when you wish to save time keying in this text, you key in the letters and press the function key to insert the text. This is useful for the beginning or ending of letters, where the text may be the same every time.
	Other ways of using shortcuts are to record macros to perform simple tasks that you do on a daily basis.
	Macros are recordings of actions you take which you save with specific names. Macros can then be played back either using a menu, the keyboard shortcut, an icon or a button.

Shortcut keys in Microsoft Word®

Ctrl+A	Select all – everything on the page.
Ctrl+B	Make **bold** highlighted selection.
Ctrl+C	Copy selected text.
Ctrl+E	Align selected text to the centre.
Ctrl+F	Open the Find and Replace box.
Ctrl+I	Make *italic* highlighted selection.
Ctrl+K	Insert link.
Ctrl+L	Align to the left of the screen.
Ctrl+M	Indent the paragraph.
Ctrl+P	Open the print window.
Ctrl+R	Align to the right of the screen.
Ctrl+U	<u>Underline</u> highlighted selection.
Ctrl+V	Paste.
Ctrl+X	Cut selected text.
Ctrl+Y	Redo the last action performed.
Ctrl+Z	Undo the last action performed.
Ctrl+Shift+*	View or hide non-printing characters.
Ctrl+left arrow	Move one word to the left.
Ctrl+right arrow	Move one word to the right.

Ctrl+up arrow	Move to the beginning.
Ctrl+down arrow	Move to the end of the paragraph.
Ctrl+Del	Delete word to right of cursor.
Ctrl+Backspace	Delete word to left of cursor.
Ctrl+End	Move the cursor to the end of the document.
Ctrl+Home	Move the cursor to the beginning of the document.
Ctrl+1	Single line spacing.
Ctrl+2	Double line spacing.
Ctrl+5	1.5 line spacing.
Ctrl+Alt+1	Change text to heading 1.
Ctrl+Alt+2	Change text to heading 2.
Ctrl+Alt+3	Change text to heading 3.
Alt+Ctrl+F2	Open new document.
Ctrl+F2	Display print preview.
Shift+Insert	Paste.
Shift+F3	Highlighted text will change from upper to lower case or a capital letter at the beginning of every word. Keep repeating and it scrolls around these options.
Shift+F7	Run a thesaurus check on the word.
Alt+Shift+D	Insert the current date.
Alt+Shift+T	Insert the current time.
F1	Open Help.
F3	Run Autotext.
F4	Repeat the last action performed.
F5	Open the Find and Replace box.
F7	Spell and grammar check selected text and/or document.
F12	Save as.
Shift+F12	Save.
Ctrl+Shift+F12	Print the document.

The mouse can also be used to perform quick actions. Examples of mouse shortcuts are:

MOUSE SHORTCUTS	DESCRIPTION
Click, hold, and drag	Selects text from where you click and hold, highlighting to the point you drag and let go.
Double-click	Within a word, selects the complete word.
Triple-click	In the margin, selects the whole document.
Ctrl+Mouse wheel	Zooms in and out of document.

Watch the demonstration to see how this works.

1.1   Demonstration

> **Worked Example A2.1**
>
> 1 Open a new blank document.
> 2 Select **View** → **Toolbars** → **Customise** → **Commands** tab → **File**.
> 3 Look for **Close** on the right side of the dialog box by scrolling down the list. Click and drag the close icon to your toolbar next to the second icon on your toolbar (Open).
> 4 When you release the mouse button, your new icon will be on the toolbar.
> 5 Close the document using the new icon – you do not need to save this file.
> 6 Open a new blank document and the icon should still be on your toolbar.

> **Task A2.1**
>
> 1 Open a new blank document.
> 2 Key in the following text:

Yours sincerely
[2 spaces]
Joseph Booth
Operations Director

> 3 Highlight the text.
> 4 Select **Insert** → **Autotext** → **New**. Type **JB** and click **OK**.
> 5 Close the document – do not save.
> 6 Open a new blank document.
> 7 Type JB, press the function key F3 and your closing text should appear.
> 8 You can create several recordings of standard text and save with simple key letters.
> 9 Check what is already saved – you may wish to use some of the defaults. Select **Insert** → **Autotext** → **Autotext** and check through this dialog box.
> 10 Close any open files – there is no need to save.

A2.1.1 Macros

At Level 1 it is expected that you can run pre-set macros – at the higher levels you will create and edit macros. A macro is an automated routine of functions that is recorded together so that when you click a button or use a keyboard shortcut, the mini program is run. Some macros are created to spell check, save and close a document.

> **Worked Example A2.1.1**
>
> 1 Open the file **macro.doc**.
> 2 The toolbar has been customised and shows the macro button **Project.NewMacros. symbol**, which allows the macro symbol to be inserted when clicked.

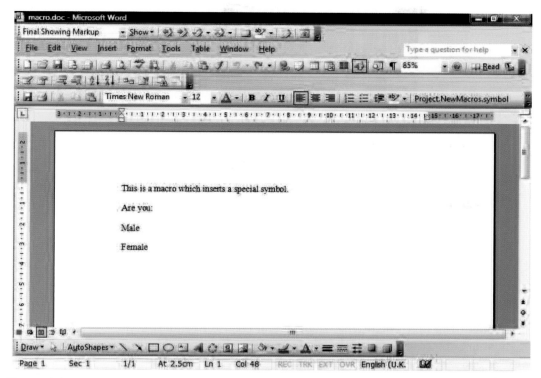

Figure 1.1

3   In the document, you are asked the question 'are you male or female?' Click the
    Project.NewMacros.symbol button next to where you want to place your answer
    and insert the symbol.
4   Save and close the document as **macro2.doc**.

Now it's your turn to have a go.

Task A2.1.1

---

1   Open the file **macro1.doc**.
2   Run the save and print macro button (**Tools** → **Macro** → **Macros** → **Save and Print**
    → **Run**) – this will spell check the document, save it and print out a copy.
3   Close the open document.

A2.1.2 Templates

A template is created to store the formatting options for documents. A template means that
when new documents are opened, they store the formatting options, which means that
documents produced are in the company style and are professional looking.

View the demonstration to see how this is done.

1.2   Demonstration

Worked Example A2.1.2

---

1   Open the file **template.doc**.
2   Click on **Format** → **Styles and Formatting** tab. You will see that the template has
    saved the following styles:

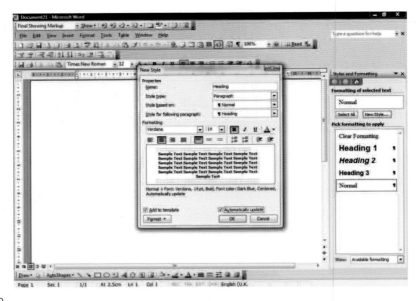

Figure 1.2

3   Highlight the text 'This is the heading' and choose Heading1 style.
4   Highlight the text 'Subhead1' and choose Heading2 style.
5   Save and close the file as **styles.doc**.

Task A2.1.2

1   Open the file **Escape Travel.doc**.
2   Click on **Format → Styles and Formatting** tab. You will see that the template has saved the following styles:

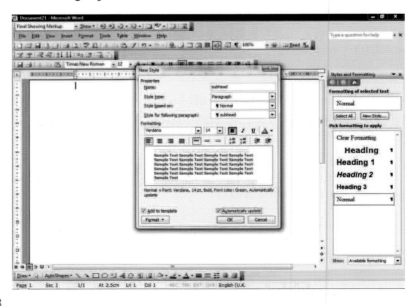

Figure 1.3

3   Highlight the text 'Escape Travel Ltd' and choose Heading1 style.
4   Highlight the address and choose Heading2 style.
5   Highlight the telephone number and fax number and choose Heading3 style.
6   Save and close the file as **travel.doc**.

Use automated routines that aid efficient processing or presentation

Complete planned tasks using IT

In this section you will create the solution. The following instructions work through the production of the newsletter. In this worked example, the solution will include using different styles, creating shortcuts, running a pre-set macro and using a template.

> **Worked Example A2.3**

You will now create your solution. You have been asked to create a solution using the **dogs.doc** file and some free clipart images to advertise a new dog walking business. You need to produce an eye-catching newsletter. You should:

- plan the task
- produce at least two pages
- include graphics
- include automated routines (e.g. using shortcuts)
- edit the text (formatting)
- insert a simple table
- use spellchecking, save and print the document.

1. Open the file **dogs.doc** that you have been provided with.
2. For the newsletter, it has been agreed that you should use word processing software and the skills listed above.
3. Insert at least two images that you have found. In a suitable location, click **Insert → Picture → From File**.
4. The file contains a number of set styles. Use these to format the newsletter attractively.
5. Add a table to the prices so that it is displayed neatly. Merge appropriate cells and add suitable headings.
6. Spell check the document.
7. Save the newsletter as **newsletter.doc**.
8. Print and close the file.

A3: Review the selection and use of IT tools to make sure that tasks are successful

Review outcomes to make sure they meet the requirements of the task and are fit for purpose

Decide whether the IT tools selected were appropriate for the task and purpose

As you work through the task, you will need to gather information and decide whether the IT tools and techniques are appropriate for your solution and whether they have allowed you to meet the intended outcome. It is a good idea to keep a log of the IT tools you have used so that you can review them against your plan to see if you did actually use the IT tools that were planned or whether you changed these as the solution was developed.

> **Worked Example A3.1**
>
> 1   Keep a log of the IT tools that have been used when producing the task.
> 2   Produce a brief review to show what tools and techniques were used and whether any changes were needed.

Suggested answer

Example: When producing the newsletter I used the tools that I had listed in the plan. I found that the tools I had planned to use were appropriate for the task and allowed me to complete the solution. The report took me an hour to complete and this included the checking that I undertook.

A3.3   Identify the strengths and weaknesses of the completed task

Once the solution has been created, you should analyse your strengths and weaknesses in the production of the newsletter. Think about these in terms of laying out the newsletter, using different formatting tools, accuracy of the final product, the structure and style, quality of the end product and how clear the information has been presented for the audience.

This could be completed using a SLOT analysis (Strengths, Limitations, Opportunities and Threats).

> **Worked Example A3.3**
>
> 1   Now that you have completed the solution, review your strengths and weaknesses in the following areas:
>   a   format and layout
>   b   accuracy
>   c   structure, style and quality
>   d   clarity for audience.

Suggested answer

Example: I found that my strength in completing the solution was that I was able to follow the organisational house style, but I found that weaknesses were experienced and it was very frustrating as Word kept creating new styles and the formatting at the end took some time to complete. I proofread my work and I also used spell check to check it for accuracy and my line manager confirmed that this met the requirements. The structure of the newsletter was in line with my line manager's requirements and he was pleased with the final outcome. The information was clearly presented.

A3.4   Identify ways to make further improvements to work

Think about how you could improve your work further, based on the review. What mistakes did you make?

Now that the solution has been created, you should check that it has met the original requirements and that it is fit for purpose. This could be evidenced by including draft copies of the newsletter, checking the plan to see whether requirements were met, checking with the line manager to confirm that the report has met the requirements and reviewing any mistakes and what impact they have had on others. You should also identify what new techniques have been learnt.

Worked Example A3.4

Suggested answer

Example: When producing the solution I did have a problem with the styles in Microsoft Word®. In future I am going to find out how I could set my template more securely so that only changes requested by me could be instigated. I only had to ask my line manager for clarification once and I learnt how to convert text to table, which was quick and easy to do.

Thinking about the newsletter, produce a brief description of the following items:

1 draft documents
2 review against initial plan
3 avoiding affecting other people's work
4 the effect of your own mistakes on others
5 learning new techniques

Suggested answer

Example: When producing the newsletter, because I was not fully familiar with the data, I initially struggled to find out exactly what information should be included. It took some time to produce the first draft and I have included this with my evidence. The draft shows the checking that I have undertaken and it also shows amendments that I made before presenting the final report to my line manager. I have checked my plan and I followed this with no problems. The newsletter has been reviewed by my line manager and he is very pleased with it – he suggested that I could have used 1.5 line spacing instead of double line spacing to display the report more effectively. I did not make any mistakes that impacted on others when completing this task and I learnt how to convert text to table by using the tool in Word.

Mini Assignment

You and some friends have decided to create new designer individual T-shirts and have decided to launch your own business. You want to create a leaflet that you can post to local houses to market your new service. The leaflet will give the householders information about the service and the costs involved.

You have been provided with a number of files to help you produce this solution. You will need to decide on the type of software to use to produce this solution and also what files to include. The solution will be printed out and posted to houses in the local area. You can source any additional information and images yourself. Ensure that any information or images you use are copyright free. Suggested software could be Word® or PowerPoint®.

You will have a consistent house style and format across the solution and the logo should be shown on the top right of any screen. You will need to decide what shortcuts to set up, customise any user interface and record any necessary macros.

The following file has been provided:

Tshirt.doc

Use the internet and carry out research to find copyright free images.

In the solution you may need to consider:

- number of pages
- layout of newsletter
- content of newsletter
- fonts, style, size and colour
- alignment
- background colour
- page numbering
- any word art
- suitable images.

Before you start, create a suitable plan for the solution.

Produce the solution and present it to your line manager.

Once you are working through your solution you need to answer the following questions:

1 What is the purpose of using IT?
2 What methods, skills and resources are required to complete the task successfully?
3 Show a plan of how you are going to create the leaflet using IT to achieve the required purpose and outcome.
4 What IT system did you choose and why? What software application have you chosen and how does this meet your needs and purpose?
5 What IT system and software have you chosen? Why is this appropriate for the task?
6 What automated routines have you used to improve productivity?
7 How have these automated routines helped with producing the newsletter efficiently?
8 How did you complete the planned task using IT?
9 How did the finished newsletter meet the requirements in terms of matching requirements and fitness for purpose?
10 How appropriate were the IT tools you selected for the newsletter? Did they meet the purpose?
11 What are the strengths of the final work?
12 What are the weaknesses of the final work?
13 How could you improve the work further? If you were to produce the newsletter again what would you do differently?
14 What new techniques have you learnt?

Level 2

This unit will develop your knowledge, understanding and skills relating to the use of IT. You will plan and review your use of commonly used IT tools for work activities that are at times non-routine or unfamiliar. As a result of reviewing your work, you will be able to devise solutions in the use of IT tools in order to improve work productivity. The solution you will create will require some preparation, clarification or research before it can be planned and it will involve a number of steps.

An example could be to create a spreadsheet to automate the price list update in a sales or accounts business context using Microsoft Office® software.

This unit contains a number of IT solutions that can be created using different software packages.

By working through the **Overview**, **Worked Examples**, **Tasks** and **Consolidations** in this chapter, you will demonstrate the skills required for Improving Productivity Using IT Level 2:

Examples are provided as a demonstration of what to do. These demonstrations are based on the Microsoft Office® 2003 suite. Review the **Overview** in each section and then watch any demonstrations in the **Worked Example** before commencing any **Tasks**.

If you are familiar with the topic covered, move onto the **Tasks** in each section of this chapter.

Throughout the **Worked Example** sections, the demonstrations relate to a word processing solution. A mini assignment is included at the end of each chapter. This can be used for additional practice only and is based on a presentation scenario.

You will need to download files from the Hodderplus Website (www.hodderplus.co.uk/itq). You will need to copy these to your file area so that you can use them during the exercises in this chapter.

ELEMENT The competent person will…	PERFORMANCE CRITERIA To demonstrate this competence they can…	KNOWLEDGE To demonstrate this competence they will also…
IPU: B1 Plan, select and use appropriate IT systems and software for different purposes	B1.3 **Plan how to carry out tasks** using IT to achieve the required purpose and outcome B1.5 Select and use IT systems and software applications to complete planned tasks and produce effective outcomes	B1.1 Describe the **purpose for using IT** B1.2 Describe what methods, skills and resources will be required to complete the task successfully B1.4 Describe any **factors that may affect the task** B1.6 Describe how the purpose and outcomes have been met by the chosen IT systems and software applications B1.7 Describe any **legal or local guidelines or constraints** that may apply to the task or activity
IPU: B2 Review and adapt the ongoing use of IT tools and systems to make sure that work activities are successful	B2.1 **Review ongoing use** of IT tools and techniques and change the approach as needed B2.5 **Review outcomes** to make sure they match requirements and are fit for purpose	B2.2 Describe whether the **IT tools selected** were appropriate for the task and purpose B2.3 Assess the **strengths and weaknesses** of final work B2.4 Describe ways to make further **improvements to work**
IPU: B3 Develop and test solutions to improve the ongoing use of IT tools and systems	B3.3 **Develop solutions** to improve own productivity in using IT B3.4 Test solutions to ensure that they work as intended	B3.1 Review the benefits and drawbacks of IT tools and systems used, in terms of business productivity and efficiency B3.2 Describe **ways to improve** productivity and efficiency

B1 Plan, select and use appropriate IT systems and software for different purposes

In this section you will find out about the task that you will complete. You will describe its purpose, plan how you will carry out the task, select the software and describe why you have chosen this.

B1.1 Describe the purpose for using IT

Before you start any task, you need to find out who the information is for and what the purpose of the task is. You need to know when it should be finished, what information to include and where it will be used, for example, on screen, posted or printed.

> **Worked Example B1.1**

You have been asked to carry out a research project by the Parkview Academy into absence management and you have been asked by the HR Manager to produce a report for current line managers, detailing the new procedure for reporting absences and to update them with current absence statistics. Your report should include the key requirements about how to deal with absence and the new procedure that has been approved in the minutes.

In order to complete this task, you have been provided with a number of files.

The first file **absence.doc** contains details of the absence policy.

The second file **minutes.doc** contains an extract of the updated information.

The third file **absence.csv** contains the statistical data we have and names/departments of line managers.

The HR Manager would like to send out this report by email to line managers by Friday. From the information you have been provided with, you will need to decide what information to include in your report.

1　Write an introductory statement describing what the information is for, when it must be finished, what information needs to be included and where it will be used.

Suggested answer

Example: I have been asked by the HR Manager to produce a report by Friday which will be circulated by email to line managers in the organisation. I have been asked to include the updated guidance on absence management and some statistics on staff absence. This report is to be presented to line managers for their comments. Once they have reviewed the report they will write back to HR with details of how they plan to cut absence in their section. The report will include statistics which have been produced in Excel®.

B1.2 Describe the methods, skills and resources required to complete the task successfully

Now that you have been informed what the task will be, you need to describe what methods, skills and resources will be required to complete it.

> Worked Example B1.2

1   When producing the absence report, you will need to include a number of resources:
   a List the computer resources (hardware and software) required to complete this task.
   b What methods will you use to complete the task?
   c What skills will be required to complete the task?

Suggested answer

Example: When producing the absence report, I will need to have access to a computer and printer. I will be using a colour laser printer which we have in the office as this will allow the graphs to be printed in colour. I have decided to use Microsoft® Word® and integrate the statistics from Microsoft® Excel® when I have produced the relevant graphs and charts. I have decided to produce the report in Microsoft® Word® as this will allow me to create different styles and apply these throughout the report. It will also allow me to import the spreadsheet data in appropriate places. I will open the statistics in Microsoft® Excel® and I will format the information so that it looks professional and then I will produce graphs for each department to show the absences to date. I will use mail merge to incorporate names and department fields into the supporting documentation that will be sent out with the report. I have read through the files I have been provided with and I will decide which information to include in the report. I will need to be competent at using Microsoft® Word® and be able to use styles, mail merge and importing data so that the report can be produced professionally. I will need to set up a page layout, import text/data, import images and import the graphs/charts from Microsoft® Excel®. I will also need to use appropriate numbering, styles and headers and footers. I will need to use a wide range of Level 2 skills for word processing and spreadsheets.

B1.3 Plan how to carry out tasks using IT to achieve the required purpose and outcome

You are ready to plan how you will carry out the tasks. A plan is crucial when considering any kind of project. It will allow you to make decisions about the structure and layout and style and format of the solution and a description of automated features to be used.

A plan shows you what you hope to achieve and it lists the steps that you will take to complete the solution. A table or a flowchart is a good way to present this information.

Worked Example B1.3

1 Create a plan to produce the HR report.

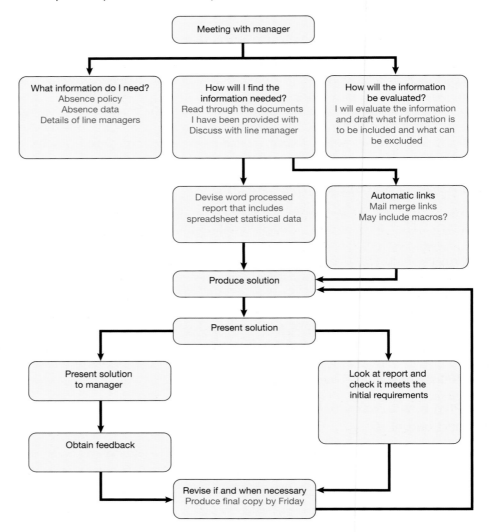

Suggested answer

Example: The report will include text, images and spreadsheet graphs. The structure and layout will include:

- *at least two pages*
- *content of pages*
- *details of where graphics will be included*
- *index/table of contents*
- *front cover and images*
- *text covering the revised absence management procedures*
- *numbered paragraphs*
- *mail merge used*
- *statistical graph.*

As I may be required to create another report in the future, I will create a standard template for the report.

I will also create a standard letter, which can be used to mail merge the report.

Company house style is to use Verdana 11 font so I will use this for the body text. Any subheadings will be emboldened.

B1.4 Describe any factors that may affect the task

At this stage, consideration should be made of any factors that may affect the task. This could include access to information, any steps you need to take before starting the task, what time you have available, whether you need any additional budget or resources and what the audience needs.

Worked Example B1.4

Below are some factors that may affect the task.

1   Factors affecting the absence management report could include:
   a   Access to information – this should be OK as I have managed to get some files from my line manager which contain the information I need to complete the task.
   b   I need to read through the files before I start the task and highlight the information I think would be useful in completing this task.
   c   I need to think about my time – I have to finish the report today so I think this will take me about an hour to complete so I need to use my time wisely.
   d   I don't need any additional budget or resources.
   e   The audience needs the report to be readable and professionally produced today.

B1.5 Select and use IT systems and software applications to complete planned tasks and produce effective outcomes

B1.6 Describe how the purposes and outcomes have been met by the chosen IT systems and software applications

You need to describe why the software applications are appropriate and fit for purpose. For example, why is Microsoft Word® more appropriate when producing a report than Microsoft Publisher®, and why not use a database? Think about how you would complete this task if you did not have access to a computer. What benefits are there of using IT over manual methods for preparing, processing and presenting the information? What are the limitations? How will this meet needs, and the required levels of quality and accuracy? How can using IT streamline business processes or increase productivity? What difficulties do people have when using IT?

Worked Example B1.6

1   Describe why you have selected the IT system and software applications you have and discuss why these are appropriate to meet the requirements of the task.

Suggested answer

Example: I decided to use my laptop instead of my PC as I have Microsoft Office® 2003 on this and I am more familiar with this IT system. I have decided to use Microsoft Word® as this is a professional word processing package and it will allow me to use various tools and techniques so that I can produce reports. I could use Microsoft Publisher® but I feel it would be more difficult to lay out the pages as a report and include fields to use mail merge.

The benefits of using IT are that I can save the information regularly and come back to it later. I can make changes to the report more easily, quicker and more accurately than doing this by hand. Editing is easier with a computer than by hand and I can use the spell check tool to check my work. The limitation in using IT is that the computer may crash. If I don't save it properly I could lose my work or the file could become corrupt so I will make sure that I save the file regularly and keep backup copies as I work through my document. I will also need to consider health and safety and make sure that I work safely at my workstation so this will mean that I will take regular breaks, ensure that my workstation is set up correctly and that my seat provides me with the appropriate support. Using a computer allows the report to be produced more professionally than writing by hand.

B1.7   Describe any legal or local guidelines or constraints that may apply to the task or activity

When completing the solution, you need to ensure that you comply with any data protection, copyright, software licensing, organisational house style or branding guidelines.

When completing the solution, you must comply with the following legislation:

- Data Protection Act – this act regulates how data is stored and processed by organisations. This means that any person or organisation that holds data (apart from a personal address book) is liable to comply with regulations. The act defines eight principles which you must follow. Further information can be found at **www.ico.gov.uk/for_organisations/data_protection_guide.aspx**

- Copyright, Designs and Patents Act 1988 – this act protects intellectual property rights and covers literary, dramatic, musical, artistic works, sound recordings, broadcasts and films. The rights cover how the original information is broadcast or reproduced. This means that, in most cases, permission must be sought from the originator before any materials can be reproduced. Further information can be found at **www.opsi.gov.uk/acts/acts1988/UKpga_19880048_en_1.htm**

- Computer Misuse Act 1990 – this act was introduced to make it illegal to unlawfully access computer systems and use the data for inappropriate purposes. Therefore, if someone accesses your computer using your login and password, and impersonates you, for example in a chat room, they can be prosecuted under the act. Also, if someone tries to access your computer data by 'phishing', they can also be prosecuted under the act. Further information on phishing and viruses can be found later in this book or at **www.opsi.gov.uk/acts/acts1990/UKpga_19900018_en_1.htm**

As a user of data you must ensure that you comply with legislation and keep all the data secure. The information for the absence management report will be subject to data protection and can only be processed and used for this purpose. The organisation's logo will be subject to copyright and cannot be reproduced without the organisation's consent. You should also keep your login and password secure during the solution so that no one accesses information unlawfully.

It is very important for organisations to keep data secure and most organisations now have a data protection office that monitors and deals with requests under the requirements of the law. For example, in a Human Resources department, staff will be required to view the details of their personnel files by submitting a subject access request. Some organisations charge for this information and this covers photocopying charges. The HR department would have to copy the information within a required timescale, and the data protection office would oversee this. They would also ensure that data was not held longer than it needed to be, and that it was processed in line with requirements and was not being used for a different purpose.

Copyright is a big area where problems can arise; some students copy and paste information from websites and pass it off as their own. Some universities have purchased special software which allows them to review assignments electronically and check to see how much is the candidate's own work and how much is from the internet. Digital recordings, e.g. songs, films and DVDs, are becoming huge areas of concern because files are uploaded to the internet and then downloaded without the originator's permission. Some large companies are now trying to have additional information in place which protects them from this abuse.

Computer 'hacking' is also a big problem and it can lead to identify theft – several people have had their identify stolen, which has allowed fraudsters to get loans or mortgages fraudulently in someone else's name using the stolen details. This is a growing area of concern and also includes the cloning of cash cards.

The absence management report will include confidential data, which may be subject to data protection and therefore this data should be kept secure and not disclosed to unauthorised users. Computers should be locked with a password so that other people cannot see the data. The files are copyright of the author and publishers. However, this should not cause a problem when completing this task.

The organisational house style and branding guidelines are to use font Verdana 11 and to include the company logo on the right-hand side of each document.

Worked Example B1.7

1   List the legal aspects that you will need to consider when completing this IT solution.

Suggested answer

Example: I will need to consider health and safety, data protection, copyright and organisational house style when completing this task. I will make sure I take regular breaks; I will ensure that my computer is locked if I take a break. I will ensure that I use the information so that it does not breach copyright legislation and I will use the organisational guidelines I have been provided with.

B2: Review and adapt the ongoing use of IT tools and systems to make sure that activities are successful

B2.1   Review ongoing use of IT tools and techniques and change the approach as needed

B2.2   Discuss whether the IT tools selected were appropriate for the task and purpose

As you work through the task, you will need to gather information and decide whether the IT tools and techniques are appropriate for your solution and whether they have allowed you to meet the intended outcome. It is a good idea to keep a log of the IT tools you have used so that you can review them against your plan to see if you did use the IT tools you planned to or whether you changed these as you developed the solution.

> **Worked Example B2.1**

1 Keep a log of the IT tools that you use when producing the task.
2 Produce a brief review to show what tools and techniques you use and whether you needed to make any changes.

Suggested answer

Example: When producing the report I used the tools that I had listed in the plan, however instead of embedding the spreadsheet I decided to import it so that it can be updated regularly.

I found that the tools I had planned to use were appropriate for the task and allowed me to complete the solution. The report took me an hour to complete and this included the checking that I undertook.

B2.3 Assess the strengths and weaknesses of final work

Once the solution has been created, you should analyse your strengths and weaknesses in the production of the report. Think about your strengths and weakness in terms of laying out the report, using different formatting tools, the accuracy of the final product, the structure and style, the quality of the end product and how clear the information has been presented for the audience.

This could be completed using a SLOT analysis (Strengths, Limitations, Opportunities and Threats).

> **Worked Example B2.3**

1 Now that you have completed the solution, review your strengths and weaknesses in the following areas:
   a format and layout
   b accuracy
   c structure, style and quality
   d clarity for audience.

Suggested answer

Example: I had a discussion with my line manager to assess the strengths and weaknesses of the final work.

Strengths:
- *I was able to complete the work in the time allocated.*
- *I followed organisational house style.*
- *The report was professionally produced and used consistent styles throughout.*
- *I was able to import the spreadsheet data.*
- *I created bar charts to show the absences across the different departments.*
- *I spell-checked the work.*

Weaknesses:
- *The styles kept changing when I was amending the data in Microsoft® Word® and this was very frustrating.*
- *I should have proofread my work in addition to spell-checking it, because the spell check did not pick up words that I had typed correctly but did not make sense.*
- *I should have spent more time checking my work.*

B2.4 Describe ways to make further improvements to work

Think about how you could improve your work further, based on the review. Think about the quality of information used, how useful your plan was, how appropriate the report was for the intended audience and what effect your mistakes had on others you worked with.

> **Worked Example B2.4**

How could you have completed the work more efficiently and effectively and what new techniques could you use?

Suggested answer

Example: When producing the solution I did have a problem with the styles in Microsoft Word®. In future I am going to find out how I could set my template more securely so that only changes requested by me could be instigated. The absence procedure was useful and the statistics were accurate. I followed and made no changes to the plan. I did make one or two mistakes with formatting but this didn't effect anyone I worked with.

B2.5 Review outcomes to make sure they match requirements and are fit for purpose

Now that the solution has been created, check that it has met the original requirements and that it is fit for purpose. This could be evidenced by including draft copies of the report, checking the plan to see whether requirements were met, checking with the line manager to confirm that the report has met the requirements and reviewing any mistakes and what impact they have had on others. It is also good to note any new techniques learnt.

> **Worked Example B2.5**

1 Thinking about the HR report, produce a brief description of the following items:
   a quality of the information used
   b draft documents
   c review against initial plan
   d review by line manage
   e effect of own mistakes on others.

Suggested answer

Example: When producing the HR report, because I was not fully familiar with the data I initially struggled to find out exactly what information should be included. It took some time to produce the first draft and I have included this with my evidence. The draft shows the checking that I have undertaken and it also shows amendments that I made before presenting the final report to my line manager. I have checked my plan and I followed this with no problems. The report has been reviewed by my line manager and he is very pleased with this – he suggested that I could have used 1.5 line spacing instead of double line spacing to display the report more effectively. I did not make any mistakes that impacted on others when completing this task.

B3: Develop and test solutions to improve the ongoing use of IT tools and systems

B3.1 Review the benefits and drawbacks of IT tools and systems used in terms of productivity and efficiency

B3.2 Describe ways to improve productivity and efficiency

Now that the solution is complete, you need to review the benefits and drawbacks of using the IT tools identified and how these have impacted on business productivity. Following the review, you should suggest ways of how productivity and efficiency could be improved.

Worked Example B3.2

1 List the benefits of the IT tools and systems used in terms of productivity and efficiency.
2 List the drawbacks of the IT tools and systems used by yourself and others in terms of business productivity.
3 Describe ways to improve productivity and efficiency.

Suggested answer

Example: One of the benefits on my own productivity of the IT tools I used was that I used numbered paragraphs and was able to create a contents page very quickly and effectively. Each time that I changed the data, I could very easily update the contents page links, which saved a lot of time. One of the drawbacks of the IT tools used was that I had problems initially with the styles – once I created a template with dedicated styles this worked more efficiently. To improve productivity and efficiency, I have saved the report as a template which includes pre-defined styles. In future when I create documents that would be used regularly, I would save these. Using IT saves time and using shortcuts makes it quicker than producing documents by hand and the IT report is more professional.

B3.3 Develop solutions to improve own productivity in using IT

In this section you will create the solution. The following instructions work through the production of the absence management report. In this **Worked Example** the solution will include a suitable template with styles and a macro created to save and print the report.

Watch the following demonstration to see how the report was created.

1.3 *Demonstration*

Worked Example B3.3

You will now create your solution. First, it is good practice to define the styles you will use in the report and also create a template.

1 Create a new Microsoft Word® document.
2 Create the following three styles – one for heading, one for sub-heading and one for body text.
3 Click on **Format** → **Styles** → **New Style** → **Heading**. Change the font to Verdana, 14, blue and bold. Centre this text. Click **Add to Template** → **Automatically update**.

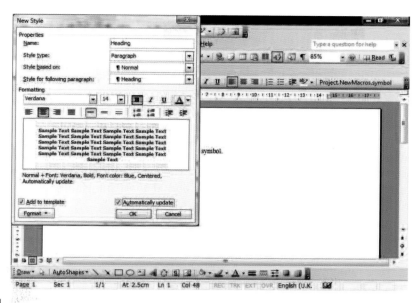

Figure 1.4

4 Repeat this step and create a new style for the subheading: Verdana, 14, green and bold. Left-align the text. You will need to include a number as the subheadings will be numbered items. Click on **Format** → **Numbering**. Choose a number style. Click on **OK** twice. Add to the template and automatically update.

5 Repeat and create a new style for body text: Verdana, 12, justified text.

6 Repeat and create a new style for numbered items. Name this **Numbers** – it should be Verdana, 12, justified text.

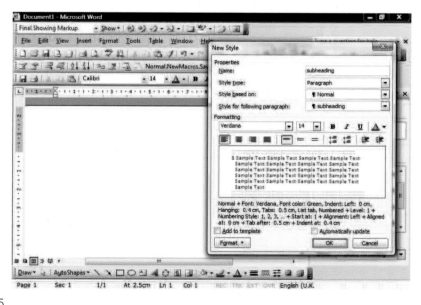

Figure 1.5

7 Click **File** → **Save As**. Change the Save As type to **Document Template**. Save this as **report.dot**. Close the file.

8 To create a new document using the template, click on **File** → **New** → **On my computer**. Choose **report.dot**.

9 Insert the file **absence.doc**. Click **Insert** → **File** → **absence.doc**.

10 Apply the body text style to the text in the report. Highlight all of the text and click on **Format → Styles and formatting**. The style pane will open. Click on **body text**. This style will be applied to the body text.

11 Repeat this and apply the subheading/numbers style to appropriate items.

12 Apply the heading style to the title of the report.

13 Spell check the report to ensure that there are no errors.

14 Save the report as **draft1.doc**.

15 Open the **minutes.doc** file and copy and paste any appropriate text into your report. Apply any formatting to this text.

16 Open the **absence.csv** file and either import the table or create a graph to import this data into your report. You will need to add at least one sentence of your own to describe the data that you are importing.

17 Add any headers/footers and automatic fields.

18 Ensure that the report is formatted correctly on the page.

19 Insert a front cover and add an appropriate title.

20 Insert another blank page, which can be used as an index page.

21 Type in the subheading **Contents**.

22 Click on **Insert → Reference → Index and Tables**. Where it says **Show levels**, change this to **1 → Options**. Remove the tick from 'heading 1' and scroll down the list until you find 'subhead' style and type in **1 → OK**. Click **Modify** and modify the font for TOC1 to Verdana 12 and colour light blue with double line space. Click **OK → OK → OK**.

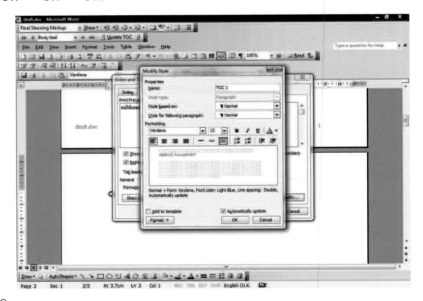

Figure 1.6

23 The Table of Contents will now be displayed on page 2. If you make any changes to the report and need to update the table of contents, right-click on the contents index and click **update field.**

24 Insert the company logo as instructed in the company organisational house style.

25 Check through the report and ensure that it is professional and it meets requirements.

26 Create a macro that records save, spell check and print. Click on **Tools → Macro → Record new macro**. Name this **Save** and click **OK**. Record the following steps – click on **Save**, spell check and print. Stop recording the macro.

27 Save the report as **final.doc** and present it to your line manager for feedback.

28 Create the mail merge labels that can be added to the report. Click on **Tools** →
Letters and Mailings → **Mail Merge** → **Labels** → **Next: Starting document** →
Label Options. Choose a suitable size for the labels. Click **OK** → **Next: Select
recipients** → **Browse**. Find the file **merge.xls**. Click **Open** → **Sheet1$** → **OK** → **OK**
→ **Next: Arrange your labels** → **More items** → **Department**. Click on **Insert**
→**Line Manager** → **Insert** → **Close** → **Next: Preview your labels** → **Complete
the merge** → **Edit individual labels ...**→ **All** → **OK**. All labels will be shown.

30 Save and close all open files and the software.

B3.4　Test solutions to ensure that they work as intended

Now that the solution has been created, you need to check and test it to ensure that it
works as intended. This will be evidenced through the production of the solution to ensure
that the plan has been followed, organisational house style has been followed and template
used and stored to improve efficiency in the future.

A good way to test the solution is to draw up a test plan and measure it against the original
requirements. An example test plan and evidence of testing is shown below.

TEST	OUTCOME
Produce a report for current line managers of at least two pages in length	Report is four pages in length
Does it include: • New procedure for reporting absence? • Current statistics? • How to deal with absences?	Yes
Use house style	Consistent house style throughout
Consistent spacing and layout	No – I will have to go back and amend so that the white spacing is consistent throughout the document, because in places, especially around the graphs/charts, there is more space below the chart than above it.
Proofread and spell checked	Spell checked – needs to proofread
Include the statistics from Excel®	Yes
Produced by Friday	Yes
Imported images look professional	Yes
Numbering consistent	Yes
Include headers and/or footers	Yes
Did the mail merge work?	Yes
Does it include a contents page and front cover?	I need to add a front cover

Now that the solution has been tested, the amendments will be made as identified above.

Worked Example B3.4

1   Produce a brief discussion of how the solution has been tested to ensure that it works as intended.

Suggested answer

Example: When the solution was created I checked back to the scenario to ensure that I had met all the requirements. I then printed out the solution and had it checked by my line manager as well as checking it myself and I was pleased that it had met final requirements.

Mini Assignment

You have been asked by your line manager to create a solution for Porchester Zoo. Porchester Zoo has been reviewing its marketing materials and it has been suggested that they require a software solution that will allow visitors to the zoo to electronically find information about the different animals.

You have been provided with a number of files to help you produce this solution. You will need to decide on the type of software to use to produce the solution and also what files to include. The solution is to be displayed on screen and this should be taken into consideration. You are required to create a multimedia product and plan this to achieve the required purpose and outcome.

The Porchester Zoo house style is to have a consistent format across the onscreen solution and for the logo to be shown on the top right of any screen. You will need to decide what shortcuts to set up, customise any user interface and record any necessary macros.

The following files have been provided:

elephants1.jpg

elephants2.jpg

elephants3.jpg

gorilla.jpg

tiger.jpg

tiger1.jpg

giraffe.jpg

Use the internet and carry out research into these different animals and add any appropriate text to your onscreen display.

In the solution you may need to consider:

- number of slides
- content and layout of master slide
- content of slides
- fonts, style, size and colour

- alignment
- background
- number of bullets per slide
- hyperlinks to other slides/presentations
- hidden slides
- customised show
- timings.

Produce the solution and present it to your line manager.

Now answer the following questions.

1 What is the purpose of using IT?
2 What methods, skills and resources will be required to complete the task?
3 What factors will affect the task?
4 What IT systems and software applications are appropriate for the purpose?
5 What IT systems and software applications did you choose to meet the purpose and outcome for the task?
6 What legal or local guidelines have affected the task?
7 Describe the ongoing use of IT tools and techniques.
8 What tools and techniques did you change to complete the task?
9 Were the tools and techniques appropriate for the task and purpose?
10 What are the strengths and weaknesses of the final work?
11 In what ways would you improve the work further?
12 Describe the outcomes in terms of matching to requirements and fitness for purpose.
13 Describe the benefits and drawbacks of IT tools and systems used by yourself and others, in terms of business productivity.
14 Describe the ways in which you could improve productivity and efficiency.
15 How has the solution improved your own productivity in using IT?
16 What tests did you carry out to ensure that the work was as intended (e.g. shortcuts, customised interface, macros).

2

Using the Internet

This unit will develop your knowledge, understanding and skills relating to the use of the internet.

You will produce an assignment that allows you to carry out effective searches on the internet.

By working through the **Overview**, **Worked Examples**, **Tasks** and **Consolidations** in this chapter, you will demonstrate the skills required for Using the Internet Level 1:

ELEMENT The competent person will…	PERFORMANCE CRITERIA To demonstrate this competence they can…	KNOWLEDGE To demonstrate this competence they will also…
INT: A1 Connect to the internet	A1.2 **Access the internet** or intranet	A1.1 Identify different types of **connection methods** that can be used to access the internet
INT: A2 Use browser software to navigate web pages	A2.1 Use **browser tools** to navigate web pages A2.3 Adjust **browser settings** to meet needs A2.4 Use browser help facilities	A2.2 Identify when to change browser settings to aid navigation
INT: A3 Use browser tools to search for information from the internet	A3.1 Select and use appropriate **search techniques** to locate information A3.3 Use **references** to make it easier to find information another time A3.4 **Download** and save different types of information from the internet	A3.2 Outline how **information meets requirements**
INT: A4 Use browser software to communicate information online	A4.1 Select and use tools and techniques to **communicate information** online A4.2 Use browser tools to share information sources with others A4.3 **Submit information** online using forms or interactive sites	A4.4 Identify opportunities to post or publish material to websites
INT: A5 Follow and understand the need for safety and security practices when working online	A5.3 Work responsibly and take appropriate **safety and security precautions** when working online A5.4 Keep personal **information secure** A5.5 Follow relevant **laws, guidelines and procedures** for the use of the internet	A5.1 Identify the **threats to user safety** when working online A5.2 Outline how to **minimise internet security risks** A5.4 Identify the **threats to user safety** when working online

Step by step examples are provided as a demonstration of what to do. These demonstrations are based on Microsoft Internet Explorer® 7. Review the **Overview** in each section and then watch the demonstrations in the **Worked Examples** before commencing any **Tasks**.

If you are familiar with the topic covered, move onto the **Tasks** in this chapter.

Consolidation exercises are provided throughout the chapter for extra practice.

Throughout the **Worked Example** sections, the demonstrations relate to finding information relating to mobile phones. The **Tasks** relate to downloading tunes from the internet.

There are **Consolidation** exercises throughout this chapter which relate to cycling.

A **Mini Assignment** is included at the end of this chapter and this can be used for additional practice.

A1 Connect to the internet

A1.1 Identify different types of connection methods that can be used to access the internet

The internet is a network of global computers that provides accessible information through a series of computers connected together and which communicate using telephone lines.

The internet evolved from ARPANET, a military system in the USA, which was used during the 1960s.

Information is transmitted through the network and passes through specialised hardware known as 'routers'. Each router decides on the most efficient path for the information to take.

To access the internet, you need to have specific computer equipment. This will include:

- a computer

- a modem

- access to a telephone line.

Currently in the UK, access to the internet is either by using dial-up or broadband.

Dial-up is access to the internet via a telephone line where a modem is connected to a telephone line. Dial-up is now usually used by travellers or in remote areas of the country where broadband is inaccessible. Dial-up uses a telephone connection and, when connected to the internet, the telephone line is in use. An engaged tone will be heard by someone if they are trying to ring you at the same time. With dial-up, you will be charged the same as a telephone call for the minutes that you use.

Broadband allows access to the internet but it splits the telephone signal into channels so that when you are on the internet, your phone line remains free and not engaged. Broadband has become popular but speed of connections are dependent on location (although in some areas of the country very fast speeds are available). However, the further you live from the local telephone exchange, the weaker the broadband signal you receive. Data is transmitted over the telephone line but it is handled by ADSL (asymmetric digital subscriber line), which allows data to be transmitted much faster than dial-up. It is worth finding out from your broadband provider the maximum speeds that can be accessed to make sure you are not charged for higher speeds.

Once you have the correct equipment of a computer, modem and telephone connection, you will need to make sure that your computer runs up-to-date operating software allowing access to the internet.

You need to load internet browser software onto your computer. Most operating systems, for example Microsoft Windows®, come with an internet browser. Microsoft Windows® operating software (e.g. XP) comes with Internet Explorer® 7. There are different versions of Internet Explorer® available and also other internet browsers. For the purpose of this unit, however, we will use Internet Explorer®, which is the web browser included with the Microsoft Windows® operating system.

In addition to connecting one computer to a telephone line in order to connect to the internet, there are other ways for computers to access the internet, including:

- LAN
- VPN
- modem
- router
- wirelessly.

Figure 2.1 LAN

Figure 2.2 Modem and router

LAN is a local area network. This means a network of local computers are connected together, either using wires or wirelessly and this is useful for a home, small office or a school. A LAN allows users to access resources that are part of the network, for example shared printers, software and scanners.

VPN is a virtual private network and this is a computer network where some of the network connections are to larger networks, for example the internet. It allows users to log in to the network remotely, for example from home, while travelling or when at head office. The head office will usually host the LAN.

A modem is used to send data over a telephone line. The modem transfers the data into a signal that can be processed by the telephone line. The receiving modem translates the signal back to digital data. Modems are available wirelessly or wired.

A router is used to send messages across a network. A router makes sure that the data is sent to the correct destination and that it doesn't go where it isn't needed. The router joins networks together allowing information to pass from one to the other. Information should be protected via a firewall.

Wireless connections allow computers to connect to a network without the use of wires. Data is transmitted using radio frequencies rather than through wires. Wireless connections are useful for small home offices or when working on mobile devices.

Task A1.1

1   Find out and note down the computer equipment that you have access to.
2   Note down the browser software and version number you will be using.
3   Find out whether you are using dial-up or broadband to access the internet.

A1.2 Access the internet or intranet

Once you have all the required hardware and software, you need to decide on an internet service provider (ISP). An ISP is a company, for example BT or Sky, that 'sells' you the requirements to connect to the internet using telephone line connections. You pay a company for this service and they will offer you email accounts, internet speeds and limit the amount of information that you download. For home users, the company will usually provide internet connection via broadband or dial-up.

Once you have signed up with a company, they will allocate you a user name and password and this will allow you access to internet services and an email account. You must keep these details secure so other users cannot log in and access your account.

The intranet is an internal network of computers. Most organisations host an intranet that allows staff secure access to resources that the company want available to staff internally but do not want to publish externally. You will require a login and password to access the intranet. Nowadays mobile phones allow internet access through a mobile phone package and also allow you to download/send/receive emails.

Task A1.2

1 Carry out some research on the internet into the services provided by different internet service providers (ISPs).
2 Note your findings.
3 Find out whether your organisation hosts an intranet.

A2 Use browser software to navigate web pages

A2.1 Use browser tools to navigate web pages

When you open an internet browser there are various tools available, which allow you to navigate web pages.

On opening Internet Explorer®, you will be met with a screen similar to that shown below.

Figure 2.3

Figure 2.4

Watch the demonstration.

 **2.1** *Demonstration*

A2.1.1 Open browser

> **Worked example A2.1.1**
>
> 1   Click on the **Start** button in Microsoft Windows®.
> 2   Click the Internet Explorer® icon.
> 3   On the home page find the back button.
> 4   Find the forward button.
> 5   Find the refresh button.
> 6   Find the home button.
> 7   In the search bar, type in **ISP** and view the search results.

> **Task A2.1.1**
>
> 1   Click on the **Start** button in Microsoft Windows®.
> 2   Click the Internet Explorer icon.
> 3   On the home page find the back button.
> 4   Find the forward button.
> 5   Find the refresh button.
> 6   Find the home button.
> 7   In the search bar, type in **ISP** and view the search results.

A2.1.2 Browser tools

The address bar in Internet Explorer® shows the web address of the page accessed, for example, the web address of Google is **www.google.co.uk** – this is shown in the address bar (see Figure 2.3).

Google is one of many search engines available on the internet. You use a search engine to search for information that is hosted on the internet. A search engine will look at the search words that you key in and display what it thinks are the best matches.

A URL is known as a uniform resource locator – www.google.co.uk is an example of a URL. This can be typed directly into the address bar.

The first part of the URL identifies the protocol to use – for example **www** (World Wide Web).

The second part specifies the domain name – for example, **google**.

The final part of the URL shows the country – for example, **co.uk.**

Domain names can be purchased so web addresses can be hosted at specific addresses, for example iTQ 2009. This is a domain name purchased by the author.

Once you carry out a search in Google, you then follow the links to the pages you want to access. For example, if you wanted to search for mobile phones you could key "mobile phone" directly into a search engine and then follow the links to one of the websites to see the different features of a mobile phone.

Watch the demonstration.

🖱 2.2 | *Demonstration*

> **Worked Example A2.1.2**

1 Open your internet browser and in the search engine type in "**latest mobile phone**".
2 Click on one of the links that has been returned by the search engine and follow it to see what some of the stores are advertising as the latest mobile phones.
3 Close your browser.

Now it's over to you.

> **Task A2.1.2**

1 Open your internet browser and in the search browser type in "**downloadable tunes**".
2 Click on one of the links and follow it to see what songs you can buy and download.
3 Close your browser.

A2.2 Identify when to change settings to aid navigation

A2.3 Adjust browser settings to meet needs

Some of the settings in Internet Explorer® can be changed to help navigate faster around the internet. The security settings and home page can be changed.

Some websites have 'pop-up windows' which are usually a form of advertising and they are designed to capture email addresses. Some web pages open a new window to display the advert when the pop-up blocker is selected. Internet Explorer® allows the user to decide whether or not to allow or block a pop-up window. Some pop-up windows may cause a security risk and you will need to decide whether or not to access this information.

Watch the demonstration.

🖱 2.3 | *Demonstration*

> **Worked Example A2.2**

1 Open Internet Explorer® and click on **Tools → Internet Options**. (Note: if you can't see the **Tools** menu, press **Alt** on the keyboard and this should be shown.)
2 In the home page key in **www.disney.co.uk → Apply → OK**.
3 Close your browser.
4 Open your browser. The home page **Disney.co.uk** should be displayed.

1 Click on **Tools → Internet Options → Security** tab.
2 The Internet Zone should be selected as **Medium-high**. (The security level slide can be moved either up or down and the security level will change.) Click **OK** to save any changes.
3 Type "**Ask.com**" in your search box. (Ask is another search engine like Google but it stores information in a different way. Carry out a search on **Ask.com** for latest mobile phones and see if the results are different from the search you did earlier.)
4 Navigate to **www.techsmith.com** and follow the link to Downloads, Free Trials and then Free Camtasia Studio Trial – you should get a pop-up message at the top of your screen.

Figure 2.5

Click on the pop-up blocker bar to allow pop-ups.

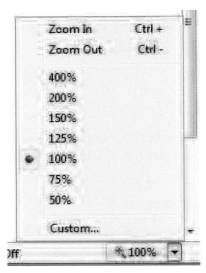

Figure 2.6

5 The settings for the pop-up blocker can be changed by clicking on **Tools** from the menu bar → **Pop-up Blocker** → **Pop-up Blocker Settings** → type in **www.techsmith.com** → **Add** → **Close**.

6 To change the size of the screen you are viewing, click the **Zoom** button. This is shown at the bottom right of the Internet Explorer® screen. You should see a magnifying glass with **100%** next to it. Click on this to zoom in and zoom out, changing the screen size.

7 AutoComplete is a facility that stores information that you type into web form fields – this can make it quicker to fill in the same information again. To change the AutoComplete options, click on **Tools** → **Internet Options** → **Content** tab. Under AutoComplete, click **Settings** and select **Web addresses**, **Forms**, **User names and passwords on forms** and **Prompt me to save passwords** check boxes. Click **OK** twice.

Now it's over to you.

Task A2.2

1 Open Internet Explorer® and click on **Tools** → **Internet Options**. (Note: if you can't see the **Tools** menu, press **Alt** on the keyboard and this should be shown.)

2 In the home page, key in **www.hodderplus.co.uk/itq**, click **Apply** and **OK**.

3 Close your browser.

4 Open your browser and your new home page should be **www.hodderplus.co.uk/itq**.

5 Click on **Tools** → **Internet Options** → **Security** tab.

6 The Internet Zone should be selected and **Medium-high**.

7 Type "**Ask.com**" in your search bar. Carry out a search on **Ask.com** for the latest tunes available for download.

8 Navigate to **www.geosites.com** and a pop-up blocker will be displayed. Click the options to **Temporarily allow pop-ups** and see what changes it makes to the web page.

9 Change the zoom setting to 75%.

10 Change the AutoComplete settings so that Internet Explorer® stores information that you type into web form fields.

A2.2.1 Privacy

Within Internet Explorer there is a privacy tab which mainly allows you to manage cookies. Cookies are small text strings that are stored on your computer and when you revisit a web page, the cookie tells the web saver. This saves you time, as you do not need to key in your address. Cookies are safe. If you click on **Tools** → **Options** → **Privacy** you can change the level of settings for cookies. The default setting is medium.

A2.4   User browser help facilities

Internet Explorer® includes a comprehensive help section, which allows you to search for various topics and get help.

Watch the demonstration.

2.4   *Demonstration*

Worked Example A2.4

1 Open Internet Explorer®.
2 Click on **Help** from the menu. (Click **Alt** if **Help** not shown.)
3 Click **Contents and Index**.
4 In the help search bar, type **pop-up**. You should get two results – click on the first one and read the FAQ about pop-ups.
5 Close your browser.

Task A2.4

1 Open Internet Explorer®.
2 Click on **Help** from the menu. (Click **Alt** if **Help** not shown.)
3 Click **Contents and Index**.
4 In the help search bar, click **AutoComplete**. You should get ten results – click on the first one and read about **Using AutoComplete**.
5 Close your browser.

Consolidation

1 Carry out a search for cycling holidays. Follow one of the links to find further information.
2 Change your home page to **www.microsoft.com**.
3 Zoom the page so that 100% is displayed.
4 Use **Help** to search for '**privacy**' and read the first returned result.
5 Close the internet browser.

A3: Use browser tools to search for information from the internet

A3.1   Select and use appropriate search techniques to locate information

When you input words into a search engine, you get hundreds of pages displaying the search results, some of which are not really related to what you are looking for. There are a number of different search engines that make finding information easier by using search spiders. Another way to make searches more effective is to use keywords. Keywords are words or phrases that are keyed into a search engine to look for information contained in a website. The search engine spiders look at the keywords and display the sites that they think relate best to the information requested.

To make searches more effective, you can use special characters and punctuation, for example:

Space	A space means 'and' in Google. If you type in '**South America**' it will be interpreted as South 'and' America. If you key '**South America**' into Google, you will get approximately 173,000,000 results.
–	The minus sign means to exclude words, e.g., **South America – weather**. This brings up 54,300,000 results in Google.
''	Quotation marks around text interpret it as a phrase, e.g. **South America – weather 'atlas'** brings the search to 1,690,000 results.
OR	OR searches for pages with either of the words in, e.g. **South America OR Africa – weather 'atlas'** brings up 43,000,000 results.

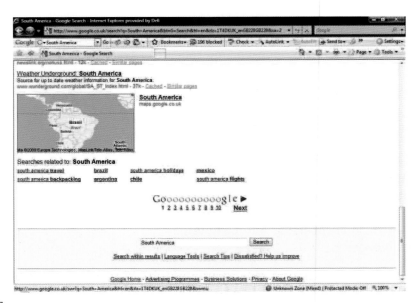

Figure 2.7

In Google, there is an option at the bottom of the page to 'Search within results'.

This allows you to narrow down the search results again, and search only within the results you have been presented with, as shown in Figure 2.8.

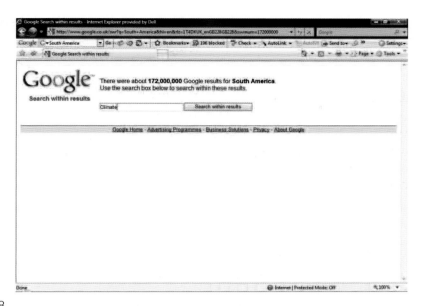

Figure 2.8

These are the results:

Figure 2.9

Searches can include relational operators, for example > **greater than** or < **less than**. You could, for example, type into Google **Interest rate <3%** and about 78,600,000 results will be displayed.

Some search engines allow you to ask questions, for example **Ask.com** and **Askjeeves.com.** If you load Ask.com, you could ask **what is iTQ?** and Ask.com will display the results:

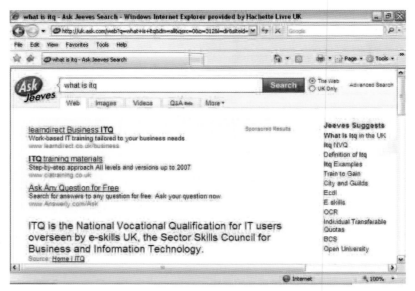

Figure 2.10

Watch the demonstration.

2.5   Demonstration

Worked Example A3.1

1   Open Internet Explorer® and navigate to **www.google.co.uk**.
2   Search for **mobile phones** and click **Search within results** and type in **3G**.
3   Now type in the search bar **<£100** and search.
4   Navigate to **www.ask.com** and type in **what is 3G?** Access one of the pages to find out what 3G is.
5   Close the browser.

Over to you.

Task A3.1

1   Open Internet Explorer® and navigate to **www.google.co.uk**.
2   Search for **best selling downloads** and click **Search within results** and type in **>2008**.
3   You should get search results of about 16,600,000.
4   Navigate to **www.ask.com** and type in **what is the advantage of downloading tunes?** Navigate to one of the answers.
5   Close your browser.

A3.2   Outline how information meets requirements

When searching for information on the internet, displayed results may not be reliable or accurate. There is a vast amount of information available and it can all be posted anonymously. Any information you find should be evaluated before it is used. When you visit certain pages, you should review the URL to find out whether or not it is a personal page or an educational/commercial website. Also consider who 'published' the page. How up-to-date is the information? Many web pages show the date published. It is important if the date on the website is old because the information could be out of date or the author may have since abandoned the site.

Some websites allow anyone to update web pages and this may not be reliable, for example, wikis. Sometimes by 'googling' a sentence from a website, you can see whether or not it has been taken from elsewhere.

Once you have carried out your search, you need to decide whether the information you have received is sufficient, current, reliable and accurate and how it meets your requirements – sometimes you will need additional searches.

A3.3 Use references to make it easier to find information another time

History

Within Internet Explorer® there is a history list, which makes it easy to find and return to websites that you have visited in the past. The History records every page visited. To find a web page that you visited yesterday, click on the Favourites button and click on the History drop-down arrow. Click on the day and select the page you want to vistit. The settings for the history list can be changed so that it stores fewer days in the history.

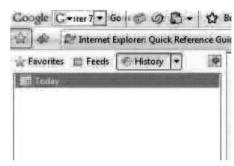

Figure 2.11

Favourites

Internet Explorer® can store useful web pages in a favourites folder. This folder 'bookmarks' the web page (URL) and stores it in the Favourites folder, which makes it easy to retrieve. To store web addresses in the Favourites folder, click on the **Favorites** button → **Add to Favorites**.

Within the Favourites folder, sub-folders can be created so that you can store similar web pages together. To arrange favourites into folders:

Click **New Folder** → **Add**.

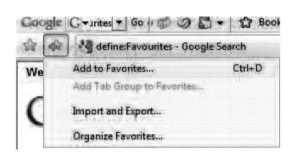

Figure 2.12

Bookmarks

Bookmark is another name for favourites and is used by different internet browser packages. A bookmark does exactly the same thing as favourites and stores web page locations (URLs) that can be quickly retrieved.

Log useful sites

You may decide that instead of using favourites you want to log useful sites. This can be done by creating a table in word and recording all the details of the website.

Watch the demonstration.

2.6 Demonstration

Figure 2.13

Worked Example A3.3

1 Open your internet browser and carry out a Google search for **internet mobile phone.**

2   Select one of the results displayed.
3   Save this link in your favourites folder.
4   Close the internet browser.

Task A3.3

1   Open your internet browser and carry out a Google search for **download UK Chart**.
2   Select one of the results displayed.
3   Save this link in your favourites folder.
4   Close the internet browser.

A3.4   Download and save different types of information from the internet

A variety of different types of information and files can be downloaded and saved. A webpage can be downloaded by **File → Save As** and the file is saved to your computer.

Images, text, sound, games, video, TV and music can also be downloaded and saved. Sometimes you might need special software to download TV programmes or video files and you may need to follow any instructions on screen. Remember that copyright may apply to these items and you should consider this before using files inappropriately as some files are not available free for general use.

Web pages and websites can also be downloaded and saved. To save a web page click on **File → Save as**. To download a website you will probably require special software.

Watch the demonstration to see how this is done.

2.7   *Demonstration*

Worked example A3.4

1   Open your internet browser and navigate to **www.hodderplus.co.uk/itq**.
2   On this site you will find various resources – the information on this site is copyright of the author.
3   Find the image **B241** and download it to your work area.
4   Find the text **Welcome to the OCR iTQ Levels 1 and 2 website**. Copy and paste this into a new Word document.
5   Find the sound file **B241sound** and save this to your work area.
6   Find the video file **B241video** and save this to your work area.

7   Carry out a Google search and search for "**free games**". Pick a site, for example
    http://play.clubpenguin.com/miniclip.htm – this allows you to access and play
    this game.
8   Navigate to **www.bbc.co.uk** and select **iplayer** – this is software that allows you to
    download and watch the TV on your computer. If you are at home and are able to
    do this, download and select a programme to watch.
9   Close your browser.

Now it's your turn to have a go.

Task A3.4

1   Open your internet browser and navigate to **www.hodderplus.co.uk/itq**.
2   On this site you will find various resources – the information on this site is
    copyright of the author.
3   Find the image **elephant**. Download and save this to your local area.
4   Find the text **African Elephants population has been reduced by poaching**. Copy
    and paste this into a new Word document.
5   Find the sound file **clip2.wav**.
6   Find the video file **PorchesterZoo.mpb**.
7   Carry out a Google search and search for "**free games**". Access and play the game.
8   Navigate to **www.bbc.co.uk** and select **iplayer**. This is software that allows you to
    download and watch the TV on your computer. If you are at home and are able to
    do this, download and select a programme to watch.
9   Close your browser.

Consolidation

1   Carry out a search on the internet for **African Elephants**. You will get approximately
    3,210,000 search results. Carry out an advanced search on the habitat of African
    elephants, which will produce fewer results.
2   Navigate to one of the pages and add this to your favourites.
3   Check the copyright of the information and copy and paste some of the text into a
    Word document.
4   Find a suitable image (check copyright) and add this to your Word document.
5   Carry out an effective search for an African elephants' habitat video. Access the
    video and play the file.
6   Close the internet browser.

A4: Use browser software to communicate information online

A4.1　Select and use tools and techniques to communicate information online

There are various tools that can be used to communicate information online. Information can be transmitted via email, blogs, instant messaging or podcasts.

Email

Email means electronic mail and allows you to send and receive messages. It also allows you to add file attachments. Microsoft Outlook® is an example of an email software package. Some of the internet search engines also have 'freebie' email, for example, googlemail, yahoomail, and so on.

Blog

A blog is a website maintained by an individual who adds information containing news or events on a particular subject. Blog entries are displayed in reverse chronological order so that the latest posting is shown at the top of a list. www.blogger.com is a website that allows you to create a blog. Visit this website. Choose a popular topic and create your own blog.

Instant messaging

Instant messaging is real-time communication whereby you can communicate with more than one person at any one time by typing information directly into the messaging system. It is very much like having a conversation on the phone as messages are sent and received instantly. There are various messaging systems available that allow you to register and communicate with other users. This can be useful for online conferencing.

Podcasts

A podcast is a multimedia file or digital recording that is broadcast over the internet. It can be used for lectures, music, radio shows or announcements.

A4.2　Use browser tools to share information sources with others

It is easy to share information with other users on the internet. There are various software packages available, which allow you to send a web page link by email. In Internet Explorer® it is easy to send a link by email. Click on **File** → **Send** → **Link by E-mail**. The URL from the web page will then be sent to an email address you specify.

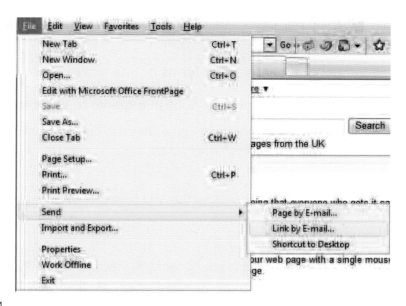

Figure 2.14

Alternatively, you can send the whole web page by email. This is useful, although some users may have trouble accessing the web page due to security settings in Microsoft Outlook®.

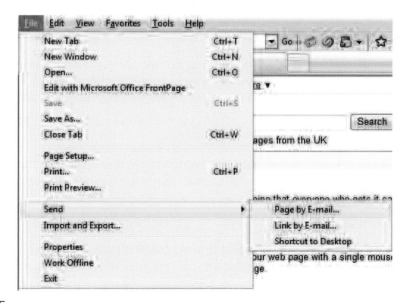

Figure 2.15

If you have relatives abroad, one useful feature of the internet is that it allows you to share photos. There are various software programs available for download that allow you to upload pictures to the internet. It is advisable to upload and store these to a secure area so that your photographs are not accessed by unauthorised users.

You can share your Microsoft Outlook® calendar with other people or you can use another calendar where you can create a web page that allows you to browse through your calendar (e.g. Google calendar). This is a useful resource if you travel a lot and need to access information when you are away from home.

A4.3   Submit information online using forms or interactive sites

A4.4   Identify opportunities to post or publish material to websites

The internet is useful to fill in and submit forms online. This can be useful when buying goods or registering your details to access a web page.

Ratings/reviews

Ratings allow you to score products or services that you have purchased online. Various websites ask you to add scores for services, for example ebay and Amazon.

Recommendations

Some websites may be recommended to you or come via other websites. Check the dates of any links and whether the recommendations are biased, for example, are they part of some kind of advertising?

Wikis

A wiki is a page or collection of web pages that is designed so that anyone who accesses it can contribute or modify the content. This means that generally the pages are constructed by users and therefore should not be classed as providing the 'definitive answer'. Wikipedia is an example of a wiki.

Discussion forums

A discussion forum is where users with the same interest can exchange ideas, post questions or offer answers/help on relevant subjects over the internet. There are many discussion forums available and they are sometimes useful if you are looking for answers to questions.

Interactive sites

An interactive website interacts with the user through either text-based or graphical user interfaces – these can be games or websites that have been designed to encourage learning.

Internet netiquette

Netiquette stands for internet etiquette and is good practice that should be observed when using all parts of the internet. Any guidelines should be read when you register with a particular website.

A5 Follow and understand the need for safety and security practices when working online

A5.1   Identify the threats to user safety when working online

SPAM

SPAM is the sending of unsolicited bulk messages, usually via email, although SPAM can also come through search engines, blogs and wikis and by logging on to certain websites maintained by hoaxers to obtain personal details.

Malicious programs

A virus is a program that can copy itself and infect a computer. This is usually spread from one computer to another through files that contain executable code. This could be through email, floppy disk or CD.

A worm is a self-replicating computer program that uses a network to send copies of itself to other computers. A Trojan horse performs functions that allow unauthorised access to computers. Sometimes a Trojan horse can open a back door to your data on the computer that allows a hacker to control your computer by monitoring key strokes.

Spyware and adware are products that are installed onto your computer when you install software, usually shareware. Shareware software contains banner ads, which also install tracking software that can send data back to the author of the software about how the product is being used.

Rogue diallers are software programs that are installed onto a computer and disconnect your genuine internet connection and redial a premium-rate phone number instead, which means you will run up very expensive telephone bills.

Hackers and hoaxes

Hackers are people who can hack into your computer and steal personal data. They use viruses, such as Trojans, to access your computer.

Hoaxes use chain mails asking you to log in to a website or send the message onto another 10 friends for prosperity. Sometimes you might get an email claiming that your bank information needs to be updated – this is known as hoaxing or phishing because the email knows your computer's IP address and has access to personal information when you log in to their 'suspect site'.

Identify the threats to user safety when working online

You should be careful when online as various potential threats exist, for example sexual predators, identity thieves, con-artists, cyber bullies, virus writers and bogus users in chat rooms. Make sure that you don't share account information with other users, don't open files sent by people you don't know, don't post inappropriate pictures and never meet anyone in person you have met online. You can even use monitoring software to record all computer activity – especially if you want to keep track of your children's internet use!

Cyber bullying

Cyber bulling is similar to bullying at school and it is where someone is harassed via websites, text messages, instant messages or blogs. It can be where children can vote for the fattest child in school or passwords are posted so that accounts can be vandalised. Cyber bullying is on the increase and it is important that you are aware of the risk when using the internet.

Inappropriate behaviour and grooming

When children use the internet they should be kept safe and parental controls should be installed so that they can only access permitted websites. Children should also be taught about the dangers of using the internet and not knowing who they are talking to. No one should ever meet in person anyone they have met on the internet without taking appropriate security measures first. Children should also not take and upload photographs of themselves.

False identities

It is very easy on the internet to have a false identity and to remain anonymous. You can even create a fictitious identity so as to hide your real details from other users.

Financial deception

If users get hold of your personal details, they could commit identity theft, access your bank accounts and withdraw funds without you knowing about it until it is too late. You must make sure that all your details are kept secure.

A5.2   Outline how to minimise internet security risks

There are many threats to your computer when using the internet, so you must be able to protect yourself from them. The following list gives some guidelines that you should follow:

1   Install a reliable anti-virus program that can detect worms, viruses and Trojans and make sure this is updated regularly.
2   Install a firewall if you are using broadband as it helps protect your computer against malicious traffic and keeps your computer safe from attacks.
3   Don't respond to emails from people you don't know, not even by asking to be removed from their mailing list. By doing so, you are confirming your email account is active and they will keep emailing you.
4   Never log in to an email where you have been asked for your personal information, for example bank details.
5   Never send personal information via email as someone could steal your identity.

Virus-checking software

There are various different suppliers of virus-checking software and sometimes this software includes a firewall, anti-spam and adware/spyware features and offers you a full package. You should carry out research into the different products available and choose the most suitable for your computer setup.

Message attachments

Unless you are 100 per cent sure of the email sender, it is advisable to immediately delete an email and its attachment from your email inbox. If you do decide to open and view the attachment, the safest way is to save this to your computer and then open it, as your virus-checking software will then scan the file to ensure that it is safe before you open it.

When working online you will have various usernames and passwords, and sometimes a PIN. For example, an online bank account may require a unique username and password, and then ask for two or three digits from a six-digit PIN. This information must be kept secure so that hackers do not hack into your bank information and steal your money. When setting passwords, some websites show password strength, indicating how secure the password is. For a strong password, it is advisable to use a combination of letters, numbers and upper and lower case characters. For example, which of the following two passwords is the most secure?

1   John170369
2   RzB2M0c9w

The second password is more secure, because it includes random letters, numbers and upper and lower case characters. Some websites or chatrooms do not hold any personal information, and therefore do not require strong passwords: you would set the password strength against the security threat to your data.

When using various websites you can create your profile or identify and this allows the company to send you marketing materials, or other users to view your profile. You should be very careful what information you add in a personal profile and what you share with others – younger people are discouraged from giving their real names, addresses or telephone numbers to people they do not know, because you do not know the real identify of the person you are 'chatting' with, and this can be very dangerous. Sometimes it is better to withhold personal information and only upload the essential information. For example, when purchasing goods and services online, you are invariably asked if you want to store your card details: if you agree and then someone hacks into the site, this information will be readily available to the hacker.

A5.3 Work responsibly and take appropriate safety and security precautions when working online

Firewall settings

Microsoft Windows® XP and Vista both come with a firewall installed and this is turned on by default. However, if you have another firewall installed you will need to turn one of them off as they conflict with each other. The firewall restricts communication between your computer and the internet and sometimes settings have to be adjusted so that you can access the internet. You will need to read the instructions that came with your own firewall to review how to make changes.

Carry out security checks

You should carry out regular security checks and change your passwords every few weeks to ensure that they do not fall into the wrong hands. Virus software should be scheduled to run at least every few days to check your system for viruses.

Report inappropriate behaviour

Some large organisations have dedicated email accounts that you can contact should you observe inappropriate behaviour on the internet.

Interactive sites

An interactive website allows the user to interact through either text-based or graphical user interfaces. These can be games or websites that have been designed to encourage learning.

Internet netiquette

Netiquette stands for internet etiquette and is a set of guidelines that you should observe when using all parts of the internet. It is good practice to read the guidelines when you register with a particular website.

Content filtering

Various software programs are available that filter content, in particular for parents wanting to install parental control software. This software allows the user or parent to block or allow certain information or websites so that it keeps children safe from inappropriate content.

Avoid inappropriate disclosure of information

You should be careful when online as various potential threats exist, for example sexual predators, identity thieves, con-artists, cyber bullies, virus writers and bogus users in chat rooms. Make sure that you don't share account information with other users, don't open files from people you don't know, don't post inappropriate pictures, never meet anyone in person you have met online and use monitoring software to record all computer activity.

A5.4 Keep personal information secure

All personal information should be kept secure, which means that passwords should not be your date of birth, address or anything that could be easily guessed by a hacker. A good password should be at least 6–8 characters long and should include uppercase letters, lowercase letters and numbers. It is a good idea to also include symbols in your password. A secure password would be something like Mn@35xK!L5s.

When you create passwords in different sites, the site will often tell you how 'strong' your password is.

Sometimes when using online forums or discussion boards, you might decide to use fictitious alternatives to your real name, for example you might log in as njbiTQ tutor and therefore keep your personal details safe by not posting messages as yourself.

An avatar is the representation of a computer user in the form of a three-dimensional model, a picture or text. In AOL messenger, avatars are commonly referred to as buddy icons. These images are usually very small images.

A5.5 Follow relevant laws, guidelines and procedures for the use of the internet

There are various rules and regulations that have to be followed when using the internet. Some employers only allow their staff to use the internet for no more than half an hour per day; other organisations allow their employees free access. However, internet access is usually monitored. This means that if you regularly use, for example, Facebook at work, this could be monitored by the organisation's IT department and you could be disciplined and sacked for misuse of company resources.

You should read any organisation guidelines set by your employer to ensure that you comply with their requirements.

With regard to health and safety, your employer should offer you a risk assessment of your workstation when you start work. This will allow your organisation to check that you have the correct equipment – for example, that your chair is at the correct height. You should ask your employer about this when you start. Some employers also provide employees with a free eye test if they are regular users of VDUs.

Copyright

Any information posted to the internet is subject to UK copyright law. This means that the author is protected in the same way as material that is printed or available on CD. Some websites will include a statement stating whether or not any of the material is available to be used in schools. Sometimes you may need to contact the author and seek permission to use the information.

Downloading materials

If you are at home, then you can download what you wish. However, if you are at work or at school/college then downloading may be restricted – you will need to review your organisation's policy to find out what you can and cannot download.

Mini Assignment

You have been asked to arrange a day trip to a local theme park by your tutor. You will need to carry out research on the internet and present your findings to your tutor in an appropriate format.

1 Start your computer and open Internet Explorer®.
2 Carry out a search (using Google) for theme parks within 100 miles of your town.
3 Follow some of the links to pages and save these links in your favourites.
4 Carry out a search (using Ask) for theme parks within 100 miles of your town using efficient criteria.
5 Follow some of the links to pages and save these links in your favourites.
6 Compare the information you have found.
7 Find more information relating to one of the theme parks and copy and paste the text into a Word document.
8 Save two images from the website to your computer.
9 Change the pop-up windows settings to **Turn off pop-up blocker** and take a screen print.
11 Carry out a search in **Help** to find out about the phishing filter and take a screen print.
12 Access **www.blogger.com** and follow the instructions to create a blog about a topic of interest. Remember copyright and ensure that the information you post is reliable, not defamatory, and truthful.
13 Send the blog page you have created by email to your tutor to show you have done this.
14 Change the security settings in Internet Explorer® to Medium instead of Medium-high. Take a screen print to show you have done this.
15 Write an email advising your tutor how to stay safe when using the internet.
16 Access a wiki page and search for **pineapple fish**. Take a screen print of the first set of information. Click **Edit** and make a minor change. Take a screen print but do not save the changes.
17 Collate all your evidence. Close Internet Explorer®

Level 2

This unit will develop your knowledge, understanding and skills relating to the use of the internet, using tools and techniques to search for and exchange information. The tasks that you will complete may require analysis, clarification or research. You will have to select how to search for and exchange information and customise a browser to alter the home page and display data feeds from selected sites.

By working through the **Overview**, **Worked Examples**, **Tasks** and **Consolidations** in this chapter, you will demonstrate the skills required for Internet Level 2.

ELEMENT The competent person will...	PERFORMANCE CRITERIA To demonstrate this competence they can...	KNOWLEDGE To demonstrate this competence they will also...
INT: B1 Connect to the internet	B1.3 Get online with an internet connection B1.4 Use help facilities to solve internet connection problems	B1.1 Identify different types of **connection methods** that can be used to access the internet B1.2 Identify the **benefits and drawbacks of the connection method** used
INT: B2 Use browser software to navigate web pages effectively	B2.1 Select and use **browser tools to** navigate web pages B2.3 Adjust **browser settings** to optimise performance and meet needs	B2.2 Identify when to change settings to aid navigation B2.4 Identify ways to **improve the performance** of a browser
INT: B3 Use browser tools to search for information from the internet	B3.1 Select and use appropriate **search techniques** to locate information efficiently B3.3 Manage and use **references** to make it easier to find information another time B3.4 **Download**, organise and store different types of information from the internet	B3.2 Describe how well **information meets requirements**
INT: B4 Use browser software to communicate information online	B4.2 Select and use appropriate tools and techniques to **communicate information** online B4.3 Use browser tools to **share information** sources with others B4.4 **Submit information** online	B4.1 Identify opportunities to create, post or publish material to websites
INT: B5 Follow and understand the need for safety and security practices when working online	B5.2 Work responsibly and take appropriate **safety and security precautions** when working online B5.4 Manage **personal access** to online sources securely B5.7 Apply **laws, guidelines and procedures** for safe and secure internet use	B5.1 Describe the **threats to system performance** when working online B5.3 Describe the **threats to information security** when working online B5.5 Describe the **threats to user safety** when working online B5.6 Describe how to **minimise internet security risks** B5.8 Explain the importance of the relevant laws affecting internet users

Step-by-step examples are provided as a demonstration of what to do. These demonstrations are based on Internet Explorer® 7.0. Review the **Overview** in each section and then watch the demonstrations in the **Worked Example** before commencing any **Tasks**.

When you are familiar with the topic covered, move onto the **Tasks** in this chapter.

Consolidation exercises are provided throughout the chapter for extra practice.

Throughout the **Worked Example** sections, the demonstrations relate to finding information relating to recycling. The **Tasks** relate to theme parks.

A **Mini Assignment** is included at the end of this chapter.

B1 Connect to the internet

B1.1 Identify different types of connection methods that can be used to access the internet

The internet is a global network of computers providing information through a series of computers connected together using telephone lines.

The internet can be accessed by using dial-up or broadband. Dial-up is access to the internet via a telephone line and a modem is used to connect the telephone line. Dial-up is used by travellers or in remote areas of the country where broadband is not accessible. Dial-up uses a telephone connection and therefore, if someone calls when you are connected to the telephone using dial-up, they will hear an engaged tone. Like a telephone, you will be charged for the time you are connected.

Broadband allows access to the internet and telephone at the same time. Data signals are divided into channels so that when you are connected to the internet, your home phone remains free. Broadband has become the popular choice recently and in some locations very fast connection speeds are available. The information is still transmitted over the telephone line but it is handled by ADSL (asymmetric digital subscriber line), which allows faster transmission over copper telephone lines. It is worth finding out from the local telephone exchange the maximum speeds you can access in your area.

LAN means local area network and this means a network of local computers, for example in a home, office or school. This means that all users of the LAN have access to resources that are part of the network, for example shared printers, software and scanners.

VPN means virtual private network and is a computer network where links are made to a larger network (e.g. the internet). It allows staff to log in to the network from home, while travelling or working at the head office. The head office will usually have a LAN for users to log in to.

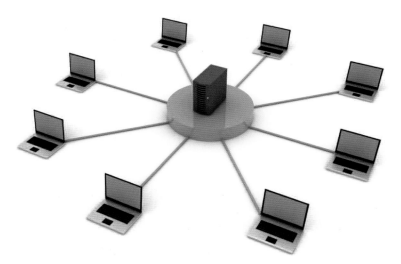

Figure 2.16 LAN

A modem is used to send data over a telephone line. The modem changes the data signal into a signal that can be processed by the phone line. The receiving modem then changes the signal back to digital data. Modems can be wired or wireless.

A router is used to send messages across a company network. The router makes sure that the information is sent to the correct destination and that it doesn't go where it isn't needed. The router joins networks together allowing information to pass from one to the other.

Figure 2.17 Modem and router

Wireless connections refer to a computer network which is wireless; that is, it works without the use of wires. Data is transmitted using radio frequencies rather than wires and this is useful for small home offices or when working on mobile devices.

Internet connections can be provided via cable connections. Cables are laid and they deliver high speed internet access and television programmes via cables rather than wireless. Some cable providers can offer very high speed internet connections through fibre optic cables.

DSL is digital subscriber line and provides data transmission through the telephone network. DSL is the term used for marketing ADSL.

Mobile phones use a wireless application protocol or WAP, which allows users to connect to the internet, but it has limited facilities. Another connection method is 3G – this is a later version of wireless technology for mobile phone users, allowing more opportunities to use the mobile network. This means users can access more websites and collect their emails while on the go.

An intranet is similar to the internet but hosts information locally and is a private network so is not accessible to unauthorised users. Company users usually have a secure login and password, which allow them to access the internal resources.

B1.2 Identify the benefits and drawbacks of the connection method used

B1.3 Get online with an internet connection

There are many advantages and disadvantages of each different type of connection method – some of these are shown below:

CONNECTION METHOD	ADVANTAGES	DISADVANTAGES
Dial-up	Can be a cheap way to connect to the internet: only pay for time spent online	Blocks your telephone line Can be expensive if used for long periods of time
Cable	High-speed internet access	Not everyone has access to cable
Broadband	Speed, stability	Accessibility and speed in certain areas
3G	Speed, stability, connection wherever you are	Accessibility varies

B1.4   Use help facilities to solve internet connection problems

By clicking on help in Internet Explorer® you can search for various options to help resolve problems.

Watch the demonstration.

2.8   *Demonstration*

Worked Example B1.4

1   Open Internet Explorer®.
2   Click on the **Help** menu. (If this is not shown, press the **Alt** key on the keyboard.)
3   Type in **connection**.
4   You should see 30 results – click on **Troubleshoot network and Internet connection problems**.
5   Close the **Help** menu.

Task B1.4

1   Open Internet Explorer®.
2   Click on the **Help** menu. (If this is not shown, press the **Alt** key on the keyboard.) Select **Contents and Index**.
3   Type in **security**.
4   You should see 30 results – click on **Change Internet Explorer Security Settings**.
5   Close the **Help** menu.

B2 Use browser software to navigate web pages effectively

B2.1   Select and use browser tools to navigate web pages

When you open Internet Explorer® you will find various tools to allow you to navigate web pages.

The screen in Figure 2.18 will be similar to that shown on your computer when you open Internet Explorer® (although the home page may be different).

Back

Forward

New Window

New tab

Click &
show history

Search

Stop

Refresh

Address bar

Figure 2.18

Watch the demonstration.

2.9   *Demonstration*

> **Worked Example B2.1 Open browser**

1   Click on the **Start** button in Microsoft Windows®.
2   Click the Internet Explorer® icon.
3   On the home page, find the back button.
4   Find the forward button.
5   Find the refresh button.
6   Find the home button.
7   In the search bar, type in **ISP** and view the search results.

Figure 2.19

B2.2   Identify when to change settings to aid navigation

A home page is the page that first loads when Internet Explorer® is opened, for example your home page could be the Microsoft website. This depends on what was set as the home page when the software was originally loaded. You can change your default home page settings so that when you open Internet Explorer® and click on the home button, it takes you to your home page. If you have created your own website, the home page could be your home page of your own website.

Auto fill or AutoComplete is a feature that you can turn on or turn off in internet Explorer. If this is turned on it allows you to automatically complete forms, for example Internet Explorer® stores the details you key into one form and remembers them so that when you complete another form, it suggests what to complete in each field.

Cookies are internet code used to track information about users, for example shopping preferences. Cookies are usually harmless and you can click to accept or reject cookies to be stored on your computer. However, if you do reject a cookie, the website you are looking at may become inaccessible.

Security settings can be changed and these can be increased or decreased depending on your own requirements. Security settings are usually set to 'Medium-high' in Internet

Explorer®, which allows access to most internet sites. If the settings are changed to 'High' then some websites may become inaccessible.

Pop-up windows are usually a form of advertising and they are designed to capture email addresses. Some web pages open a new window to display the advert when the pop-up blocker is selected 'to allow'. Internet Explorer® allows you to decide whether or not to allow or block a pop-up window. Some pop-up windows may cause a security risk and you will need to decide whether or not to access this information.

The appearance of internet pages can be changed by altering the colours, language, fonts and accessibility options. The colours can be changed from the windows default options to specific colours of your choice. The language settings can be changed from UK to US and fonts can be changed to your preference. The accessibility options allow changes to the formatting or the use of style sheets in web pages.

To change the appearance of a web page:

Click on **Tools** → **Options** and view the appearance options at the bottom of the page. Change some of the options to see what it does to your files. Privacy levels are set within Internet Explorer®. The levels can be set to low, medium or high. The default setting is medium. This protects your privacy and allows you to block or allow cookies and specific websites to have access to personal information.

A search engine is a program on the internet that allows you to search for information. There are a number of search engines including Google, Yahoo and Ask. They all store and retrieve information differently so you may wish to use more than one search engine when you are looking for information.

Zoom allows you to increase or decrease the information viewed.

Microsoft Windows® version tracker reviews and finds the latest software updates available from Microsoft and installs these onto your computer. You may sometimes find that you are asked to restart your computer because of an update – make sure you clearly follow the instructions.

Within Internet Explorer® there is a temporary file storage area which stores your browsing history and settings and temporarily stores files. The settings can be changed so that each time you load a page, Internet Explorer® checks the internet for a new page rather than using the version stored on your computer. The history can be changed so that the history length can be longer or shorter.

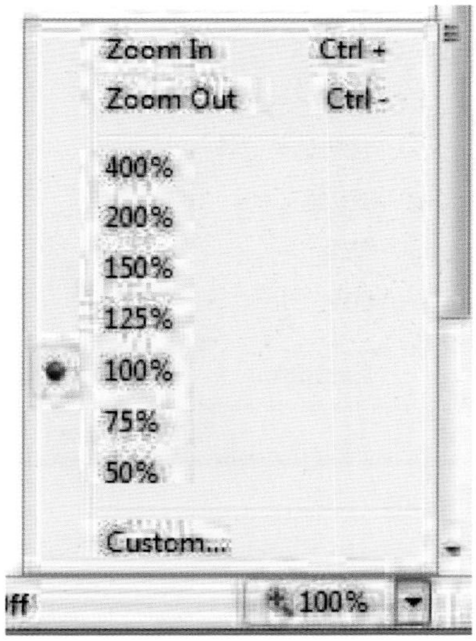

Watch the demonstration.

Figure 2.20

🖰 2.10 | Demonstration

> **Worked Example B2.2**

1 Open Internet Explorer® and click on **Tools** → **Internet Options**. (Note: if you can't see the **Tools** menu, press **Alt** on the keyboard and this should be shown.)
2 In the home page, key in **www.disney.co.uk** → **Apply** → **OK**.
3 Close your browser.
4 Open your browser and the home page **Disney.co.uk** should be displayed.

1 Click on **Tools** → **Internet Options** → **Security tab**.
2 The internet zone should be selected as **Medium-high**. (The security level slide can be moved either up or down and the security level will change). Click **OK** to save any changes.

3   Type "**Ask.com**" in your search box. (Ask is another search engine like Google but it stores information in a different way. Carry out a search on Ask.com for the latest mobile phones and see whether the results are different.)
4   Navigate to **www.techsmith.com** and follow the link to Downloads, Free Trials and then Free Camtasia Studio Trial. You should get a pop-up message at the top of your screen.

Figure 2.21

Click on the pop-up blocker bar to allow pop-ups.

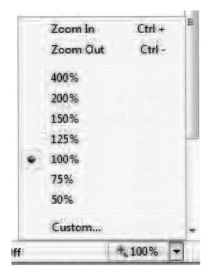

Figure 2.22

The settings for the pop-up blocker can be changed by clicking on **Tools** from the menu bar → **Pop-up Blocker** → **Pop-up Blocker Settings**.

Type in **www.moneysupermarket.com**.

Add → **Close**.

5   To change the size of the screen you are viewing, you can click the Zoom button. This is shown at the bottom right of the Internet Explorer® screen – you should see a magnifying glass with 100% next to it. By clicking on this, you can zoom in and zoom out to change the screen size.
6   AutoComplete is a facility that stores information that you type into web form fields – this can make it quicker to fill in the same information again. To change the AutoComplete options, click on **Tools** → **Internet Options** → **Content** tab.

Under AutoComplete, click **Settings**.

Select web addresses, forms, user names and passwords on forms and prompt me to save passwords check boxes. Click **OK** twice.

7   Change the temporary file storage history to two days. Click on **Tools** → **Internet Options** → **Settings** → change the **History** to 2 days.

Now it's over to you.

Task B2.2

---

1 Open Internet Explorer® and click on **Tools → Internet Options**. (Note: if you can't see the Tools menu, press **Alt** on the keyboard and this should be shown.)
2 In the home page, key in **www.hodderplus.co.uk/itq**. Click **Apply** and **OK**.
3 Close your browser.
4 Open your browser and your new home page should be **www.hodderplus.co.uk/itq.**
5 Click on **Tools → Internet Options → Security** tab.
6 Select **Medium-high** on the internet zone.
7 Type **Ask.com** in your search bar. Carry out a search on **Ask.com** for latest tunes available for download.
8 Navigate to **www.geosites.com** and a pop-up blocker will be displayed. Click the option to **Temporarily Allow Pop-ups** and see what changes it makes to the web page.
9 Change the zoom setting to 75%.
10 Change the **AutoComplete** settings so that Internet Explorer® stores information that you type into web form fields.

B2.3 **Adjust browser settings to optimise performance and meet needs**

B2.4 **Identify ways to improve the performance of a browser**

Internet Explorer® allows you to work on and offline while accessing the pages you want. Work offline while you are reading the pages and then log back online to access other pages. This can save money for users using dial-up!

History

Within Internet Explorer® there is a history list that makes it easy to find and return to the web sites that you have visited in the past. The History records every page you have visited. To find a web page you visited yesterday, click on the **Favourites** button and then on the **History** drop-down arrow. Click on the day and select the page to visit. You can change the settings for the history list so that it stores fewer days in the history.

Favourites

Internet Explorer® can store useful web pages in a favourite's folder. This folder 'bookmarks' the web page (URL) and stores it in the Favourites folder which makes it easy to retrieve. To store web addresses in the Favourites folder, click on the **Favorites** button → **Add to Favorites**.

Figure 2.23

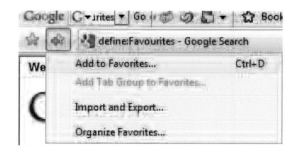

Figure 2.24

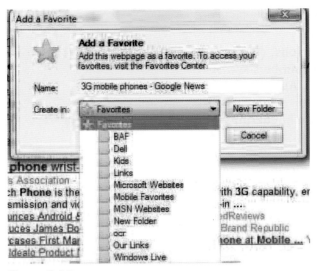

Figure 2.25

Within the Favourites folder, you can create sub-folders so that you can store similar web pages together. To arrange favourites into folders:

Click **New Folder** → **Add** to save in the favourites list.

Bookmarks

Bookmark is another name for favourites and is used by different internet browser packages. A bookmark does exactly the same as favourites and stores web page locations (URLs) that can be quickly retrieved.

Delete cache

Cache stores the temporary internet files. These are files, folders, pages you have visited and information downloaded which are temporarily stored on your computer. This allows browsing to be quicker as pages can be loaded from this folder. To clear, click on **Tools** → **Internet Options**. Click the General tab and go to **Browing History** → **Settings and new settings** → **OK** → **Delete**. Choose **Delete files** → **Close**.

Consolidation

1 Open Internet Explorer® and change your home page to **www.hodderplus.co.uk/itq**.
2 Carry out a search and find the eskills website home page.
3 Bookmark this page.
4 Check for software updates by clicking on **Tools** → **Windows Update**.
5 Follow any instructions on screen.
6 Close Internet Explorer®.

B3: Use browser tools to search for information from the internet

B3.1 Select and use appropriate search techniques to locate information efficiently

When you key words into a search engine, you will get hundreds of pages displaying the search results, some of which are not really related to what you are looking for.

There are a number of different search engines that make finding information easier by using search spiders. Another way to make searches more effective is to use keywords. Keywords are words or phrases that are keyed into a search engine to look for information contained in a website. The search engine spiders look at the keywords that have been inserted and displays the sites that they think relate the best to the information requested. Some search engines ignore common words such as 'where', 'the' and 'how'. By putting double quotes around words, the search engine searches for the exact words in the order given, for example, "Nicola Bowman" will search for Nicola Bowman but will ignore all instances of 'Nicola J Bowman'.

If you want to exclude words, you can add the minus sign, for example "African Elephants – habitat" will exclude all search results that include the word habitat.

If you want to search exactly for information you can add a + immediately before a word (no space after the +). This tells the search engine to match the word precisely.

To make searches more effective, you can use special characters and punctuation, for example:

Space	A space means 'and' in Google and if you type in **South America**, it will be interpreted as South 'and' America. If you key this into Google, you will get approximately 173,000,000 results.
–	The minus sign means to exclude words, for example **South America – weather** – this brings up 54,300,000 search results in Google.
"	Quotation marks around text interpret it as a phrase, for example **"South America – weather atlas"** brings the search results to 1,690,000.
OR	OR searches for pages with either of the words in, for example **South America OR Africa – weather 'atlas'** – this brings up 43,000,000 search results.
+	+ searches exactly for what has been input.

In Google, there is an option at the bottom of the page to **Search within results**.

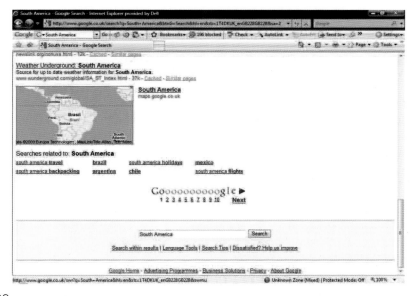

Figure 2.26

This allows you to narrow down the search results again, only looking within the results that Google has displayed. For example:

Figure 2.27

Results are shown below:

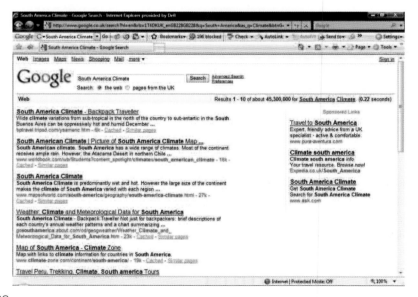

Figure 2.28

Searches can include relational operators like > **greater than** or < **less than**. For example, you could type into Google **Turkey** and <**30 degrees** and about 121,000 results will be displayed.

Some search engines like **Ask.com** and **Askjeeves.com** allow you to ask questions. If you load **Ask.com**, you could ask 'What is it' and the site will display the results.

Watch the demonstration.

 **2.11**   *Demonstration*

Worked Example B3.1

1 Open Internet Explorer® and navigate to **google.co.uk**.
2 Search for **mobile phones**, click **Search within results** and type in **3G**.

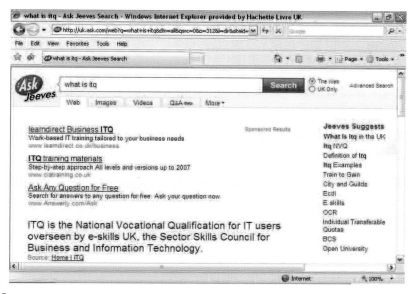

Figure 2.29

3 Now type in the search bar **<£100** and search.
4 Navigate to **Ask.com** and type in **what is 3G**. Access one of the pages to find the answer.
5 Close the browser.

Over to you.

Task B3.1

1 Open Internet Explorer® and navigate to **google.co.uk**.
2 Search for **best selling downloads** and click **Search within results** and type in **>2008**.
3 You should get search results of about 16,600,000.
4 Navigate to **Ask.com** and type in **what is the advantage of downloading tunes**. Navigate to one of the answers.
5 Close your browser.

B3.2 Describe how well information meets requirements

You need to be aware that when you search for information on the internet, displayed results may not be reliable or accurate.

There is a vast amount of information available and a lot of it may have been posted anonymously. You should evaluate any information you find before you use it. When you visit a new site, review the URL to find out whether or not it is, for example, a personal page or an educational/commercial website. Also consider who 'published' the page. How up-to-date is the information? Many web pages show the date published. Make sure you check to see if the date is very old because information could be out of date or the author may have since abandoned the site.

Some websites allow anyone to update web pages and this may not be reliable, for example, on wikis. Sometimes by searching on a sentence from a website, you can see whether or not it has been taken from elsewhere.

Once you have carried out your search, you need to decide if the information you have received is sufficient, current, reliable and accurate and how it meets your requirements – sometimes you will need additional searches. Remember that any information you do find is someone else's work and therefore you should read through it and synthesise and re-write it in your own words. Otherwise, this is not your own work and is known as plagiarism.

B3.3   Manage and use references to make it easier to find information another time

History, favourites and logs are covered in Level 1 on page 41. RSS and data feeds are covered on page 69.

B3.4   Download, organise and store different types of information from the internet

You can store information using bookmarks.

You can download and save different types of information and files. Do this by clicking **File → Save As** and save the file to your computer.

You can also download and save images, text, sound, games, video, TV and music. You might need special software to download TV programmes or video files and you will need to follow the instructions on screen. Remember that copyright may apply to these items and you should consider this before using the files inappropriately. Some files are not available to use without charge.

Watch the demonstration to see how this is done.

🖱 2.12 | *Demonstration*

Worked example B3.4

1 Open your internet browser and navigate to **www.hodderplus.co.uk/itq**.
2 On this site you will find various resources – the information on this site is copyright of the author.
3 Find the image **B241** and download it to your work area.
4 Find the text **Welcome to the OCR iTQ Levels 1 and 2 website**. Copy and paste this into a new Word document.
5 Find the sound file **B241sound** and save this to your work area.
6 Find the video file **B241video** and save this to your work area.

7 Carry out a Google search and search for **free games**. Pick a site such as **http://play.clubpenguin.com/miniclip.htm** – this allows you to access and play this game.
8 Navigate to **www.bbc.co.uk** and select iplayer – this is software that allows you to download and watch the TV on your computer. If you are at home and are able to do this, download and select a programme to watch.
9 Close your browser.

Now it's your turn to have a go.

Task B3.4

1 Open your internet browser and navigate to **www.hodderplus.co.uk/itq**.
2 On this site you will find various resources – the information on this site is copyright of the author.
3 Find the image **elephant**. Download and save this to your local area.
4 Find the text **African elephants population has been reduced by poaching**. Copy and paste this into a new word document.
5 Find the sound file **clip2.wav**.
6 Find the video file **PorchesterZoo.mpg**.
7 Carry out a Google search for **free games**. Pick a site, access and play the game.
8 Navigate to **www.bbc.co.uk** and select **iplayer**. This is software that allows you to download and watch the TV on your computer. If you are at home and are able to do this, download and select a programme to watch.
9 Close your browser.

Consolidation

1 Search on the internet for a holiday to Spain where the temperature will be less than 32 degrees. Then carry out an advanced search that will produce fewer results and and include results that show the habitat.
2 Navigate to one of the pages and add this page to your favourites.
3 Check the copyright of the information and then copy and paste some of the text into a Word document.
4 Find a suitable image (check copyright) and add this to your Word document.
5 Carry out an effective search to find a copyright-free video of Spanish holidays. Access the video and play the file.
6 Close the internet browser.

B4: Use browser software to communicate information online

B4.1 Identify opportunities to create, post or publish material to websites

B4.2 Select and use appropriate tools and techniques to communicate information online

Blog

A blog is a website (usually) maintained by an individual, who adds information about news or events on a particular subject. Blog entries are displayed in reverse-chronological order so that the latest posting is shown at the top of a list. An example is **www.blogger.com**. This site allows you to create a blog. You can visit the site, create an account and choose a popular topic to create your own blog.

Instant messaging

Instant messaging is real-time messaging where you can communicate with more than one person at any one time by typing information into the messaging system. It is very much like having a conversion on the phone as messages are sent and received instantly. There are various messaging systems available. You need to register and then you can communicate with other users – this can be useful if you want to have an online conference.

Podcasts

A podcast is a multimedia file or digital recording that is broadcast over the internet. It can be used for lectures, music, radio shows or announcements.

FTP

FTP stands for file transfer protocol and this allows files to be transferred and uploaded/downloaded from computers to a network or website. There are various free versions of ftp software. You can download and install these onto your computer, which makes it simpler to upload files to the internet.

HTTP

HTTP stands for hypertext transfer protocol and is a language used by computers when transferring documents to the World Wide Web.

VOIP

VOIP stands for Voice Over Internet Protocol. This allows you to make/receive telephone calls using broadband internet rather than a traditional telephone line. This is usually cheaper than using a telephone line.

Watch the demonstration.

 **2.13** *Demonstration*

> Worked example B4.1

Create blog

1 Access **www.blogger.com** and click on **Create your blog now**.
2 Create an account by following the onscreen instructions.
3 Choose an appropriate topic and launch your blog.

Podcast

1 Carry out a search for **BBC radio podcasts**.
2 Access the Radio 1 podcast. Choose one of the podcasts shown and listen to this by clicking **Download episode**.
3 Save the file to your computer and then open it from the **My documents** folder.
4 Close the window.

Instant messaging

1 Using Google, search for **MSN web messenger**.
2 Disable the pop-up blocker so that you can access the site.
3 Sign in and see whether you can find any friends to have an online chat with.
4 Close the internet browser window.

> Task B4.1

Create blog

1 Access **www.blogger.com** and click on **Create your blog now**.
2 Create an account by following the onscreen instructions.
3 Choose an appropriate topic and launch your blog.

Podcast

1 Carry out a search for **Guardian podcasts**.
2 Access one of the news stories shown and listen to it.
3 Save the file to your computer and then open it from the **My documents** folder.
4 Close the window.

Instant messaging

1 Using Google, search for **Google Messaging (Google Talk)**.
2 Create an account and sign in to see whether you have any friends who are online.
3 Save and close the internet browser window.

B4.3 Use browser tools to share information with others

It is easy to share information with other users on the internet. Internet Explorer® allows you to send a web page link by email.

Click **File** → **Send** → **Link by E-mail**. The URL from the web page will then be emailed to the email address you entered.

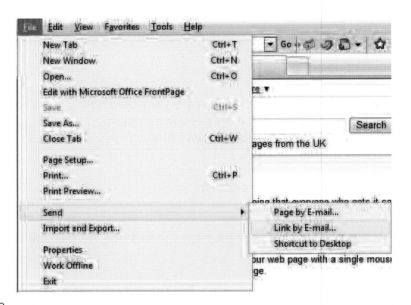

Figure 2.30

Alternatively, you can send the whole web page by email. This is useful, although some users may have trouble accessing the web page due to security settings in Microsoft Outlook®.

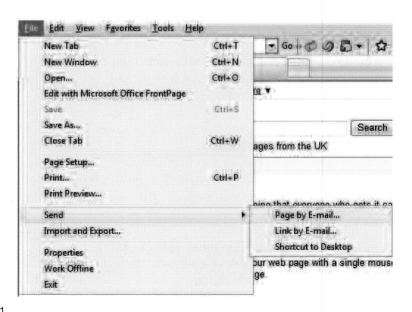

Figure 2.31

Sharing photos

Photos can be shared with others over the internet. There are various software programs available for download that allow you to upload your pictures to the internet. It is advisable to upload and store these to a secure area so that your photographs are not accessed by people other than your friends and relatives.

Sharing calendar

You can share your outlook calendar with other people or you can use another calendar where you can create a web page that allows you to browse through your calendar (e.g. Google calendar). This is a useful resource if you travel a lot and need to access information when you are away from home.

Data feeds

Data feeds or RSS feeds allow you to stay up to date with information you have subscribed to. You need an RSS reader to check feeds and read the latest articles that have been added. You need to decide what information you want to receive. For example, carry out a search for BBC weather feeds. Select one and then subscribe to this feed.

Watch the demonstration.

2.14 | *Demonstration*

> **Worked Example B4.3**

1 Open Internet Explorer® and carry out a search for **RSS news feeds.**
2 Navigate to the news feeds from the BBC web page.
3 Choose a feed from the right of the page.
4 Click **Subscribe to this feed.**

> **Task B4.3**

1 Open Internet Explorer® and carry out a search for **RSS financial feeds.**
2 Navigate to the Financial feeds from the **FT.com** web page.
3 Choose a feed and subscribe to this feed.

B4.4 Submit information online

The internet is used for filling in and submitting forms online – this can be useful when buying goods or when registering your details to access a web page.

Recommendations

Some pages may be recommended to you by friends or be linked to from other websites. You need to treat all websites with care and ensure that you only access appropriate websites.

Wikis

A wiki is a page or collection of web pages that is designed so that anyone who accesses the page can contribute or modify the content.

Discussion forums

A discussion forum is where people with the same interest can exchange ideas, post questions or offer answers/help on relevant subjects electronically over the internet. There are many discussion forums and they are sometimes useful if you are looking for answers to questions. If you want to find out about the iTQ, for example, there is an ICT Skill for life website.

Watch the demonstration.

2.15 Demonstration

Worked Example 4.4

1 Carry out a search for the ICT Skill for life website.
2 Locate the ITQ and ITQ for Life forum.
3 Log in as a guest.
4 Review the general discussion about iTQ.
5 Close the window.

Task 4.4

1 Carry out a search for the ICT Skill for life website.
2 Locate the ITQ and ITQ for Life forum.
3 Log in as a guest.
4 Review 'Discuss the New Nos for IT'.
5 Close the window.

Interactive sites

An interactive website allows the user to interact through either text-based or graphical user interfaces. These can be games or websites that have been designed to encourage learning.

Internet netiquette

Netiquette stands for internet etiquette and is a set of guidelines that you should observe when using all parts of the internet. It is good practice to read the guidelines when you register with a particular website.

B5 Follow and understand the need for safety and security practices when working online

B5.1 Describe the threats to system performance when working online

SPAM

SPAM is the sending of unsolicited bulk messages, usually via email, although SPAM can also be generated through using search engines, blogs and wikis.

Malicious programs

A virus is a program that can copy itself and infect a computer and is usually spread from one computer to another through files that contain executable code. This could be through email, floppy disk or CD.

A worm is a self-replicating computer program that uses a network to send copies of itself to other computers. A Trojan horse performs functions that allow unauthorised access to the computer. Sometimes the Trojan horse opens a back door that allows a hacker to control the user's computer.

Spyware and adware are products that are installed onto your computer when shareware software is installed. The product can contains banner ads, which also install additional tracking software that sends data back to the author of the software.

Rogue diallers are software packages that are installed onto your computer. When you connect to the internet, these diallers disconnect you and then redial a premium-rate phone number instead, running up extensive telephone bills.

Hackers and hoaxes

Hackers are people that can hack or steal crucial data from accounts using data that is stored on your computer. They use viruses and Trojans to access your computer.

Hoaxes may use chain mails that take up time and bandwidth. Sometimes you might get an email claiming that your bank information needs to be updated. This is known as a hoax or phishing because the email sender knows your IP address and when you log in to their 'hoax' site they can access your valuable personal information and use it to log in to the correct website.

B5.2 Work responsibly and take appropriate safety and security precautions when working online

Firewall settings

Microsoft Windows® XP and Vista both come with a firewall installed and this is turned on by default. However, if you have another firewall installed you will need to turn one of them off as they can conflict with each other. The firewall restricts communication between your computer and the internet and you sometimes have to adjust your settings so that you can access the internet. You will need to read the instructions that came with your own firewall to review how to make changes.

To check the Windows firewall settings, click on **Start** → **Control Panel** → **Change settings**.

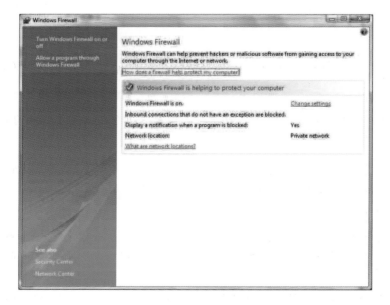

Figure 2.32

Report inappropriate behaviour

Some large organisations have dedicated email accounts that you can contact should you observe inappropriate online behaviour or if you receive phishing emails.

Content filtering

Various software programs are available that filter content, in particular for parents wanting to install parental control software. This software allows the user or parent to block or allow certain information or websites so that it keeps children safe from inappropriate content.

Avoid inappropriate disclosure of information

You should be careful when online as various potential threats exist, for example sexual predators, identity thieves, con-artists, cyber bullies, virus writers and bogus users in chat rooms. Make sure that you don't share account information with other users, don't open files from people you don't know, don't post inappropriate pictures, never meet anyone in person you have met online and use monitoring software to record all computer activity.

Proxy servers

A proxy server is a go between for the user requesting information and another resource (e.g. a webpage). The proxy server filters information against pre-defined rules and allows/denies the request.

B5.3 Describe the threats to information security and integrity when working online

All personal information should be kept secure – no password should be your date of birth, address or anything that could be easily guessed by a hacker. A good password should be at least 6–8 characters long and should include uppercase letters, lowercase letters and numbers. It is a good idea to also include symbols in your password. A secure password would be something like Mn@35xK!L5s.

When you create passwords in different sites, they may tell you how 'strong' your proposed password is.

Sometimes, when using online forums or discussion boards, you might decide to use a fictitious alternative to your real name. For example, you might log in as njbiTQ tutor and therefore keep your personal details safe and not post messages using your own name.

An avatar is a representation of a computer user in the form of a three-dimensional model, a picture or text. In AOL, messenger avatars are commonly referred to as buddy icons. These images are usually very small.

B5.4 Manage personal access to online sources securely

B5.5 Describe the threats to user safety when working online

Abusive behaviour

Sometimes when visiting discussion forums or websites that can be updated by users, you might be aware of abusive behaviour. You should report any abusive behaviour to the web hoster.

Cyber bullying

Cyber bulling is similar to bullying at school and it is where someone is harassed via websites, text messages, instant messages or blogs. It can be where children can vote for the fattest child in school or passwords are posted so that accounts can be vandalised. Cyber bullying is on the increase and it is important that you are aware of the risk when using the internet.

Inappropriate behaviour and grooming

When children use the internet they should be kept safe and parental controls should be installed so that they can only access permitted websites. Children should also be taught about the dangers of using the internet and not knowing who they are talking to. No one should ever meet in person anyone they have met on the internet without taking appropriate security measures first. Children should also not take and upload photographs of themselves.

False identities

It is very easy on the internet to have a false identity and to remain anonymous. You can even create a fictitious identity so as to hide your real details from other users.

Financial deception

If users get hold of your personal details, they could commit identity theft, access your bank accounts and withdraw funds without you knowing about it until it is too late. You must make sure that all your details are kept secure.

B5.6 Describe how to minimise internet security risks

There are various tools available which enable you to minimise the risks to internet security. Virus-checking software, anti-spam software, parental controls and firewalls treat messages, files, software and attachments from unknown sources with caution and may even block sites.

Virus-checking software

There are various different suppliers of virus-checking software and sometimes this software includes a firewall, anti-spam and adware/spyware features – in other words it offers you a full package. You should carry out research into the different products available and choose the one most suitable for your computer setup.

Message attachments

Unless you are 100 per cent sure of the email sender then it is advisable to immediately delete an email and its attachment from your email inbox. If you do decide to open and view the attachment, the safest way is to save it to your computer and then open it, as the virus program will scan the file to ensure that it is safe before it is opened.

B5.7 Apply laws, guidelines and procedures for safe and secure internet use

B5.8 Explain the importance of the relevant laws affecting internet users

There are various rules and regulations that have to be followed when using the internet. Some employers only allow their staff to use the internet for half an hour per day; other organisations allow their employees free access but internet access may be monitored. This means that if you regularly use websites at work, this may be monitored by the organisation's IT department and you could be disciplined and sacked for misuse of company resources.

You should read any organisation rules set by your employer to ensure that you comply with their requirements.

With regard to health and safety, you should carry out a risk assessment of your workstation. This will allow you to check that you have the correct equipment, for example, that your chair is at the correct height. Ask your employer about this when you start work and carry out these assessments when working at home also. Some employers provide employees with a free eye test if they are regular users of VDUs.

Copyright

Any information posted to the internet is subject to UK copyright law. This means that the author is protected in the same way as they would be if they wrote material printed in books or available on CD. Some websites include a statement where it states whether or not any of the material is available to be used in schools. Sometimes you may need to contact the author and seek permission to use the information.

Downloading materials

If you are at home then you can download what you wish. However, if you are at work or at school/college downloading may be restricted. Review the policy to find out what you can and cannot download.

Digital rights

Digital rights protect the author/publisher of digital material against it being downloaded and copied illegally.

Consolidation

1   Describe three threats to your computer when working online.
2   Describe three actions you need to take to ensure that you work safely online.
3   Describe two threats to data security when working online.
4   Describe how to manage your personal details online.
5   Describe how to minimise internet security risks.
6   List two laws that keep you safe when using the internet.

Mini Assignment

In this Mini Assignment, you will practice all the skills you have learned throughout this chapter.

You have been asked by your supervisor to carry out a variety of tasks on the internet.

Task 1

1   Change the appearance of Internet Explorer® by changing the colours so they are different from the Microsoft Windows® colours.
2   Change the fonts to Verdana.
3   Delete the files that are currently held in the temporary folder.
4   Change the home page to **www.hodderplus.co.uk/itq.**
5   Check security settings so that all zones are reset to default level.

Task 2

1   Use a search engine to search for products/services available in the local community to encourage recycling. Use effective search criteria and bookmark the page.
2   Use a different search engine to see if you get different results.

3 Bookmark the page.
4 Search within the results to see if you get anything different.
5 Create a one-page document using text and image files to send to your supervisor.
6 Create a blog about recycling in your area.
7 Subscribe to an RSS feed about recycling.
8 Access a wiki website and find some information about recycling. Take a screen print before you start. Add some information you have found about recycling in your area. Save and close the wiki. Take another screen print to show the changes.
9 Carry out a search to find a recycling discussion forum in the UK. Follow links to various websites. Choose a website and register to access the discussion forum. Post a relevant message and take a screen print.
10 Present all your evidence to your supervisor.

Task 3

1 Carry out a search on Google to find an image-hosting internet website.
2 Choose a suitable image-hosting website. Register your details and then save photographs of your family and friends. Take a screen print to show you have done this.
3 Carry out a search to find a hosting program which will allow you to share your Microsoft Outlook® calendar free of charge. Follow the instructions on screen.
4 Take screen prints and save these to your folder.

Task 4

1 Describe inappropriate behaviour and grooming on the internet.
2 Describe the guidelines relating to health and safety.

3

Using Email

This unit will develop your knowledge, understanding and skills relating to the sending and receiving of emails. You will be able to use basic email software facilities to send and receive email messages with file attachments. You will be required to store email messages.

By working through the **Overview**, **Worked Examples**, **Tasks** and **Consolidations** in this chapter, you will demonstrate the skills required for Using Email Level 1:

ELEMENT The competent person will...	PERFORMANCE CRITERIA To demonstrate this competence they can...	KNOWLEDGE To demonstrate this competence they will also...
EML: A1 Use email software tools and techniques to compose and receive messages	A1.1 Use software tools to **compose and format email** messages A1.2 Attach files to email messages A1.3 **Send** email messages A1.5 Use an **address book** to store and retrieve contact information	A1.4 Identify how to **stay safe** and respect others when using email
EML: A2 Manage incoming email effectively	A2.1 Follow **guidelines and procedures** for using email A2.3 Read and respond to email messages appropriately A2.5 **Organise and store** email messages A2.6 Respond to common **email problems**	A2.2 Identify when and how to **respond** to email messages A2.4 Identify what messages to delete and when to do so

Step-by-step examples are provided to demonstrate what to do. These demonstrations are based on Microsoft® Outlook® 2003. Review the **Overview** in each section and then watch the demonstration in the **Worked Example** before commencing any **Tasks**.

If you are familiar with the topic covered, move on directly to the **Tasks**.

The **Worked Examples** relate to working in an HR department of a small business. The **Tasks** relate to working for a local animal sanctuary.

The **Consolidation** exercises relate to arranging a music festival.

A **Mini Assignment** is included at the end of each chapter, which can be used for additional practice.

Download the **Email Level 1** files from the Hodderplus website (www.hodderplus.co.uk/itq) before you start the unit, so that you can use them when working through this chapter.

A1 Use email software tools and techniques to send and receive messages

Microsoft® Outlook® is a personal information management (PIM) program that allows you to send/receive emails, maintain a calendar, add notes and maintain contacts. For the purpose of this unit you will be using Outlook® to send and receive messages. When you run Outlook® your window will look similar to that shown in Figure 3.1; however, this will depend on how your copy of Outlook® has been set up.

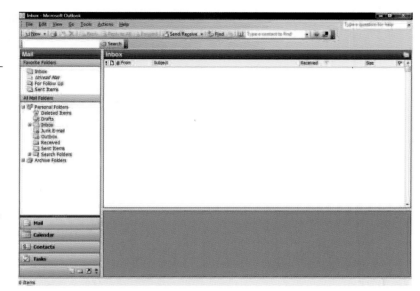

Figure 3.1

A1.1 Use software tools to compose and format email messages

The default settings for font size and colour are automatically used when you compose new messages. The default settings can be changed. You can format paragraphs by changing line spacing and you can check spelling before sending messages.

Watch the demonstration to see how this is done.

🖱 3.1 | Demonstration

Worked Example A1.1

1 Open Microsoft® Outlook®.
2 Click the **New Mail Message** button.
3 Type the email address **enquiries@itq2009.com**.
4 Also include your own email address – you need to send a copy of the message to yourself so you can complete the future tasks.
5 Type the subject **Administrator (A101)**.
6 Type the following message in the message box:

With reference to your email requesting a copy of the Recruitment pack (A101) for the role of administrator in our sales department, I have pleasure in enclosing the pack attached to this email.

Regards

HR Administrator

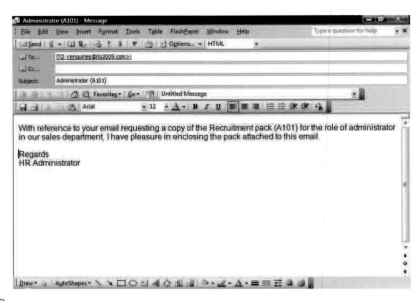

Figure 3.2

7 Highlight all of the message text and change this from the default setting to Tahoma font size 10.
8 Change the colour of the text 'HR Administrator' to blue.

Figure 3.3

Figure 3.4

9 Carry out a spell check by clicking the spell check button. Change any words that have been misspelt.
10 Click **File** and **Close**, and choose to save the changes to this message in the draft folder so that you can send it later.

Now it's your turn to have a go.

Task A1.1

1   Open Microsoft® Outlook®.
2   Click the **New Mail Message** button.
3   Type the email address **animalsanc@itq2009.com** and send a copy to yourself.
4   Type a subject – **Donations**.
5   Type your message in the message box:

Thank you for your recent donation with which you kindly agreed to adopt Daisy Duck for 3 months. Your donation is very welcome and we will send you regular updates to show how Daisy is getting on at the sanctuary. If you require any additional information or photos of Daisy, please do not hesitate to contact me.

Regards

Caroline

6   Highlight all of the message text and change it to Arial size 14.
7   Change the colour of the text 'Daisy Duck' to green.
8   Carry out a spell check by clicking the spell check button.
9   Click **File** and **Close**, and choose to save the changes to this message in the draft folder so that you can send it later.

A1.2   Attach files to email messages

Files can be 'attached' to an email message to be sent to other people. For example, you might want to send a colleague a copy of a document that you have drafted. Instead of printing it and handing it to them, you could attach it to an email and send it.

Watch the demonstration to see how this is done.

3.2   *Demonstration*

Worked Example A1.2

1   Click the drafts folder (where you stored a copy of the email you created in the previous worked example).
2   Double-click to open the email message.
3   Click the **Attach** button on the Outlook® toolbar.
4   Select the file **A101.doc** from your work area.

Figure 3.5

5 Click the **Insert** button.
6 Check that you have attached the correct file.
7 Save the email in the drafts folder once again.

Now you have a go.

Task A1.2

1 Click the drafts folder (in which you stored a copy of the email you created in the previous task).
2 Double-click to open the email message.
3 Click the **Attach** button on the Outlook® toolbar.
4 Select the file **Daisy.doc** from your work area.
5 Click the **Insert** button.
6 Check that you have attached the correct file.
7 Save the email in the drafts folder once again.

A1.3 Send and receive email messages

A1.3.1 Send email messages

Once you have composed an email message (including the recipient and subject), it is ready for you to send. You will need an Outlook® account (with a username and password) to be able to send and receive email messages. It is best to check with the administrator to make sure you have an account and find out what your login details are. When sending a message you must show To, Subject and message text. However, you can also copy other people into the message (this is covered later).

Watch the demonstration to see how this is done.

3.3   Demonstration

Worked Example A1.3.1

1 Having drafted your email, you need to check that the address, subject and the message text are correct before sending your message.
2 Double-click to open the **Administrator (A101)** message in the drafts folder. Check all the details are correct.
3 Click the **Send** button.
4 Click the **Send/Receive** button to check that the message has been sent correctly. You can also check the **Outbox** folder and **Sent Items** folder.

Now it's your turn to have a go.

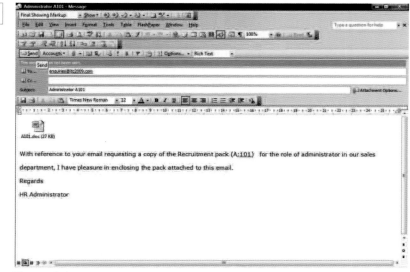

Figure 3.6

Task A1.3

1 Having drafted your email, you need to check that the address, subject and the message text are correct before sending your message.
2 Double-click to open the **Donations** message in the drafts folder. Check all the details are correct.
3 Click the **Send** button.

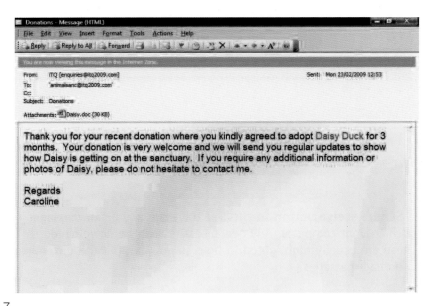

Figure 3.7

4 Click the **Send/Receive** button to check that the message has been sent correctly. Check the **Outbox** folder and **Sent Items** folder to show the message has been sent.

A1.3.2 Receive email messages

Now that you are able to send an email message you need to know how to receive email messages. When you click the **Send/Receive** button, Outlook® will download to the **Inbox** folder any new messages from your Internet Service Provider. You can download these automatically by clicking **Send/Receive Auto check every 15 minutes**.

Watch the demonstration to see how this is done.

3.4   Demonstration

Worked Example A1.3.2

1   Click the **Send/Receive** button to check if there are any email messages to be downloaded to your computer. Any new messages will be downloaded to the **Inbox** folder. These are usually highlighted in bold so you can tell the difference between read and unread messages.

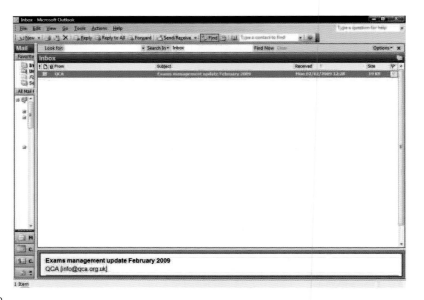

Figure 3.8

Now it's your turn to have a go.

Task A1.3.2

1   Click the **Send/Receive** button to check if there are any email messages to be downloaded to your computer. Any new messages will be downloaded to the **Inbox** folder. These are usually highlighted in bold so you can tell the difference between read and unread messages.

A1.3.3 Reply to an email

When you receive a message it may have been addressed just to you or it may have been also addressed to other people. When you are ready to reply to a message decide whether to reply to just the sender or to send a reply to everyone that was originally included in the message.

Figure 3.9 shows an example of **Reply** and Figure 3.10 shows an example of **Reply to All**.

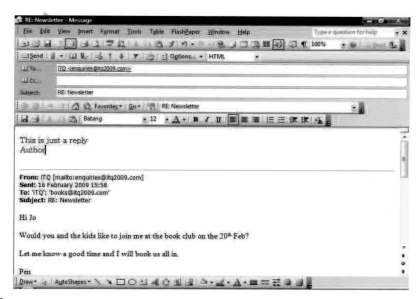

Figure 3.9

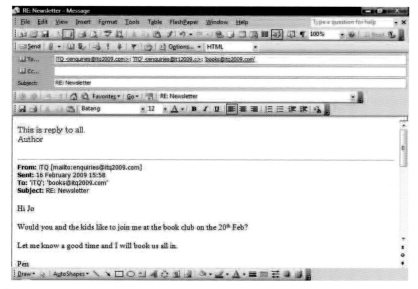

Figure 3.10

Watch the demonstration to see how this is done.

 **3.5** | **Demonstration**

Worked Example A1.3.3

1　Open the email **Administrator (A101)**.
2　Click to open the email message and send a reply.
3　Reply with the text shown in Figure 3.11.

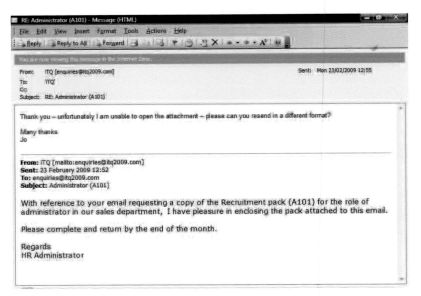

Figure 3.11

4   Click the **Send** button.

Now it's your turn to have a go.

Task A1.3.3

1 Open the email **Donations** and send a reply to the message.
2 Click to open the email message.
3 Reply with the text shown in Figure 3.12.

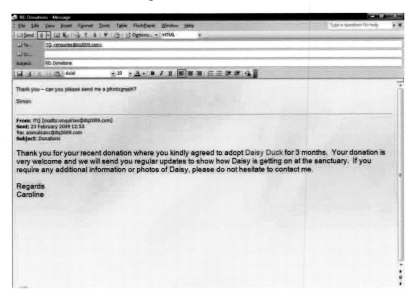

Figure 3.12

4 Click the **Send** button.

A1.3.4 Forward an email

Sometimes you might want to forward an email to someone else because you think it is important and they would benefit from reading it or because it was not for you anyway.

Watch the demonstration to see how this is done.

3.6 **Demonstration**

Worked Example A1.3.4

1 Open the email **Administrator (A101)**.
2 Forward it to **paul@itq2009.com**.
4 Type the message text:

I thought this might interest you – any questions, come back to me.

Hazel

5 Click the **Send** button.

Now it's your turn to have a go.

Task A1.3.4

1 Open the email **Donations**.
2 Forward it to **enquiries@itq2009.com**.
3 Type the message text:

I have made a donation for Daisy Duck – do you fancy contributing as well so that we can support the sanctuary for more than three months?

Karen

4 Click the **Send** button.

A1.3.5 Opening an email attachment

You sent a message in previous tasks that contained an email attachment. However, what do you do if you receive an email that contained an attachment? When you receive an email from someone who you do not know that contains an attachment, you should be careful about opening it. Viruses and other malware can be transmitted by file attachments to emails. The safest way to deal with emails with attachments that you receive from a sender unknown to you is not to open the attachments, but to save them to your computer. Make sure that you have virus-scan software installed first and that the file is scanned and clean before opening it.

Watch the demonstration to see how this is done.

3.7 **Demonstration**

Worked Example A1.3.5

1 Double-click to open the email **Administrator (A101)**.
2 Click **File → Save Attachments**, and then save the documents in your work area.
3 You can then open the saved attachment in the same way as you would open any file.

Now it's your turn to have a go.

Task A1.3.5
---

1   Open the email **Donations**.
2   Save the file to your work area.
3   Open the file from your work area.

A1.4   Identify how to stay safe and respect others using email

Staying safe when using email is very important. It is essential that none of your own personal information is disclosed to anyone when sending emails. Email is not a secure format to transmit information, for example you would not send a company your debit card details via email because it could be viewed by others.

When composing an email you should use appropriate text in the message and add an appropriate subject line so that the receiver knows what the message is about before they open it. While you might use text message abbreviations and emoticons in an email message to a friend, it is inappropriate to send them in a business email. You should choose an appropriate font, size and colour (for example, a message in capital letters could be viewed as shouting). Sending an email in capital letters using red font would certainly be inappropriate. Think about what you are saying in your emails before you send them. Once you have sent them they are very difficult to retrieve. You should re-read and spell check a message before sending it.

If you are sending information to several people think about using **cc** and **bcc**. The letters refer back to when typewriters were popular:

■ **'cc'** means carbon copy, which indicated that the typist had placed a sheet of carbon paper between two pieces of ordinary paper, so that two copies of the document were produced. Nowadays, when using email, 'cc' is used if you want to send a message to one person and send a copy of the message to someone else. For example, you might want to send some information to one person and let another person know that you have done this. Instead of sending two separate messages, the second person is 'copied in', using 'cc'.

■ **'bcc'** means blind carbon copy, which indicates that the first person you have addressed the message to does not know that you have sent a copy of the message to someone else. This enables you to hide the other person's email addresses from all the other people you are sending the message to. For example, if I send an email message to a group of learners and do not want to disclose their email addresses to the others in the group, I would send myself a message and 'bcc' everyone else into the message. This keeps everyone else's email addresses private and respects their confidentiality.

Before sending any message you should consider whether it is appropriate to reply to just the person you are sending the message to or whether you should send it to all.

Watch the demonstration to see how this is done.

3.8   *Demonstration*

Worked Example A1.4

1 Create a new message to **managers@itq2009.com**.
2 Click the **Cc...** button under the **To...** button in the message and type your own email address.
3 Add bcc to **paul@itq2009.com**.
4 Type the message shown in Figure 3.13.

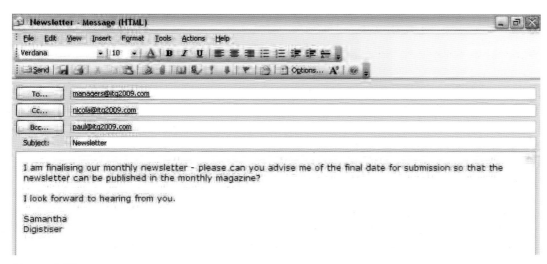

Figure 3.13

5 Click the **Send** button.

Now it's your turn to have a go.

Task A1.4

1 Create a new message to **publisher@itq2009.com**.
2 Click the **Cc...** button under the **To...** button in the message and send a copy of the message to yourself.
3 Add a bcc to **supervisor@itq2009.com**.
4 Type the message shown in Figure 3.14.

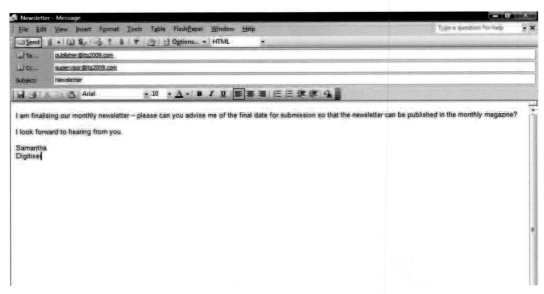

Figure 3.14

5 Click the **Send** button to send the message.

A1.5   Use an address book to store and retrieve contact information

A1.5.1 Use an address book

An address book (**Contacts** in Outlook®) stores the names, addresses, telephone numbers and email addresses of your contacts for easy retrieval. It is a good idea to store the email addresses of your contacts in the Microsoft® Outlook® address book so you can quickly look up contact details for future messages. Over time your contacts list can become very crowded so it is good practice to routinely delete any unwanted contact details.

Watch the demonstration to see how this is done.

3.9   *Demonstration*

Worked Example A1.5.1

1 Click the **Contacts group** button or click the **Address Book** button on the toolbar.
2 Click the **New** button.

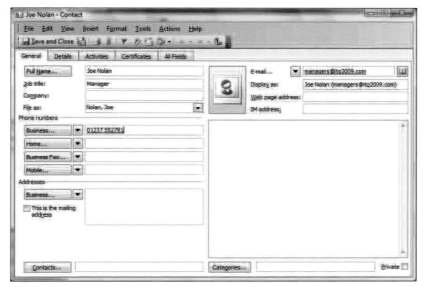

Figure 3.15

3 Type the details shown in Figure 3.15.
4 Click the **Save and Close** button.
5 To retrieve an email address from the address book, click **Mail → New → To...** to open the address book.
6 Select the names of the recipients, in this case **Joe Nolan**, and click the **To...** button.
7 Add the subject **Grievance hearing**.
8 Type the message shown in Figure 3.16.

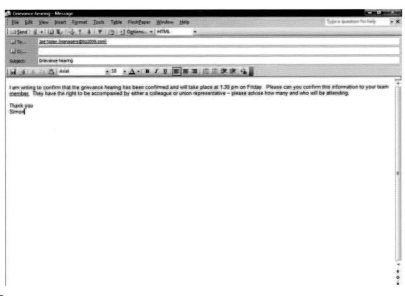

Figure 3.16

10 Send the message.

Now it's your turn to have a go.

Task A1.5.1

1 Click the **Contacts group** button or click the **Address Book** button on the toolbar.
2 Click the **New** button.
3 Type the details shown in Figure 3.17.

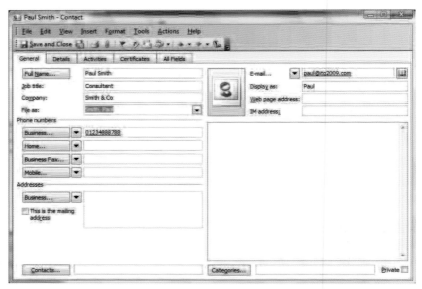

Figure 3.17

4 Click the **Save and Close** button.
5 To retrieve an email address from the address book, click **Mail** → **New** to create a new message.
6 Click the **To...** button to open the address book.
7 Select the names of the recipient, in this case **Paul Smith**, and click the **To...** button.
8 Type the message shown in Figure 3.18.

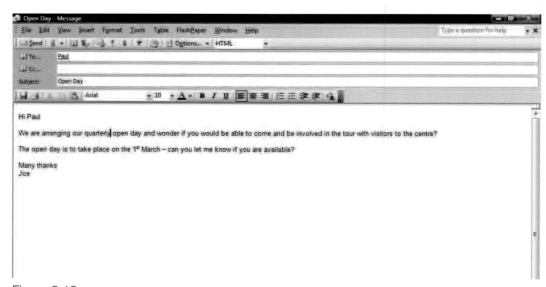

Figure 3.18

9 Send the message.

A1.5.2 Edit contacts

Once you have added contacts to your address book you may need to change or add to their details, for example, their name, address, telephone number or email address.

Watch the demonstration to see how this is done.

3.10 | **Demonstration**

> **Worked Example A1.5.2**

1 Click the **Contacts group** button or click the **Address Book** button on the toolbar.
2 Find the entry for **Joe Nolan**.
3 Add the address **51 Camberwell Square, Coventry, CP1 4PQ**.
4 Save and close the changes.

Now it's your turn to have a go.

> **Task A1.5.2**

1 Click the **Contacts group** button or click the **Address Book** button on the toolbar.
2 Find the entry for **Paul Smith**.
3 Add the address **21 Richmond Court, Bishop Auckland, Co Durham, DL15 9QQ**.
4 Save and close the changes.

A1.5.3 Creating a distribution list

The Contacts list in Outlook® lets you create a distribution list. A distribution list is a list of email contacts that are grouped together so that you can easily locate their details or you can email the group without having to type in each group member's individual email address. For example, I could set up a distribution list containing the contact details of all my learners for a particular class. I could then select the distribution list when I want to send an email to the whole class rather than individually having to select them from the address book.

Watch the demonstration to see how this is done.

3.11 | **Demonstration**

> **Worked Example A1.5.3**

1 Click the **Contacts group** button or click the **Address Book** button on the toolbar.
2 Click **New → Distribution list**.
3 Add the name **wedpmstudents**.
4 Click **Select Members → OK → Save and Close**.
5 Check that the distribution lists works by creating the message in Figure 3.20.

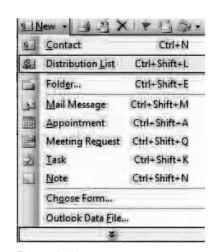

Figure 3.19

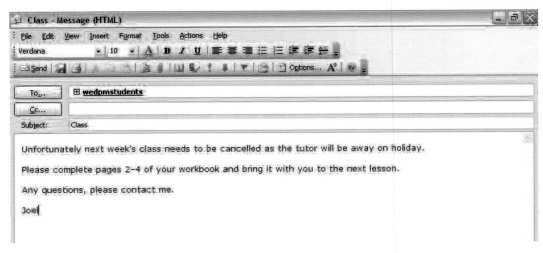

Figure 3.20

6   Send the message.

Now it's your turn to have a go.

Task A1.5.3

1   Click the **Contacts group** button or click the **Address Book** button on the toolbar.
2   Click **New** → **Distribution list** → Add the name **Adoptions** → Select **Members** →
    OK → **Save and close**.
3   Check that the distribution list works by creating the following message:

*Thank you for your recent donation to adopt an animal. I attach the latest copy of our
quarterly newsletter which gives information on our new additions to the sanctuary.*

The Editor

4   Attach the file **newsletter.doc**.
5   Format the message so that it uses a different font, size and colour of text from the
    default settings (Figure 3.21).

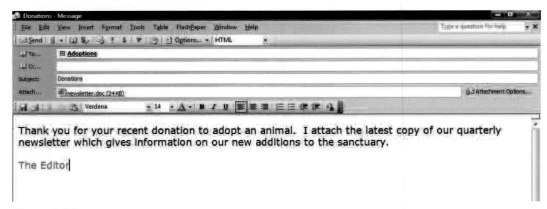

Figure 3.21

6   Send the message.

Consolidation

You have been asked to send and receive emails to promote the launch of a musical festival.

1 Compose an email message to **editor@itq2009.com**.
2 Add the subject **Durham Musical Festival**.
3 Type the message text as follows:

Thank you for your enquiry about the Durham Music Festival which will take place at the Cricket Club in June next year. Preliminary arrangements have been agreed, however once we receive formal confirmation I will send you further details.

Thank you

The Editor

4 Attach the file **music.doc** to your message.
5 Send a copy of the message to yourself by using **cc** so that you will receive a copy of the message to use in later tasks.
6 You should now have received a copy of the message that you sent yourself with the file attachment.
7 Open the file **music.doc** and save this to your file area as **festival.doc**.
8 Create a distribution list which will hold all the email addresses of those people that have requested information relating to the festival. Call the distribution list **durhamfestival** and add the following email addresses:
Joe Vickers joe@itq2009.com
Sophie Totten sophie@itq2009.com
9 Create an email to the members of the 'durhamfestival' distribution list and give it the subject heading **latest performers**.
10 Type the following message:

We are pleased to announce that Quiet Boys *will be performing at the Durham Festival in June next year.*

Watch this space for further announcements.

The Editor

11 Format the message using appropriate font style, size and colour of text.
12 Send the message.

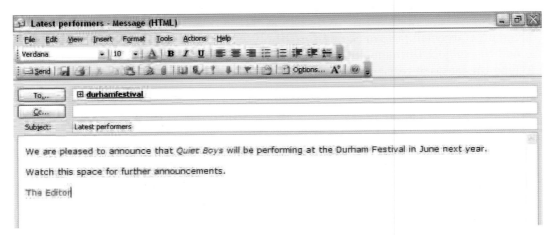

Figure 3.22

A2 Manage incoming emails effectively

The **Inbox** folder will start to fill up once you send and receive emails regularly. One way of organising messages is by creating new folders to store them, for example you may decide that all of your emails relating to **iTQ** should be stored in a folder named iTQ rather than in the **Inbox** folder.

A2.1   Follow guidelines and procedures for using email

You may have to follow set procedures at work when using email, for example you may only be able to send private emails at lunchtime or you may be restricted to 30 minutes' access per day. Some organisations' email servers block certain words that are not allowed for use in emails. If these words are used, then they are automatically picked up by the server and the employer might want to discuss their use with the employee. Ask your employer about the regulations that apply to you at work when sending and receiving emails and ask for a copy of the guidelines.

Another procedure to follow is copyright. This means that you cannot copy and paste information from the internet or take someone else's work and use it as your own. This includes text, graphics, sounds and video files. If you do want to use any copyright material you should obtain the author's permission first.

Email netiquette is 'network etiquette' and it means good practice on how you should communicate with others when using email. You should communicate effectively with others while using email and you should not overuse capital letters and red fonts or send spam or chain mail messages which can clog up the email system.

Each email account has a unique combination of username and password for login security reasons. This means that only the authorised user can access their email messages. You should review your password regularly to ensure that other users have not managed to work out what your password is or hacked into your account.

A2.2 Identify when and how to respond to email messages

A2.3 Read and respond to email messages appropriately

You need to decide when and how to respond to messages. Some users log on to their email account twice a day – once in the morning and once in the afternoon. Some users have a day a week where they do not answer emails because they find it interrupts their work, however other users respond immediately and have their account open all the time. You need to adopt an approach that is best for you – replying at least once a day is good practice and if you are out of the office you should ask your supervisor about adding an out-of-office reply so that the sender knows you are unavailable to reply in person. It is important that you very carefully read and re-read both sent and received messages to ensure that the message conveyed is that intended and that any message that is received is understood; sometimes you can very quickly read an email message that has been received but completely misunderstand the content.

You may need to allocate time to find information before you are able to respond to some emails. This time might be needed to carry out research on the internet or to get files from another team member. When sending and replying to emails, you need to decide carefully whether or not to copy anyone else into your reply. Sometimes you might decide to send a copy of an email to yourself so that you can file it in a specific folder instead of keeping it in the sent folder; however, you may also decide to send a copy of a message to your line manager to keep them informed of your progress. Emails, like any form of business correspondence, should be carefully planned and drafted, checked and double-checked before being sent.

A2.4 Identify what messages to delete and when to do so

If you receive lots of email messages your inbox will soon fill up and you may not be able to receive new messages until you have deleted some old ones. Sometimes a message will appear in Outlook® prompting you to delete old messages.

It is good practice to organise messages into folders and delete them regularly to prevent the inbox becoming too full, and to plan how often you will do this. Another way to maintain an efficient inbox is to archive email messages – have a word with your supervisor to find out how to do this.

Watch the demonstration to see how this is done.

3.12 Demonstration

> **Worked Example A2.4**

1 Highlight the email **Administrator (A101)** in the Inbox folder.
2 Press the **Delete** key on your keyboard.
3 Your message is deleted and will have been placed in the **Deleted Items** folder.
4 Click to open the **Deleted Items** folder to check that the message you deleted has been placed there.

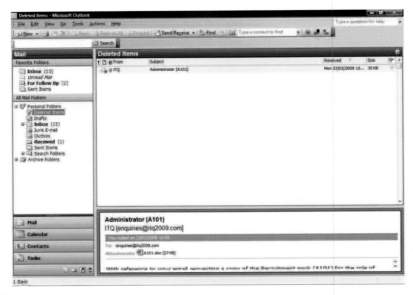

Figure 3.23

5   Right click the file in the **Deleted Items** folder and select **Empty "Deleted Items" Folder** to permanently remove the message.

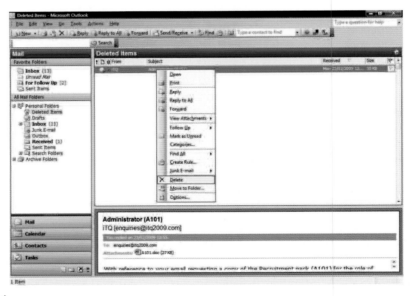

Figure 3.24

Task A2.4

1   Click the email **Donations**.
2   Press the **Delete** key on your keyboard.
3   Open the **Deleted Items** folder.
4   Delete the message from the **Deleted Items** folder.

A2.5 Organise and store email messages

One way to organise emails is to create folders and sub-folders. You can then move the messages from your inbox. You can also set your computer to back up your emails regularly. This backup should be to a removable storage device. For example, you can set your outlook folder to back up three times a week to a removable storage device which can be retrieved if needed. In addition to emails you should also back up your address list or contacts so that if something does happen to your computer you can retrieve this information.

Watch the demonstration to see how this is done.

 3.13 | **Demonstration**

> Worked Example A2.5

1 Click **File → New → Folder....**
3 Type the name **iTQ** for the new folder. This new folder will be created as a sub-folder of the inbox.
4 Click **OK.**
5 Move the messages you have received about your iTQ by dragging and dropping them into the new folder.

Now it's your turn to have a go.

> Task A2.5

1 Click the **Personal Folders** folder in the Microsoft® Outlook® Folder List.
2 Click **File → New → Folder....**
3 Type the name **iTQ** for the new folder.
4 Click **OK.**
5 Move the messages you have received about your iTQ by dragging and dropping them into the new folder.

Figure 3.25

A2.6 Respond appropriately to common email problems

Email mailboxes are set up to only send and receive messages of up to a certain size, for example some email accounts do not allow messages to be sent or received that are over 5 MB. This means that if you are trying to send messages and any files over 5 MB in size the file may have to be compressed. If, after compressing the email with its attachments, the file size is still over 5 MB then you may have to find another way to send the message.

Other problems with email include spam, junk, chain-mails and phishing.

Spam is an unsolicited email that is sent to numerous email addresses. Spam messages are commonly advertisements for products or services. Sending the same message to lots of users is very cheap for the sender and some companies sell email addresses to spammers.

A form of spam is junk email from unknown senders who have obtained your email address to send you inappropriate messages. Microsoft® Outlook® and some Internet Service

Providers allow junk and spam emails to be moved into a dedicated folder. We will not be covering this in the Level 1 unit, but you may wish to find out how to do this to prevent viewing inappropriate messages.

A chain-mail message asks you to forward it to, say, 10 friends, with some form of future prosperity often being the promised reward. These messages clog up your inbox and should be deleted.

Phishing is where someone tries to acquire personal, sensitive information (e.g. usernames, credit card details, etc.) via email as they masquerade as a trustworthy company. For example, you might receive an email from what looks like your bank asking you to update your internet account login details. However, these are fraudulent emails because banks do not email their customers for these details. If you were to click the link in the email and log in the sender would be able to obtain your login details. It is important that you do not click any of the links in these emails and enter any details because the user will then will be able to log in as you.

Mini Assignment

In this Mini Assignment you will practise all the skills you have learnt throughout this chapter.

1 Compose a new message to the editor at the Animal Sanctuary. His email address is **editor@itq2009.com**.
2 Add your own email address in the cc field.
3 Add the subject **Newsletter**.
4 Carry out research on the internet and save a copy of an image of Girls Aloud, making sure you comply with any copyright legislation.
5 Type in the following text using suitable font, size and colour and netiquette guidelines:

I have been advised today that Girls Aloud *have agreed to perform at the Festival. They will perform a number of their latest songs and be on stage for about 40 minutes.*

I attach an image I have downloaded from the internet – before we produce this in the newsletter please can you contact artist@itq2009.com to ask for permission to reproduce this?

Any questions, please do not hesitate to contact me.

6 Add suitable closing text and attach the image file.
7 Send the message.
8 Create a new folder named **Festival**.
8 Move a copy of the message you sent to yourself into the new folder.
9 Delete any unwanted messages, including spam messages.
10 Use help to find information on how to deal with spam messages.
11 Save and close all open files.

Level 2

This unit will develop your knowledge, understanding and skills relating to the use of email. At Level 2 you will use email features including automating responses, using auto-signature, auto-archiving messages and setting message filters. It is expected that some of the messages you will send, receive and store will be unfamiliar.

By working through the **Overview**, **Worked Examples**, **Tasks** and **Consolidations** in this chapter, you will demonstrate the skills required for Using Email Level 2:

ELEMENT The competent person will...	PERFORMANCE CRITERIA To demonstrate this competence they can...	KNOWLEDGE To demonstrate this competence they will also...
EML: B1 Use email software tools and techniques to send and receive messages	B1.1 Select and use software tools to compose and format email messages, including with attachments B1.3 Send email messages to individual groups B1.5 Use an address book to organise contact information	B1.2 Determine the message size and how it can be reduced B1.4 Determine how to stay safe and respect others when using email
EML: B2 Manage incoming email effectively	B2.1 Follow guidelines and procedures for using email B2.2 Read and respond to email messages appropriately B2.3 Use email software tools and techniques to automate responses B2.5 Organise, store and archive email messages effectively B2.6 Respond appropriately to email problems	B2.4 Describe how to archive email messages, including attachments

Step-by-step examples are provided to demonstrate what to do. These demonstrations are based on Microsoft® Outlook® 2003. Review the **Overview** in each section and then watch the demonstration in the **Worked Example** before commencing any **Tasks**.

If you are familiar with the topic covered, move on directly to the **Tasks**.

The **Worked Examples** relate to a bookshop. The **Tasks** relate to a sports club. **Consolidation** exercises, provided throughout the chapter for extra practice, relate to an online music store.

A **Mini Assignment** is included at the end of each chapter which can be used for additional practice.

Download the Email Level 2 files from the Hodderplus website (www.hodderplus.co.uk) before you start the unit, so that you can use them when working through this chapter.

B1 Use email software tools and techniques to send and receive messages

Microsoft® Outlook® is a personal information management (PIM) program that allows you to send/receive emails, maintain a calendar, add notes and maintain contacts. For the purpose of this unit you will be using Outlook® to send and receive messages. When you run Outlook® your window will look similar to that shown in Figure 3.28; however, this will depend on how your copy of Outlook® has been set up.

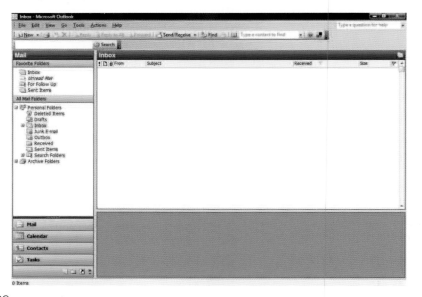

Figure 3.28

B1.1 Select and use software tools to compose and format email messages, including with attachments

When you open Outlook® you can compose and format email messages using the default settings or you can choose to format the text in your email message by changing the font, size and colour. You can also format paragraphs and carry out a spell check to ensure that your message is spelt correctly before sending.

B1.1.1 Formatting email text characters

When composing an email message you will use the 'default' settings as shown in Figure 3.29.

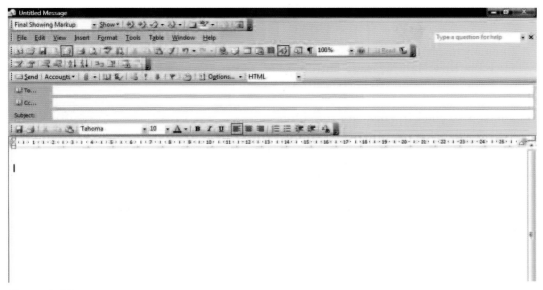

Figure 3.29

Watch the demonstration to see how this is done.

3.14 | Demonstration

Worked Example B1.1.1

1 Open Microsoft® Outlook®.
2 Click the **New Mail Message** button.
3 Type the email address **books@itq2009.com**.
4 Also include your own email address – you need to send a copy of the message to yourself so you can complete the future tasks.
5 Type the subject **Web Design**.
6 Type the message in the message box:

With reference to your online booking to reserve the above textbook, I confirm that we have now managed to obtain the latest edition from the publishers.

Please arrange to contact us to pay for and collect your book at your earliest convenience.

Regards

Administrator

7 Highlight all of the message text and change this from the default setting to Verdana font size 11.
8 Change the colour of the text 'Administrator' to blue.
9 Carry out a spell check by clicking the spell check button and correct any errors.
10 Send the message.

Now it's your turn to have a go.

> **Task B1.1.1**
>
> 1 Open Microsoft® Outlook®.
> 2 Click the **New Mail Message** button.
> 3 Type the email address **sports@itq2009.com**.
> 4 Also include your own email address – you need to send a copy of the message to yourself so you can complete the future tasks.
> 5 Type a subject **Here come the clowns!**
> 6 Type your message in the message box:
>
> *Parents/Carers/Governors*
>
> *I am pleased to let you know that the school sports club will be holding a gymnastics competition on 5th February at 9.30 a.m. Six local schools, including our Year 1 children, will be competing. Our theme is 'Here come the clowns!' Tickets are priced at £2.50 each and these will be limited to two per family in the first instance. Please contact the office to obtain your tickets.*
>
> *We look forward to seeing you and supporting the school.*
>
> *Regards*
>
> *Caroline*
>
> 7 Highlight all of the message text and change this to Arial font size 14.
> 8 Change the colour of the message text 'Here come the clowns' to green.
> 9 Carry out a spell check by clicking the spell check button and correct any errors.
> 10 Send the message.

B1.1.2 Formatting email paragraphs

You will now format the paragraphs by aligning the text.

The following are examples of text that have been aligned differently:

> This text has been left aligned – this means that lines start at the left margin and have a ragged right margin.
>
> > This text has been right aligned – this means that lines start at the right margin and have a ragged left margin.
>
> > This text has been centred – this means that lines are centred horizontally across the page.
>
> This text has been justified – this means that the text is aligned to both the left and right margins.
>
> Different width spaces are added between words so that the lines begin and end at the margins.
>
> • Bullets and numbering can be added to text to enhance the readability of the message.

Figure 3.30 shows bullets and numbering being used in an email message:

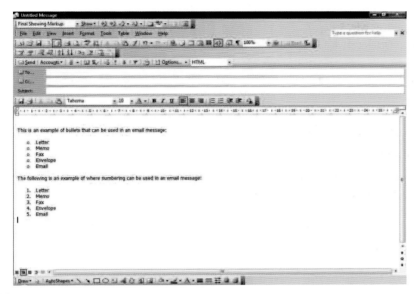

Figure 3.30

Watch the demonstration to see how this is done.

3.15 **Demonstration**

> **Worked Example B1.1.2**

1   Create a new email and address it to **books@itq2009.com**.
2   Also include your own email address – you need to send a copy of the message to yourself so you can complete the future tasks.
3   Compose the following email with the subject **Newsletter**.

Welcome to our monthly newsletter!

We have had a busy month and are pleased to announce that the following children's books are now available on loan:

- *I Hate School*
- *Bunny Cakes*
- *A Squash and a Squeeze*
- *Josie Smith in Summer*
- *Rosie's babies*

To change the bullets:

1   Click **Format** → **Bullets and Numbering...** → **Customize** → **Character**
2   Click **Customize...**
3   Click **Character...** and then choose a symbol.

If you wish to pre-order any of these books, please complete the online form.

We are offering our young readers a half-term special! One of our local authors is to visit us and is offering reading workshops at the following times on Thursday 20th:

1   *9.30–10.00 a.m.*
2   *10.30–11.00 a.m.*

3   *1.30–2.00 p.m.*
4   *2.30–3.00 p.m.*

Please sign up at the bookshop.

Regards

4   Send the email.

Figure 3.31

Now it's your turn to have a go.

Task B1.1.2

1   Create a new email and address it to **sports@itq2009.com**.
2   Also include your own email address – you need to send a copy of the message to yourself so you can complete the future tasks.
3   Compose the following email:

Trampolining for all

Our sports club has recently acquired a professional trampoline and we are offering the following classes:

■   *Beginners*
■   *Summer workshops*
■   *Elite squad*

Ring us for details of each class so we can advise you where to start!

At various times of the year we will be entering students for different trampolining competitions. The following categories are available:

1   *Under 9*
2   *Under 11*
3   *Under 13*

4   *Under 15*
5   *Under 18*
6   *Over 18*

Please sign up at the sports hall entrance.

Any questions, please do not hesitate to contact us.

Regards

4 Spell check the message and correct any errors.

You can set automatic spelling so that every message is checked before you send it.

1 Click **Tools** → **Options**.
2 Click the **Spelling** tab and tick **Always check spelling before sending**.
3 Click **Apply** → **OK**.
5 Send the email.

B1.1.3 Format options

There are three format options within Outlook®:

■ Rich text format (rtf) – text will include formatting such as bullets and alignment (Figure 3.32).

Figure 3.32

■ Plain text – text does not show any formatting such as colour and alignment (Figure 3.33).

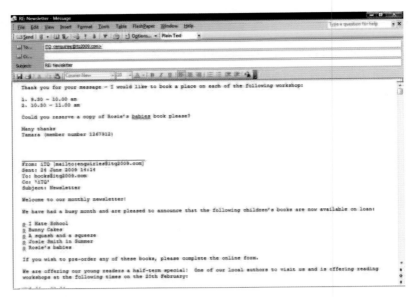

Figure 3.33

■ Hypertext mark-up language (HTML) – this is the default setting. This format supports numbering, bullets, alignment, text colours, backgrounds, pictures, sound, movies and hyperlinks (Figure 3.34).

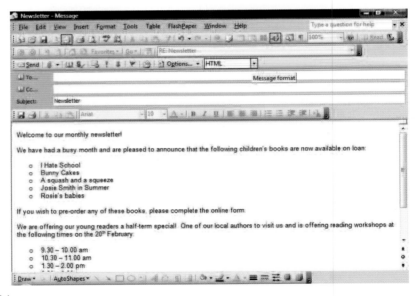

Figure 3.34

Some email servers do not allow messages that include background images and therefore the format may need to be changed to plain text. You can change the format of a new message or one that you are replying to.

Watch the demonstration to see how this is done.

3.16 Demonstration

Worked Example B1.1.3

1   Compose an email to **books@itq2009.com**.

2 Also include your own email address – you need to send a copy of the message to yourself so you can complete the future tasks.
3 Change the format to **Plain Text** by clicking the **Message Format** drop-down box.
4 Type the subject **Book Club**.

The Book Club will be closed for the next two weeks for refurbishment. We will open again at 10 a.m. on 25ᵗʰ March and the Mayor will open the new facilities.

We look forward to seeing you there.

Regards

Administrator

5 Send the message.

The default settings of how messages are replied to can be changed. For example, if you always want to display messages in plain text:

1 Click **Tools → Options…**
2 Select the **Message Format** drop-down tab and change this to **Plain Text**.
3 Click **Apply → OK**.

This will now change the default setting for outgoing mail.

Now it's your turn to have a go.

Task B1.1.3

1 Compose an email to **sports@itq2009.com**.
2 Also include your own email address – you need to send a copy of the message to yourself so you can complete the future tasks.
3 Type the subject **Trampoline Club**.
4 Change the format of the message to RTF by clicking the **Message Format** drop-down menu and changing the default setting.
5 Type the message:

The trampoline club is having a week away at the Dunfermline competition and therefore there will be no classes for the next five days.

The trampolines will be available for use during this time – please book at reception.

Regards

6 Send the message.

B1.1.4 Saving draft emails

An email can be composed and saved in the drafts folder until you are ready to send it. This is useful if further information is required or if the time to send the message is not due. This is covered in the Level one section of this chapter.

B1.1.5 Email features

Various features can be added to composed messages. For example, an automatic signature or a background image/colour can be applied automatically to every message. The page setup of messages can be changed and you can use Outlook® offline.

An email signature is a block of text that is added automatically to each message. The signature can be any text (e.g. a name, job title, telephone number, etc.). A signature could also be message text that is sent with every message, for example text which asks users not to print the email in order to save paper.

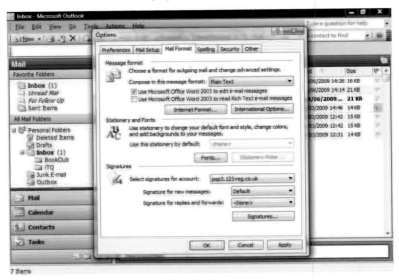

Figure 3.35

Adding a background image or colour scheme to a message can enhance its appearance. Email background images could be a company logo, block colour or suitable images that have been selected by the user from clipart or from their own images store. Before adding any background image you should consider the appropriateness of using it in a business context – sometimes just having a plain background fill colour is more appropriate.

The page setup of messages can be changed by altering the paper size, margins and page orientation. Default settings are A4 paper, portrait orientation with 2.54 cm left and right margins and 3.17 cm top and bottom margins.

You can use Outlook® to work offline, for example when travelling if there is no internet connection. You can work offline and draft emails to send all together at a later time. This is also useful if you have to pay each time you connect to the internet or if you are allowed access to it only at certain times of the day. Emails are stored in your **Outbox** (or **Drafts**) folder until you connect to work online.

Watch the demonstration to see how this is done.

3.17   *Demonstration*

Worked Example B1.1.5

1 Change the setting to work offline by clicking **File** → **Work Offline**. A message in the bottom right-hand corner of the screen shows 'offline'.
2 Create an email signature by clicking **Tools** → **Options...** and selecting the **Mail Format** tab.
3 Click **Signatures...** → **New...**
4 Type the name **default** → **Next** and type:

Administrator

Tel: 01234 889781

Opening hours – 7 days a week 10 00–16 00 hours

5 Format the signature text with a suitable font and colour.
6 Click **OK** → **Apply** → **OK**.
7 Check that the signature works by starting a new message. The signature should be displayed.
8 Add a background image to your messages. Click **Tools** → **Options...** and then select the **Mail Format** tab.
9 In the **Stationery and Fonts** section, click **Stationery Picker...** and then choose a style from the displayed list.
10 Click **OK** → **Apply** → **OK**.
11 Create a new message and check that the background colour and signature are displayed.
12 In the To field add the address: **books@itq2009.com**.
13 Also include your own email address – you need to send a copy of the message to yourself so you can complete the future tasks.
14 Change the page setup to **A4 Landscape** and change all the margins to **2.5 cm**.
15 Add the subject **Test**.
16 Type the text **This is a test message**.

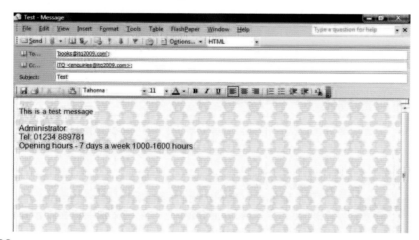

Figure 3.36

17 Change Outlook® to work online.
18 Send the message.

Get more stationery from Microsoft® Office Online

1 Click **Select from Microsoft Online** → OK.
2 Select one of the backgrounds.

Task B1.1.5

---

1 Change Outlook® to work offline.
2 Create the following email signature:

Coach

Tel: 01234 889781

Remember competition entries to be in by Friday 31st!

3 Choose suitable fonts and colours for the signature.
4 Add a background from the **Stationery Picker**.
5 Set up the page to be **A4 Landscape**.

B1.1.6 Sound, movies and hyperlinks

Sound, movies and hyperlinks can be added to messages composed and sent using Outlook®.

Sound and movies can be added to an email; however, being able to play the sound or video will depend on the recipient's computer's email settings. Always consider whether or not it is appropriate to add sound or video to any message because they will increase the message file size and also have security implications for the recipient. Sound and video, unless applicable to the content of the message, can be very annoying and detract from the message's purpose. Their use is rarely applicable in any business email.

Hyperlinks to web pages are a useful way of directing users to further information related to a message's content, however some email servers block this information because the links may pose security risks.

Watch the demonstration to see how this is done.

🖱 3.18 Demonstration

> **Worked Example B1.1.6**

1 Create a new message with the subject **Books**.
2 Add the message text:

With reference to my recent order, please can you let me know when the order will be dispatched.

To add a sound:

Figure 3.37   Sound

3 Click **View** → **Toolbars** → **Web Tools** → **Sound**.
4 Browse and choose **Sound** → In **Look**, select **Infinite** → click **OK**. To add a movie:
5 Click **View** → **Toolbars** → **Web Tools** → **Movie**.
6 Browse and choose **File** → In **Playback** options, **Look**, choose **Infinite** → Click **OK**.

To add a hyperlink:

7 Type **Visit the website www.itq2009.com** at the bottom of the message.
8 In the To field add the address: **Tamara@itq2009.com** and send the message.

> **Task B1.1.6**

1 Create a new message to **Stephen@itq2009.com** with the subject **Sports equipment**.
2 Add the message text:

We have managed to obtain some local funding and are looking to invest in some new gymnastic equipment – please can you send to me a copy of your latest brochure?

3 Add a sound file.

4   Add a movie file.
5   Add a hyperlink to **www.itq2009.com** by clicking on the **Insert** menu item. Click **Hyperlink** to open the **Insert Hyperlink** dialogue box and type in **www.itq2009.com**. Click **OK**.
6   Send the message.

Priority

Emails can be set as high or low priority – this is a useful tool if you want to make a message important or if you need a speedy reply. High priority shows a red exclamation mark on messages, so that the recipient can see that this email is important. Low priority is shown as a blue arrow pointing down. To set priority, click on the red exclamation mark or the blue down arrow.

Consolidation

1   Set the background colour for all messages to **Bears** (if this is not available choose another suitable background).
2   Create an email signature:

Customer Support

Tel: 01234 1234569

3   Type the recipients as **Chris@itq2009.com** and yourself.
4   Type the subject **Rentals**.
5   Type the message text:

With reference to your recent rental, it would appear that you have not returned the DVD within the 7-day rental period.

Please contact us and let us know when it will be returned.

I attach an invoice showing the increased fee.

Regards

6   Format the message text using appropriate font size, style and colour.
7   Add a hyperlink to **www.itq2009.com**.
8   Attach the compressed file **invoice.doc**.
9   Send the message.

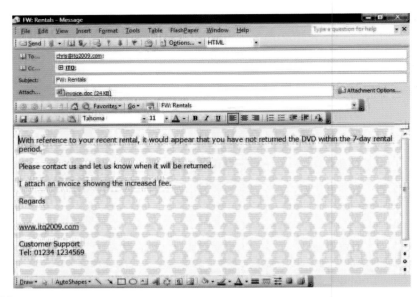

Figure 3.38

B1.2　Determine the message size and how it can be reduced

It is important that you are aware that organisations usually set a limit on the maximum message size that can be sent and received through their mail servers. For example, some email accounts might not allow messages over 5 MB to be sent, or some organisations might not allow messages to be received which are over 4 MB. If the limitations are exceeded, then you will receive a message saying that the email could not be delivered. Consequently, you will needed to find an alternative way of sending very large files.

Find out what the maximum size of messages to be sent and received are within your organisation.

To find out the size of a sent message, open the **Rentals** email from the sent folder and click **File** → **Properties**, and the message size will be displayed.

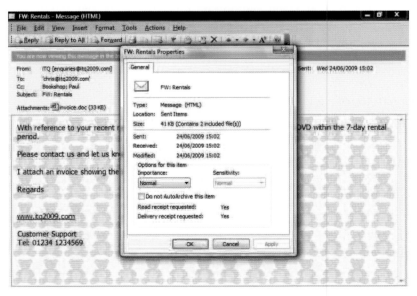

Figure 3.39

Another way to reduce the size of email attachments is to compress them using a compression utility such as **WinZip®**.

Watch the demonstration to see how this is done.

3.19 | **Demonstration**

Worked Example B1.2

1 Open the message in your **Sent Folder** with the subject **Web Design**.
2 Click **File → Properties** and check the size of the email. Close the email.
3 Compose a new message to be sent to **books@itq2009.com** and to yourself.
4 Type the subject **Book Order 1001**.
5 Type the message:

Thank you for your recent order. I confirm this has been dispatched and you should receive your book within the next five days. Attached is remittance advice showing the account paid in full.

6 Attach the compressed file **remittance1001.zip** from your file area.
7 Send the message.

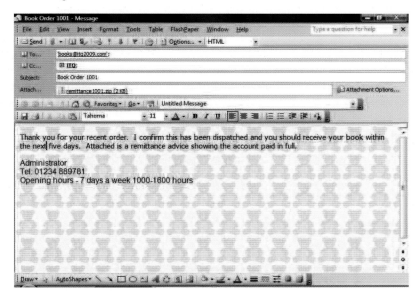

Figure 3.40

Now it's your turn to have a go.

Task B1.2

1 Compose a new message to be sent to **sports@itq2009.com** and to yourself.
2 Type the subject **Elite Squad**.
3 Type the text:

Thank you for your interest in the Elite Squad. I attach some information about training and uniforms.

If you require any further information, please contact me.

Regards

5   Attach the compressed file **Elite.zip**.
6   Send the message.

B1.3   Send and receive email messages

When you send an email message you must as a minimum include information in the **To:** and **Subject** fields as well as the message text itself. It is not business-like and it is considered bad practice to leave out either the subject or message text. Sometimes you might send an email either to yourself or to someone else you work with. You need to be careful about sending copies of email messages to other people so as not to overload their inbox with email messages that are irrelevant to them.

B1.3.1 Receive email attachments

3.20   *Demonstration*

> **Worked Example B1.3.1**

1   Open the received message with the subject **Book Order 1001**.
2   Save the compressed file to your file area.
3   Uncompress the file attachment in your file area and open the file.
4   Close all open files.

B1.3.2 Replying with history

There are different ways to reply to an email. For example, clicking **Reply** will send a reply only to the sender of the original message. Click **Reply to all** sends a reply to everyone who was originally included as recipients of the message.

You can forward a received email to a recipient not on the original recipient list. For example, you may have received an email message that is not for you, but you know who it was originally intended for, or you might need to ask a colleague's advice before you reply. It is good practice to include the reason why you are forwarding a message.

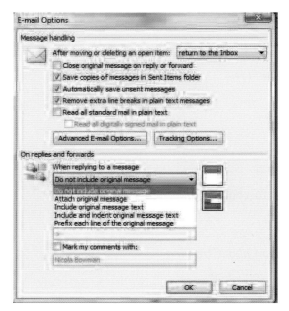

Figure 3.41

After a few emails have been exchanged on a topic, it might become difficult to remember what was typed in the previous messages. You can include in your reply all the related emails (the 'history trail'), up to the latest message. Some people find tracking messages useful, but others do not. There is an option in Outlook® to set whether or not the related original messages are included in any replies.

Watch the demonstration to see how this is done.

3.21   *Demonstration*

> **Worked Example B1.3.2**

1   Click **Tools** from the main menu → **Options** → **Preferences** tab.
2   Click the **Email Options**... button (see Figure 3.41).
3   In the **On replies and forwards** section, select how you want Outlook® to deal with history trails by selecting the option from the down-down lists.

B1.3.3 Reply and forward email

1 Open the email with the subject **Newsletter**.
2 Click **Reply to All**.

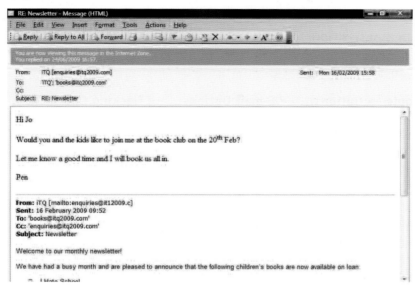

Figure 3.42

3 Type the following message text:

Hi Jo

Would you and the kids like to join me at the book club on the 20th Feb?

Let me know a good time and I will book us all in.

Pen

4 Send the message.
5 Forward the message **Book Club** to **enquiries@itq2009.com**.
6 Type the text:

Have you seen this? It might be worth looking at?

Al

7 Send the message.

Now it's your turn to have a go.

1 Forward the message **Trampoline Club** to **headteacher@itq2009.com**.
2 Type the text:

It would be good for the Year 1 children to take part in this. What do you think?

Nat

3 Send the message.

B1.3.4 Determining receipt of an email

You can set up Outlook® so that a read or delivery receipt is requested when messages are read or received, respectively, by the recipient. The delivered/read status can be set to automatically send back to the sender thereby giving an obvious indication of the status of the message.

Watch the demonstration to see how this is done.

3.22 | *Demonstration*

Worked Example B1.3.4

1   Click **Tools** → **Options...** → **E-mail Options...** → **Tracking Options...**
2   Click one of the following radio buttons: **Always send a response, Never send a response or Ask me before sending a response.**
3   Save and close any open windows.

Task B1.3.4

1   Set your copy of Outlook® to always send a read and a delivery receipt.
2   Save and close the settings.

B1.3.5 Adding a flag

You can add a flag to messages to identify them for following up. A flag on a message gives a visual reminder of the message status, for example a message flagged as 'follow up' indicates that it requires further action. Messages could also be flagged and rules added so that important messages have, for example, a blue flag – these can also be automatically transferred to a designated folder. It could be that you set priority flags on all messages sent to you from your line manager.

3.23 | *Demonstration*

Worked Example B1.3.5

1   Open the message **Book Order 1001** and click the **Follow Up** button.

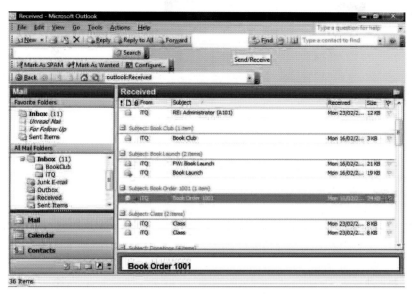

Figure 3.43

2 Click **Flag** → **Flag to: Follow up** → **Flag colour: Blue** → **Due by: 31 May** → **OK**.

You should now see a blue flag at the end of the email message title.

Now it's your turn to have a go.

> **Task B1.3.5**

1 Select the message **Here come the Clowns!** Set a flag follow up for **2 February**.
3 Choose a green flag.

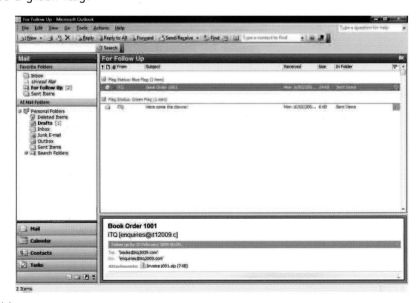

Figure 3.44

B1.3.6 Outlook® voting

You can add voting buttons to a message when Outlook® uses a Microsoft® Exchange
server. Find out if your messaging system is using an Exchange server.

Watch the demonstration to see how this is done.

 **3.24** *Demonstration*

Worked Example B1.3.6

Voting buttons only work if your email account is set up as a Microsoft® Exchange Server. They can be used to find answers to questions, a bit like answering a questionnaire. Microsoft® includes some preset buttons or you can create your own.

1 Open the message containing the voting buttons and click **Tools** → **Options**.
2 Click the **Use voting buttons** check box and choose the voting button names you want to use in the box.

B1.3.7 Reading email

Outlook® will notify you when a new message is received. You can read the message in the **Preview Pane** or you can double click it to open it and read it. If the message has an attachment, before opening it you should first save it to your user area so that the anti-virus software installed on your computer can scan it.

Watch the demonstration to see how this is done.

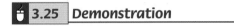 **3.25** *Demonstration*

Worked Example B1.3.7

Figure 3.45

1 Click the **Send/Receive** button on the toolbar.
2 Double click a received email in the **Inbox** to open it.
3 If there is an attachment, double click it and save it to your own file area.
4 Locate the file in your file area and open it.

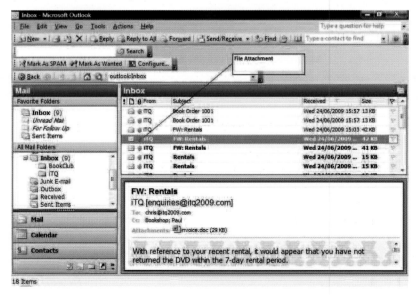

Figure 3.46

Task B1.3.7

1 Double click a received email in the **Inbox** to open it.

2   If there is an attachment, double click it and save it to your own file area.
4   Locate the file in your file area and open it.

| **Consolidation** |

You have received a message with the subject **Rentals**.

1   Forward this message to **accounts@itq2009.com** and send a copy to yourself. Add suitable message text.
2   Reply to the message by adding the message text:

Thank you for your message. The DVD was returned in the post yesterday. Please let me know when you receive it.

3   Send the message.
4   Flag the received message to review in 7 days.

B1.4   Describe how to stay safe and respect others when using email

Email is one of the easiest ways to transmit a virus so it is important to stay safe when using Outlook®. Email is not a secure method of sending personal information and you should keep all personal information safe. For example, messages can be viewed and intercepted by hackers and it is not wise to send any personal details such as credit card details by email. Any personal details should be sent only via a secure method.

Chain mails are emails that are sent and ask for the message to be sent to 10 friends in return for good health or wealth, etc. Some organisations do not allow chain emails. If you receive a chain mail, delete it.

The language used in an email should be appropriate and businesslike, for example red capital letters can be interpreted as shouting. Some emails can appear curt and short and this may not be the intended message, so you need to think about what the image and text are portraying before sending the email.

You might address a message to several people who do not know each other, and in this case you should not disclose a recipient's email address to the others. Send the message to yourself and use **bcc** (blind carbon copy) to send it to them so that email addresses are hidden.

B1.5   Use an address book to organise contact information

Outlook® includes an address book (called **Contacts**), which is an excellent way of keeping the contact details (e.g. name, address, email address and telephone numbers) up to date. The address book allows you to quickly search for the details.

B1.5.1 Creating and using a contact

🖰 3.26 | *Demonstration*

| Worked Example B1.5.1 |

1   Click **File → New → Contact**.
2   Type **Joanne Smith** in the **Full Name** box.
3   Type the following details in the boxes indicated:

Job title: **Administrator**

Company: **The Crazy Bookshop**

Business phone: **01234 79862541**

Email: **tamara@itq2009.com**

Display as: **Bookshop**

4 Click the **Save and Close** button.
5 Click **New** to create a new message.
6 Click **To...** and select **Bookshop** from the contacts list.
7 Click **OK**.
8 Type the message as shown in Figure 3.47.

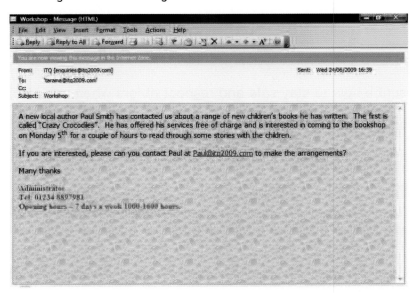

Figure 3.47

9 Send the message.

Now it's your turn to have a go.

Task B1.5.1

1 Create a new contact as follows:

Name: **Jennifer McCarthy**

Job title: **Consultant**

Company: **Own**

Business phone: **01234 7988255**

Email: **jennifer@itq2009.com**

Display as: **Jennifer**

2 Type the message as shown in Figure 3.48.

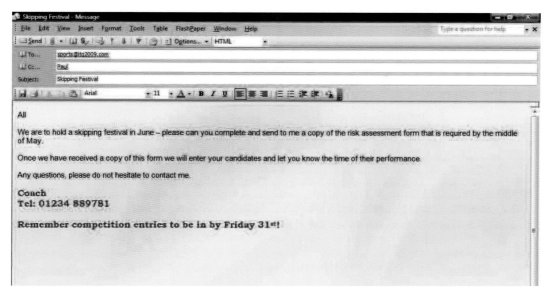

Figure 3.48

3 Send the message.

Watch the demonstration to see how to edit address book entries.

3.27 Demonstration

> **Worked Example B1.5.2**

1 Open the contact details for Joanne Smith and change the job title to Owner.
2 Save and close the changes.

Now it's your turn to have a go.

> **Task B1.5.2**

1 Open the contact details for Jennifer and change the telephone number to Tel: 01234 888788.
2 Save and close the changes.

Watch the demonstration to see how this is done.

3.28 Demonstration

You can create a distribution list that holds the details of all members of a group. For example, if you have a class of learners, you could create a distribution list for that class so that you can quickly send one message to the distribution list rather than sending separate messages to each learner.

> **Worked Example B1.5.3**

1 On the file menu click **New → Distribution List**.
2 In the Name box, type **iTQ**.
3 Click on the **Select Members...** button.

4   In the **Show names from the** drop-down box double click both entries in your address book.
5   Save and close.
6   On the file menu, click **New** → **Mail message**.
7   Click on the **To...** button and select **iTQ members**.
8   Compose the following message:

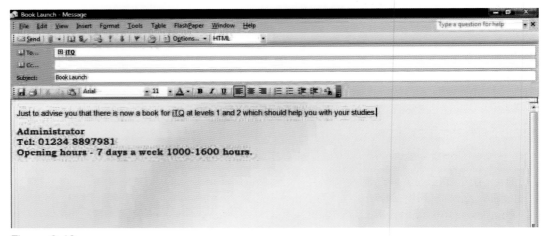

Figure 3.49

Now it's your turn to have a go.

| Task B1.5.3 |

1   Create a new Distribution List.
2   In the **Name** box, type **iTQ** and double click both entries in your address book.
3   Compose the following message:

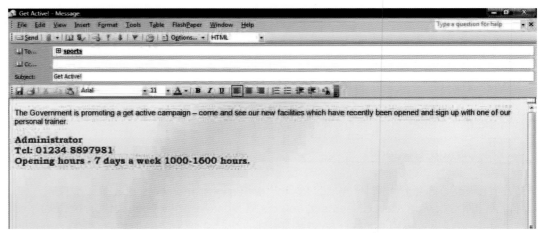

Figure 3.50

Consolidation

1   Create the following new contact details:

Full Name: **Emma Scorer**

Job Title: **Sales Assistant**

Business Tel: **01237 1234568**

Business address: **35 North End**

Bishops Way

Sunderland

SR1 6PW

Email: **SalesAss@itq2009.com**

Display as: **Emma – Sales**

2   Create the following distribution list and name it **Rentals.**
3   Add Joanne Smith, Joe Nolan, Paul Smith and Emma Scorer.
4   Compose an email to **Rentals.** Use the subject heading **New Stock.**
5   Add the following message text:

I am pleased to let you know that the new stock is now available for Rental and details are shown on our website at www.itq2009.com/rentals.

Please promote these to our customers.

Regards

Sales Manager

6   Send the message.

B2 Manage incoming email effectively

It is important that any organisational guidelines and procedures are followed when using email. Some common guidelines are:

- read messages twice before sending

- consider copyright

- advise people if you are forwarding a message to someone else

- avoid over-using capital letters

- make sure the title of the message is relevant

- keep messages short and simple

- do not send personal details.

B2.1 Follow guidelines and procedures for using email

Email netiquette means network etiquette and covers communicating effectively with others whilst using email, not over-using capital letters red fonts and not sending spam messages.

Email accounts are secured by a password and passwords will be kept secure so no one else can gain access to your mailbox.

B2.2   Read and respond to email messages appropriately

Microsoft Outlook® has settings which enable timings to be set for how often to check the email server for messages. Usually this is set at every 15 minutes – anything more frequent can cause internet traffic problems as it means that emails will be downloaded constantly.

Sometimes emails are only responded to once or twice a day: Outlook® is opened first thing in a morning, messages are replied to and then it is closed until later in the day. Some organisations also have 'email free' days. For example, staff do not respond to emails on a Friday and out of office messages are set.

An email might be received which requires information to be gathered from others. It is good practice to reply to the sender, advising them the message has been received and to let them know approximately when they will receive a reply. There is nothing worse than wondering if a message has been delivered and when to expect a reply.

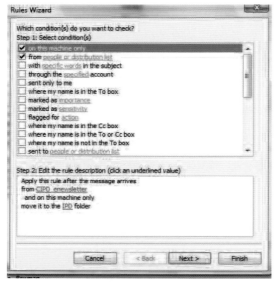

Figure 3.51

B2.3   Use email software tools and techniques to automate responses

B2.3.1 Auto Response (Out of Office)

Automatic responses allow you to send an automatic reply to a sender from your email account when you are away from the office. Some Outlook® automatic responses will only work if the email server settings are changed or you are using Outlook® via an exchange server; you will need to check if you need to do something in addition to the information provided below to get auto responses to work.

B2.3.2 Rules

A rule is another way to manage received messages. Outlook® has the facility to automatically move messages from the inbox into a specific folder. Rules can be set so that when messages are sent and received from different senders they are automatically moved into one folder. An example rule is shown in Figure 3.51:

Watch the demonstration to see how this is done.

3.29   Demonstration

Worked Example B2.3.2

1 Click on **Tools** → **Rules and Alerts** → **New Rule**.
2 Click **people or distribution list** and in the **From ->** box type **books@itq2009.com**.
3 Click **OK**.
4 Click **move to specified folder** and click on the **New...** button.
5 Name the folder **BookClub** and click **OK** → **OK**.

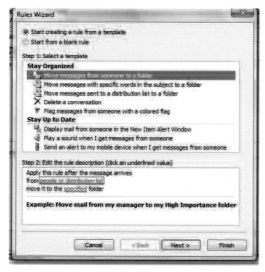

Figure 3.52

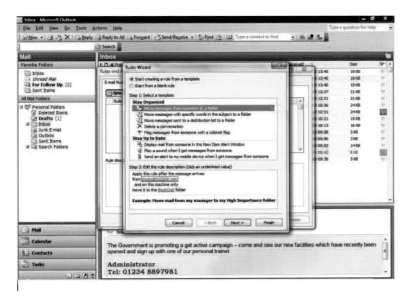

Figure 3.53

6 Click **Next** → **Next** → **Next** → **Next** → **Finish**.
7 Click **Apply** → **OK**.

Now it's your turn to have a go.

Task B2.3.2

1 Create a rule to move messages received from **sports@itq2009.com** to a folder.
2 Name the rule **Sports**.
3 Name the folder **Elite**.
4 Make all changes and save the settings.

Worked Example B2.3.2

1 Click on **Tools** → **Out of Office Assistant**.
2 Check the **I am currently Out of the Office** box.
3 In the **Auto Reply only once to each sender with the following text** box, type the following:

Thank you for your message. I am currently on holiday and will respond to any messages on my return.

4 Save and close.
5 Test the message to see it works.

Task B2.3.2

1 Create an Out of Office Assistant message. Add the following text to the message:

Thank you for your message. I am currently away at a conference and will reply on my return.

2 Save and close.
3 Test the message to see it works.

Figure 3.54

B2.3.3 Junk Email

Outlook® includes a junk email filter which scans each message to see if it could be spam. Details that are scanned could include the time when the message was sent and if the content is deemed inappropriate. The level of junk email filtering can be changed by altering the security settings in Outlook®.

In Outlook® there is a Junk E-mail folder.

To add a message to the Junk E-mail folder you can right click on the message that has been received and select **Junk E-mail** and then choose **Add Sender to Blocked Senders List**. Alternatively, you can set rules to automatically send messages to the Junk E-mail folder.

View the demonstration to see how this is done.

3.30 Demonstration

> **Worked Example B2.3.3**

1 Select an email message from your inbox. Right click on the message and click **Junk E-mail** → **Add Sender to Blocked Senders List** → **OK**.
2 Click on the Junk E-mail folder and right click on the message.
3 Click Junk E-mail → **Add Sender to Safe Senders List** → **OK**.
4 Drag and drop the message back to your inbox.

Now it's your turn to have a go.

> **Task B2.3.3**

1 Select an email message from your inbox.
2 Click **Add Sender to Blocked Senders List**.
3 Click on the Junk E-mail folder and **Add Sender to Safe Senders** List.
4 Move the message back to you inbox.

B2.4 Describe how to archive email messages, including attachments

It is common for mailboxes get full over time. It is good practice to create folders and sub-folders to store messages that are received and to set Outlook® to archive messages regularly.

Auto Archiving is a tool which is used to reduce the size of messages stored in your mailbox. You can set various options for archiving messages – for example Outlook® can archive messages every three days or every three weeks. This means that messages are moved from Personal Folders to Archive Folders so messages can still be accessed but the size of Personal Folders is reduced.

Watch the demonstration to see how this is done.

3.31 Demonstration

> **Worked Example B2.4**

1 Click on **Tools** → **Options**.
2 Click the **Other** tab and click on the **Auto Archive...** button.

3   Check the **Run Auto Archive every...** box and select **7 days**.
4   Click **OK**.

Now it's your turn to have a go.

> **Task B2.4**

1   Set Auto Archive to every 3 days.
2   Save and close all options.

B2.5 Organise, store and archive email messages effectively

One way to keep your emails organised is to create folders and sub-folders to store messages.

Watch the demonstration to see how this is done.

3.32 *Demonstration*

B2.5.1 Create folders

> **Worked Example B2.5.1**

1   Click on the **Personal Folders** link from your Microsoft Outlook® email.
2   Click **File → New → Folder**.
3   Key in the name **iTQ** and click **OK**.
4   Move one of the messages you have received about your iTQ into this folder by dragging and dropping it into the folder.

Now it's your turn to have a go.

> **Task B2.5.1**

1   Click on the **Personal Folders** link from your Microsoft Outlook® email.
2   Click **File → New → Folder**.
3   Key in the name **Trampolining** and click **OK**.
4   Move messages you have received about trampolining into this folder by dragging and dropping them into the folder.

B2.5.2 Identify what messages to delete and when to do so

Over time inboxes become full and this prevents messages being sent and received until some messages have been archived or deleted.

It is good practice to maintain good housekeeping of messages and delete messages on a regular – or even daily – basis. Decide how often messages will be deleted so that email accounts work correctly. Another way to maintain a healthy inbox is to archive email messages (covered earlier in this chapter).

Watch the demonstration to see how this is done.

3.33 *Demonstration*

Worked Example B2.5.2

1   Click on the 'test' messages in your inbox.
2   Press the DELETE key on your keyboard. Your message is deleted and will have been posted into the Deleted folder.
3   Have a look in the Deleted folder to check that the message has been deleted.

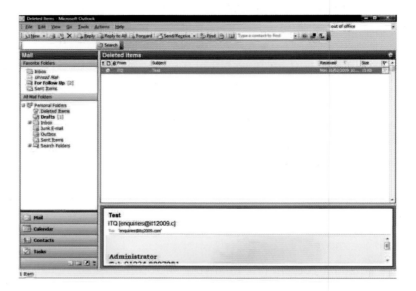

Figure 3.55

4   Every few weeks you should empty your Deleted folder to permanently remove messages. To do this right click on the **Deleted Items** folder and select **Empty Deleted Items Folder**.
5   These messages have now been permanently removed from your computer.

Task B2.5.2

1   Click on the **Trampoline Club** message in your inbox.
2   Delete this message.

Watch the demonstration to see how this is done.

3.34   *Demonstration*

B2.5.3 Backup

It is important to make regular backups of important data. Emails can be backed up by using the Outlook® **Auto Archive** feature which was covered earlier in this chapter.

Another way to make a backup file is to export the message folder to a **Personal Folders** file (.pst). This is a data file that stores your messages and other items on your computer. You can assign a .pst file to be the default delivery location for email messages. You can use a .pst to organise and back up items for safekeeping using the **Import and Export Wizard**. This creates the backup .pst file. You can then copy the .pst file onto a CD or DVD for safekeeping or to move the data to another computer with Outlook® installed.

> **Worked Example B2.5.3**

1 Click on **File** → **Import** and **Export**.
2 Select **Export to a file** and click **Next**.
3 In the list, click **Personal Folder File** (.pst) and select **Next**.
4 Click the folder that contains the messages you want to back up.
5 Under **Save exported file as**, click **Browse** and specify a name and location for your backup file.
6 Click **Finish** → **OK**.

Important: you should not export items that were created in multiple languages or in a language that is not supported by your system code page to a file type that does not support Unicode. For example, if you have items created in multiple languages in a Microsoft Outlook® Personal Folders file (.pst), you should not export the items to a Microsoft Outlook® 97–2002 Personal Folders file (.pst). The latter file type does not support Unicode. Therefore, all items that contain characters in a language other than those supported by the system code page in text fields other than the body of items, such as To, Subject, ContactName and BusinessTelephoneNumber or properties of Contact items, will be interpreted incorrectly and displayed as question marks (?) and other unintelligible text.

> **Task B2.5.3**

1 Create a backup of your inbox and **Trampoline** folder using the instructions provided above.
2 Back this up to a removable device, e.g. CD or USB stick.

B2.6 Respond to common email problems

B2.6.1 Common email problems

Mailboxes are set so that they can send and receive email messages of a certain size – for example a mailbox can be set so that email messages over 5 MB cannot be sent. This means that if any files are over 5 MB and need to be sent via email, the file attachment needs to be compressed and attached.

Other problems with email include spam, junk, chain-mails and phising.

Spam is the sending of emails to many email accounts. Spam messages usually contain commercial advertising for products or services. Sending the same message to many users is very cheap and some companies sell on email addresses to spammers.

Junk email is another form of spam – this is where messages are received from people not known to you and who have obtained your mail address. Microsoft Outlook® has features built in which allow you to direct junk and spam emails into a dedicated folder.

Chain-mails are emails that request the message be passed onto 10 friends and by doing so they may be promised prosperity. These again can clog up your inbox and should be deleted.

Phishing is a process where someone tries to fraudulently acquire sensitive information, for example usernames or credit card details. They do this by masquerading as a trustworthy company; for example emails may be received from banks asking you to log in and update details – these are always phishing emails as banks would never email to ask for these details. If you click on the link in the email then the hacker knows your email account is active and can track your keystrokes, obtaining your true login details, which they can then use to hack into your account. These emails should be added to your junk email list and deleted.

The following is an example of a phishing email:

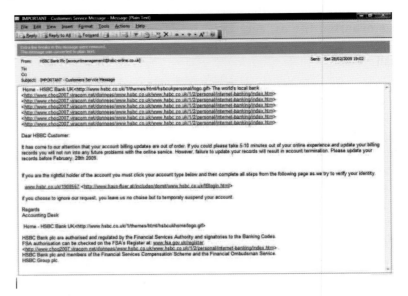

Figure 3.56

Mini Assignment

You have started to do some work for an online shopping company and they have asked you to send and receive various emails. Before you start you need to set templates for sending and receiving messages.

1 Open Outlook® and add the background file **image1**.
2 Create the email signature, using the following text:

We will respond to any messages within 48 hours – if you require a quicker response please ring 0800 00000001.

3 Change the page setup to A4 landscape and set the margins at 2.5cm all round.
4 Create a new folder in **Personal Folders** and name this **Shop**.
5 Change the read and delivery receipt so that all messages that are sent request both a read and delivery receipt. Produce a screenshot to show this has been done.
6 Add the following contacts to the address book:

Full Name: Stephen Brown
Job Title: Supervisor
Business: 01237 1234569
Business: ShopChannel
St Cuthbert's Way
Sunderland
SR1 6PW
Email: supervisor@itq2009.com
Display as: Stephen

Full Name: Joanna Boom
Job Title: Deputy Supervisor
Business: 01237 1234570
Business: ShopChannel
St Cuthbert's Way
Sunderland
SR1 6PW
Email: dsupervisor@itq2009.com
Display as: Joanna

Full Name: Roland Carlton
Job Title: Assistant
Business: 01237 123456971
Business: ShopChannel
St Cuthbert's Way
Sunderland
SR1 6PW
Email: sales@itq2009.com
Display as: Roland

7 Create a distribution list and call it **Channel**. Add Stephen and Joanna to the distribution. Create a screenshot to show this has been done.

8 Create a rule so that all messages with **Shopping** in the subject are moved to the **Shop** folder. Create a screenshot to show this has been done.

9 Set the Auto Archive so that this is run every 10 days. Take a screenshot to show this has been done.

10 Compose the following message to the Channel distribution list, with the heading **Shopping** (remember to send yourself a copy of the message):

Great News! We now have in stock a two-piece slicing set which allows you to slice different vegetables quickly and clearly without having to use a knife.

This new product is available in red, white or blue and can be ordered directly from our website. The set also includes a bowl which catches the food that has been sliced.

11 Use different font styles, colours and size of text.
12 Change the alignment of the text.
13 Add bullets to the colours of the products available.
14 Add a sound and movie file (if you have the facility to do this).
15 Add the hyperlink **www.itq2009.com/shopping**.
16 Add the zipped folder **slicer.zip**.
17 Send the message.
18 Once you have received a copy of the message, save a copy of the file attachment to your file area.

The received message should have automatically moved with the rule.

19 Flag the message for follow-up within the next 3 days.
20 Save and close all messages and Outlook®.

4

Database Software

This unit is all about creating and maintaining a simple database. You will develop your knowledge and skills relating to entering and retrieving information from databases, such as:

- names and addresses
- stock control
- time management
- event management
- running simple queries
- producing reports (using menus or shortcuts).

You will enter straightforward information in a single table database, run routine queries and product reports.

By working through the **Overview, Worked Examples** and the **Tasks** in this chapter, you will demonstrate the skills required for Database Software Level 1:

ELEMENT The competent person will...	PERFORMANCE CRITERIA To demonstrate this competence they can...	KNOWLEDGE To demonstrate this competence they will also...
DB: A1 Enter, edit and organise structured information in a database	A1.2 Create a database table for a purpose using specified fields A1.3 Enter structured data into records to meet requirements A1.4 Locate and amend data records A1.5 Respond appropriately to data entry error messages A1.6 Check data meets needs, using IT tools and making corrections as necessary	A1.1 Identify the main components of a database
DB: A2 Use database software tools to extract information and produce reports	A2.2 Run simple database queries A2.4 Generate and print pre-defined database reports	A2.1 Identify which queries meet information requirements A2.3 Identify which reports meet information requirements

Step-by-step examples are provided as a demonstration of what to do. These demonstrations are based on Microsoft Access® 2003. Review the **Overview** in each section and watch the demonstrations in the **Worked Example**. Once you have watched the demonstrations, work through the **Tasks**.

Throughout this chapter, consolidation exercises have been provided. These allow you to practise further the skills you have learned.

A1 Enter, edit and organise structured information in a database

A1.1 Identify the main components of a database

What is a database?

A database is an electronic filing system; for example, imagine you are employed as a clerical assistant at a car sales garage. Each car that is for sale has an index card, which is filed alphabetically in an index card storage box.

When a customer wants further information about a car, the salesperson goes to the index card storage box, retrieves the card and passes on the information to the prospective buyer. If any details need to be changed, these are manually written onto the index card. When the car is 'sold', the index card is marked as sold and 'archived' into a sold index card storage box.

A database works in the same way, but all the information is stored electronically. When a buyer wants details of a car, the database can be 'queried' and information about the different cars retrieved from the database for the prospective buyer. Any amendments are entered directly into the database and when the car is sold, it is marked as sold in the database. This type of electronic filing system makes it very efficient to store and retrieve data.

The main components of a database

Databases contain **tables**, **forms**, **queries** and **reports**.

A table holds the information in a basic format in a database. Each record in a database consists of a number of fields. Fields in a database are where information is stored, for example, using the cars database you may have a field 'manufacturer' and a different field named 'colour'. Each field may have different characteristics or formats and therefore different fields can be represented differently, for instance as text, numbers or currency.

See the example below, which shows a basic table and its field properties:

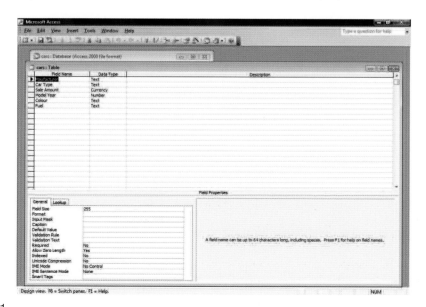

Figure 4.1

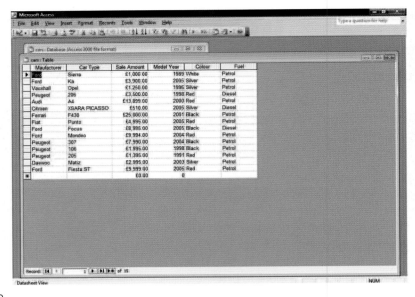

Figure 4.2

A **form** is a more 'user-friendly' way of entering the data into the database. The form is created and linked to a table and provides a graphical interface for being able to see and enter the data.

An example form is shown below:

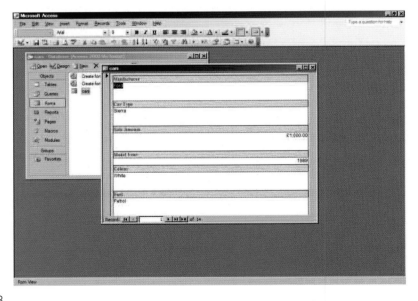

Figure 4.3

A **query** is the action you perform if you want to extract or find specific data from the database. Imagine if a customer came into the car showroom and asked to see all 'red Ford' cars. The salesperson could run a query on the database that would then show all red Ford cars.

Data extracted from the database after running such a query is shown in Figure 4.4.

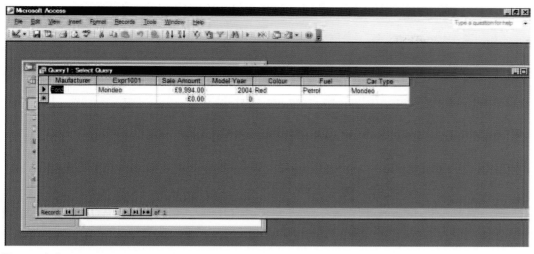

Figure 4.4

A **report** allows you to display and print your data in a professional way. Access contains a number of different report templates that you can use to adapt the way your report is produced. A report can be produced from either a table or a query. You can change the page orientation of a report, change the font style and size and add images.

An example report is shown below:

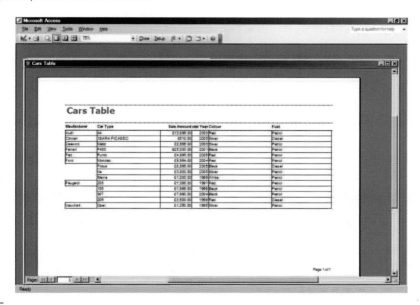

Figure 4.5

At Level 1, you will create a database table and you may also be provided with a database to:

■ enter and amend data in a database either using a table or form

■ create new records in a database table or form

■ run routine queries

■ produce pre-defined reports.

Watch the demonstration to see how this is done.

🖱 4.1 | *Demonstration*

Worked Example A1.1

1 Create a new folder in which to store your database.
2 Name the folder **carsdatabase**.
3 Copy the file **cars.mdb** to the **Carsdatabase** folder.
4 Load Microsoft Access®.
5 Open the database file **cars.mdb**.
6 In the **Table** menu you will see one table:

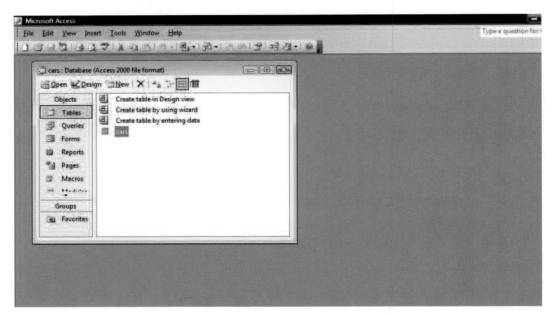

Figure 4.6

7 Click on the **Queries** tab and you will see three queries:

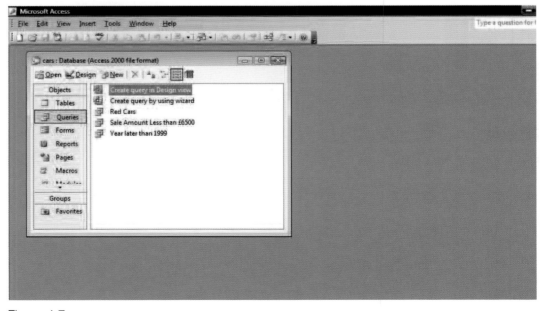

Figure 4.7

8 Click on the **Forms** tab and you will see one form:

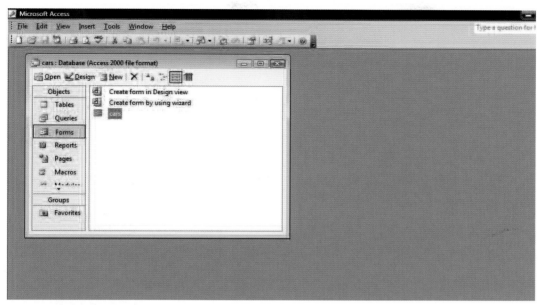

Figure 4.8

9 Click on the **Reports** tab and you will see two reports:

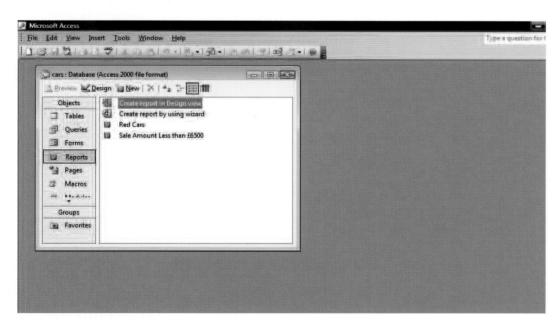

Figure 4.9

10 Close the database by clicking on the close button:

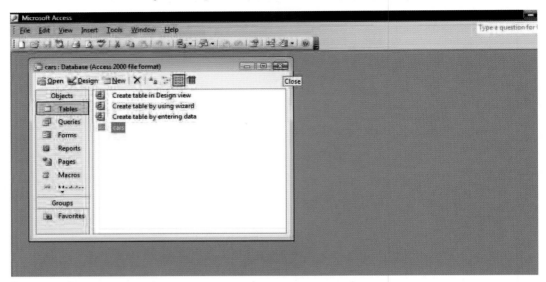

Figure 4.10

11 Exit Microsoft Access® by clicking **File** → **Close**.

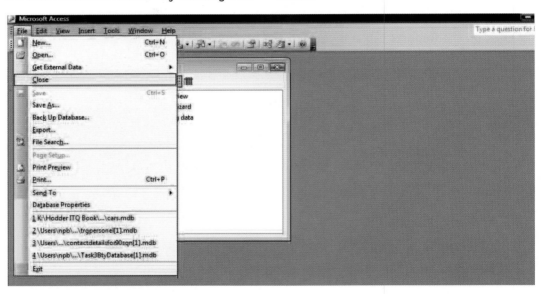

Figure 4.11

Now it's your turn to have a go.

Task A1.1

1 Create a new folder in which to store your database.
2 Name the folder **equipmentdatabase**.
3 Copy the file **equipment.mdb** to the Equipment Database folder.
4 Load Microsoft Access®.
5 Open the database file **equipment.mdb**.
6 Open each of the different tabs – table, queries, forms and reports. Review the tables, queries, forms and report tabs to familiarise yourself with a database.
7 Save and close the database and exit Microsoft Access®.

A1.2 Create a database table for a purpose using specified fields

Once you are familiar with an existing database then you are ready to create, enter and organise your own data in the database.

Now it's your turn to create a database of dental patients. Follow the instructions in the demonstration.

4.2 Demonstration

Worked Example A1.2

1 Create a new folder called **Dental.**
2 Load Microsoft Access®.
3 Click on **New.**

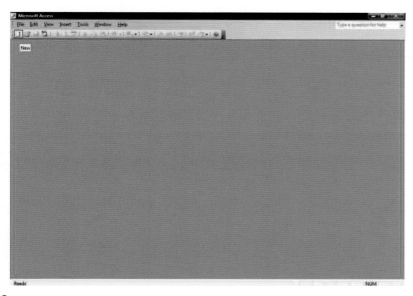

Figure 4.12

4 Click **Blank Database.**

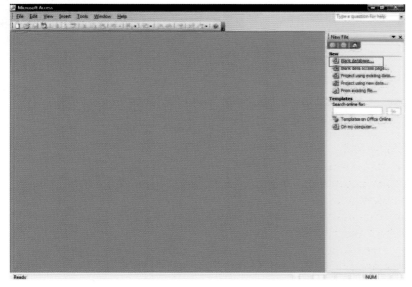

Figure 4.13

5 Open the **Dental** folder and save the database as **Dentists**.

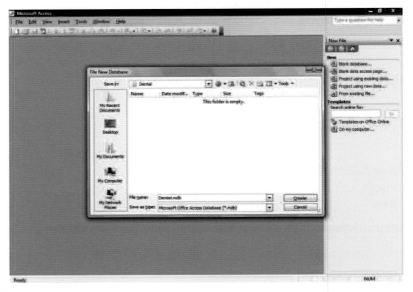

Figure 4.14

6 Click **Create** → **Design** and enter the field structure as shown below:

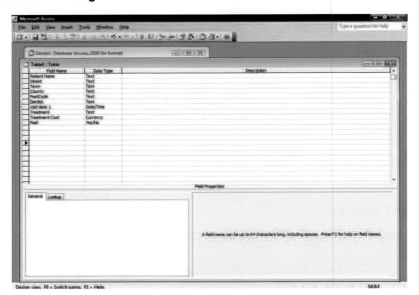

Figure 4.15

7 Click **Close** → **Yes** and enter the table name **Patients** → click **OK**.

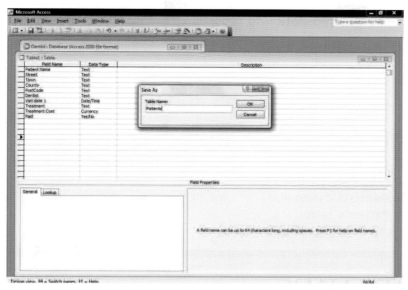

Figure 4.16

8 Select **No** (at Level 1 and Level 2 there is no requirement to create a primary key).
9 The created table is now shown.
10 Close the database.

Now it's your turn to have a go.

Task A1.2

1 Create a folder and name this **Customers**.
2 Load Microsoft Access® and create a new database and save this as **Customers**.
3 Create the following table structure:

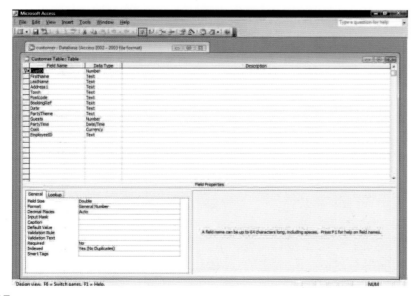

Figure 4.17

4 Save and close the table as **2009**.
5 Save and close Microsoft Access®.

Enter structured data into records to meet requirements

It is important when you enter data into a database table that any updated fields and new records are entered accurately. An updated field is where, for example, in the cars database you might change the selling price of one of the cars.

Watch the demonstration to see how a database is created.

4.3 | **Demonstration**

Worked Example A1.3

1   Open the **Dentists** database.
2   Open the **Patients** table.
3   Add the data as shown below:

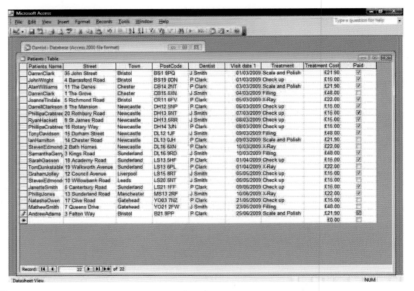

Figure 4.18

4   Save and close the table.

Task A1.3

1   Open the **customers** database.
2   Open the **2009** table.
3   Add the data as shown in Figure 4.19.

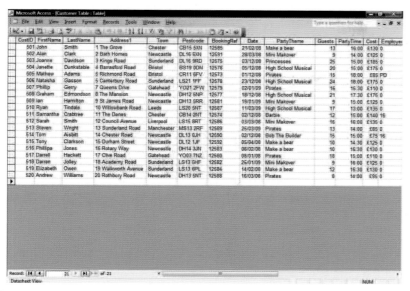

Figure 4.19

4   Save and close the table.

A1.4   Locate and amend data records

Once you have entered data into a database, you may need to change it. Data may need to be changed if one of the customers moves or you sell one of the cars. Data can be amended by keying directly into the record or carrying out a search and replace.

Like any filing system, if the information is not stored correctly it is very difficult to retrieve – a database is just the same. Imagine you were trying to find all the sales for March 2008, but you had entered the year as 2009 instead – this would mean that no records would be shown.

Search and replace is a function within Microsoft Access® 2003 and it allows you to search for data and replace it automatically with something else. For example, if you wanted to change all customers who had red cars to blue cars, you could do this using the search and replace function without having to manually replace each word on each occasion.

A wildcard character can also be used, for example if you wanted to search for party themes that start with M you could search for M* and Access® would locate all records that start with an M.

Watch the demonstration to see how this is done.

4.4   Demonstration

Worked Example A1.4

1   Open the **customers** database and 2009 table.
2   Find the following record in the database.

Customers Table											
CUST ID	FIRST NAME	LAST NAME	ADDRESS 1	TOWN	POSTCODE	BOOKING REF	DATE	PARTY THEME	GUESTS	PARTY TIME	COST
512	Sarah	Smith	12 Council Avenue	Liverpool	LS15 8RT	12586	03/03/08	Mini Makover	16	16:00	£135

3 Change the address to 121 Kirkheaton Lane, Liverpool, LS21 8PT.
4 Add the following new record:

Customers Table											
CUST ID	FIRST NAME	LAST NAME	ADDRESS 1	TOWN	POSTCODE	BOOKING REF	DATE	PARTY THEME	GUESTS	PARTY TIME	COST
521	Stephanie	Tagg	1 The Spinney	Liverpool	LS18 8QT	12593	03/03/08	Mini Makover	16	16:00	£95

1 Check that the data you have added and amended is correct.
2 Find record **508 – Graham Edmondson** and delete this record from the database table.
3 Carry out a search and replace and search for **Princesses** and replace this with **Disney Princesses.**
4 Save and close the database.

Now it's your turn.

Task A1.4

1 Open the **Sales** database from the **Sales** folder.
2 Find the following record in the database.

Sales Table							
ID	ADDRESS 1	FIRST NAME	LAST NAME	TOWN	POSTCODE	SALES REF	DATE OF SALE
4	4 Barrasford Road	Janette	Clarkson	Sunderland	SR19 0DN	12576	05/12/08

1 Change the LastName from Clarkson to Cox and change the Date of Sale to 08/12/08.
2 Add the following new record:

SALES TABLE						
ADDRESS 1	FIRST NAME	LAST NAME	TOWN	POSTCODE	SALES REF	DATE OF SALE
21 Leazes Road	Karen	Thompson	Newcastle	NE1 6TG	12593	21/03/08

1 Find record ID **15** and delete this record from the database table.
2 Carry out a search and replace and replace **Sland** with **Sunderland**.
3 Check that the data you have added and amended is correct.
4 Save and close the database table and the database.

A1.5 Respond appropriately to data entry error messages

When entering data in to a database you sometimes get error messages and these can be due to field size, data type or validation checks. They can sometimes be resolved using the help function.

The following screenshot shows an example of where text **ABC** has been entered into a numeric field. Access shows an error message and does not allow the data to be entered.

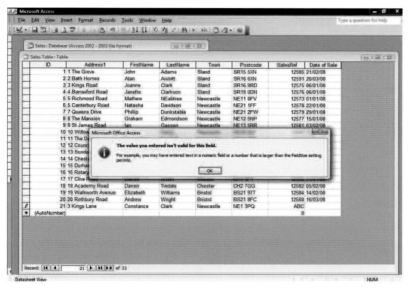

Figure 4.20

Sometimes you may need to enter data where the field size is not large enough, for example the **LastName** field below has been set to **nine** characters – if you want to enter a last name of more than nine characters, you will not be able to enter the data:

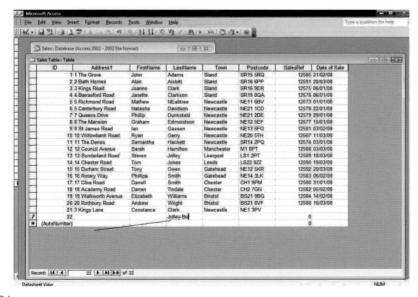

Figure 4.21

In this case Microsoft Access® will not allow you to enter any more than nine characters. To change the field size, click on **Design** and click into the **LastName** field and the **FieldSize** – change **9** to **20**.

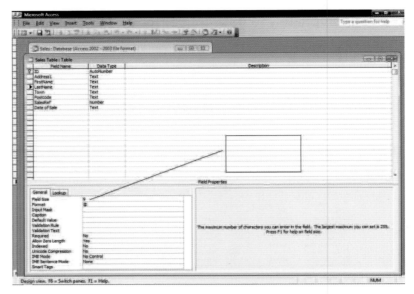

Figure 4.22

Sometimes when you get stuck in a database you can use help by clicking on **Help** and **Microsoft Access Office Help** and you can then type in a question and get an answer to your query.

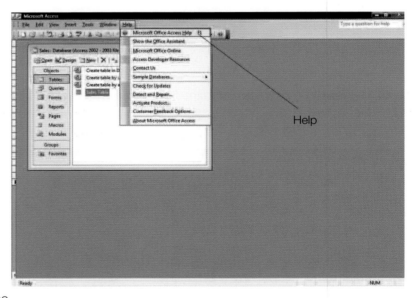

Figure 4.23

Watch the demonstration below to see how this works.

4.5   *Demonstration*

Worked Example A1.5

1   Open the **dentists** database.
2   Click on **Design** and click in the **PatientsName** field.
3   Change the **FieldSize** from **16** to **25**.

A1.6 Check data meets needs, using IT tools and making corrections as appropriate

Spell checking

Once you have entered all your data, you can then run a spell check through Microsoft Access® as a final check to make sure you have spelled all the words correctly.

Format

When setting up your database you need to check that you have the correct format assigned to each field. For example, if you set a date field as a text field in Microsoft Access®, when you query dates from the tables, these will not work.

Accuracy

When data is entered, you need to proofread it very carefully to ensure that you have copied it correctly. You could also ask one of your colleagues to check your accuracy until you are confident in what you are doing.

Consistency

Data should be entered consistently, for example, all the same words should start with a capital letter.

Watch the demonstration.

 4.6 | Demonstration

Worked Example A1.6

1 Open the **Customers** database and the **2009** table.
2 Click on the **spelling** icon and carry out a spell check (names and addresses are correct).

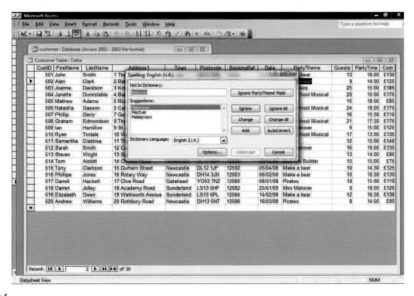

Figure 4.24

3 Proofread and check all the data in the table.
4 Check the format of each field to ensure that the correct data type has been set.
5 Check for consistency across all of the data.
4 Save and close the database table and the database.

Task A1.6

1   Open the **Dentists** table from the **Dental** folder on the CD and the **Patients** table.
2   Carry out a spell check.
3   Proofread and check all the data in the table.
4   Save and close the database table and the database.

A2 Use database software tools to extract information and produce reports

A2.1   Identify which queries meet information requirements

A query is the action you perform if you want to extract or find data in a database. Imagine if a customer came into the car showroom and asked to see all red Ford cars. The salesperson could run a query on the database which would then show him or her all the red Ford cars. In Microsoft Access® you can run different types of queries.

In addition to running a query, data can be filtered in the table. A filter allows you to keep the data intact in the table but just view the records you want. A query creates a new, smaller table with just the data you have selected in the query. However, if you need to find the same information regularly it is more efficient to create a query because you can edit it later.

You can also sort the data in the database table or in the query. Data can be sorted in ascending A–Z order. This puts the data into alphabetical order starting with A and ending with Z. For example:

Aisbitt
Biscuit
Dodds
Zion.

Data can also be sorted into descending order Z–A. This puts the data into descending alphabetical order starting with Z and ending with A. For example:

Zion
Dodds
Biscuit
Aisbitt.

Data can also be sorted in alphanumeric ascending order, for example:

Apple 21
Banana 36
Carrot 18

At Level 1, the queries that you will create will be routine.

A2.2   Run simple database queries

When trying to retrieve information from your database you can use single criteria, for example, searching for all customers in 'Durham' would be a searching on a single criterion where 'Durham' is the criterion.

You can also search on more than one criterion, for example, searching for all customers in 'Durham' who purchased a car in 'March 2008' where 'Durham' and 'March 2008' are the criterion.

You can also use different operators with search criteria to find information. For example, if you wanted to find sales where the price was less than £200 you could enter the criterion <200 and this would search for records where the sales price was less than £200. If you wanted to search for sales that were £200 or more, you would enter >=200.

The table below shows some of the different operators that can be used.

OPERATORS	DESCRIPTION
>	Greater than
<	Less than
>=	Greater than or equal to
<=	Less than or equal to

Wildcard or Like Queries

The asterisk (*), per cent sign (%), question mark (?), underscore (_), number sign (#), exclamation mark (!), hyphen (-) and brackets ([ ]) are all wildcard characters. These can be used in queries and expressions to include all records, file names, or other items that begin with specific characters or match a certain pattern. For example, if you wanted to search for sales in January 2008, you could enter */01/08 – this would search for records in January 2008.

View the demonstration to see how this works.

4.7 | Demonstration

Worked Example A2.2.1

1 Open the **Customers** database and search for customers who live in **Gateshead**.
2 Click on **Queries** → **New** → **Design View** → **OK** → **Add** → **2009**. Click **Close**.
3 Transfer all fields from the **Customers** table into the query design by double clicking on each field name.
4 In the criterion row, key in the **Town** field **Gateshead**.
5 Click on the **Run the query** icon.
6 Save and close the query as **Gateshead**.

Now it's your turn to have a go.

Task A2.2.1

1 Open the **Sales** database from www.hodderplus.co.uk/itq and search for customers who live in **Sunderland** using all fields.
2 Save and close the query as **Sunderland**.

Your answer should be similar to the one in Figure 4.25.

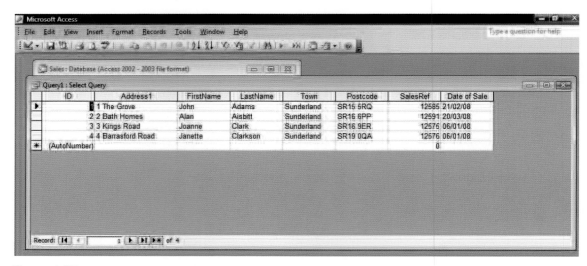

Figure 4.25

Now view the demonstration on how to create a query with more than one criterion that uses a wildcard.

Worked A2.2.2

1   Open the **Customers** database and carry out the following query.
2   Search for customers who live in Town **Gateshead** and whose **Date of Sale** was January 2008.
3   Click on **Queries** → **New** → **Design** → **View** → **OK** → **Add** → **2009**. Click **Close**.
4   Transfer all fields from the **2009** table into the query design by double clicking on each field name.
5   In the criterion row, key in the **Town** field **Gateshead** and add */01/08 into the **Date of Sale** field.
6   Click on the **Run the query** icon.
7   Save and close the query as **Gateshead sales in January**.

Now it's your turn to have a go.

Task A2.2.2

1   Open the **Sales** database and carry out the following query.
2   Search for customers who live in **Newcastle** and where the **Date of Sale = February 2008**.
3   Save and close the query as **Newcastle**.

Your answer should be similar to that shown in Figure 4.26.

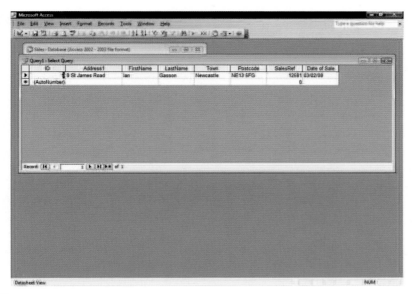

Figure 4.26

View the demonstration of how to sort data in a query.

4.8   Demonstration

Worked Example A2.2.3

1   Open the **Customers** database and carry out the following query.
2   Search for customers who have booked a **High School Musical** party.
3   Do not display the **CustomerID** field. Click the tick in the **Show** row so the tick is removed.
4   Sort the **Date** into ascending order. Click on the **Sort** and choose **Ascending**.
5   Click on the **Run the query** icon.
6   Save and close the query as **HSM Parties**.

Now it's your turn.

Task A2.2.3

1   Open the **Sales** database and carry out the following query.
2   Search for sales that have been agreed after 31 January 2008.
3   Sort the **Town** field into ascending order.
4   Do not display the **ID** field or the **SalesRef** field.
5   Click on the **Run the query** icon.
6   Save and close the query as **Sales**.
7   Your answer should be similar to that shown in Figure 4.27.

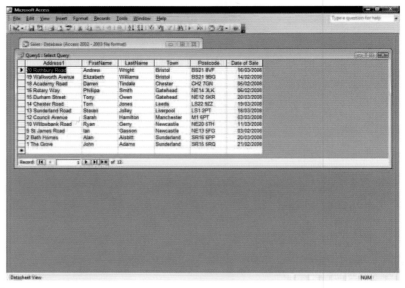

Figure 4.27

View the demonstration on how to run a filter on a database table.

4.9   Demonstration

Worked Example A2.2.4

Instead of running a query, sometimes you might want to quickly search for data in the database without creating a new query. This can be done by 'filtering' the data.

1   Open the **Customers** database and 2009 table.
2   Click on the **Town** field and click on the **Filter** icon.

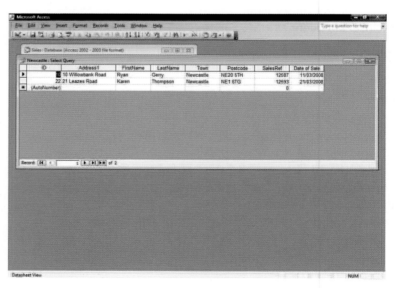

Figure 4.28

3   Choose **Newcastle**.
4   The table will now show the Newcastle records, which have been filtered.

5 Remove the filter by clicking back on the **Town** field and the **Filter** icon and choose **none**.
6 Save and close the database table without making any changes.

Now it's your turn to have a go.

Task A2.2.4

1 Open the **Sales** database table.
2 Click on the **Date of Sale** field and click on the **Filter** icon.
3 Choose **06/01/08**.
4 Click on **Apply filter** button.
5 The table will now show the sales agreed on this date.
6 Click **Remove filter**.
7 Save and close the database table without making any changes.

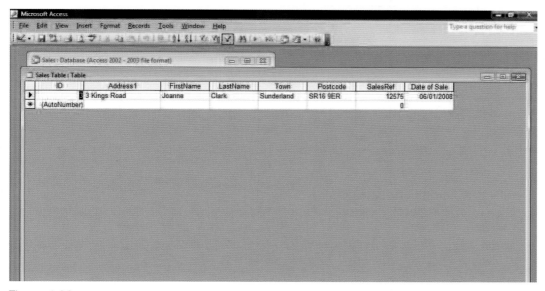

Figure 4.29

A.2.3 Identify which reports meet information requirements

A database report shows the data in either the database table or the database query professionally. In Microsoft Access® you can use the Wizard to create different styles of reports. When you are completing your iTQ, you will need to decide what reports you need to produce and how to do this. For example, you might be sending letters out to customers and you might decide to produce a report that displays the information as labels so that you can easily stick these onto the envelopes that are sent to customers.

Using menus or shortcuts

Database reports can be opened either using a menu or a shortcut. Creating the shortcuts is covered in Level 2. However, at Level 1 you should be able to open a report from a shortcut or menu.

View the demonstration to see how this works.

4.10 *Demonstration*

Worked Example A2.3

1   Open the **Sales2** database. You will see a different layout – this shows a menu for opening queries/reports.
2   Click on the **salesreport** button.
3   This opens the **salesreport** report. This has been predefined by the author of the database and makes it easier for new members of staff to operate the database.
4   Save and close the database.

Over to you.

Task A2.3

1   Open the **Cust2** database.
2   Click on the **pirate report** button.
3   This opens and prints the **Pirate** report.
4   Save and close the database.

A2.4   Generate and print pre-defined database reports

Microsoft Access® allows you to create a variety of reports to display the information from your tables and/or queries more effectively. The reports that you produce should include a range of standard templates. Reports can be customised by adding background or by changing the font styles/sizes.

Worked Example A2.4.1

1   Open the **Equipment** database.
2   Click on the **Reports** → **New** → **Report Wizard** → select the query **Location CM131** → **OK**.
3   Select all the fields to be displayed in the report by clicking on the double-headed arrow and clicking next twice. Do not sort at this point.
4   Select **block** layout and **portrait** orientation.
5   Click **Next** → **Casual** and add a title **Equipment in CM131** and then click **Finish**.
3   Your completed report will now be displayed.

Note: some of the fields may not be wide enough and the data may not be shown in full – we will amend this in a later exercise.

Over to you.

Task A2.4.1

1   Open the **Equipment** database.
2   Click on **Reports** → **New** → **Report Wizard**. Select the query **Location CM131** → **OK**.
3   Select all the fields to be displayed in the report by clicking on the double-headed arrow and click next three times. Do not sort at this point
4   Select **tabular** layout and **portrait** orientation. Click on **next**, choose **casual** and add a title **IT Equipment in CM131**, and then click on **finish**.
5   Your completed report will now be displayed.

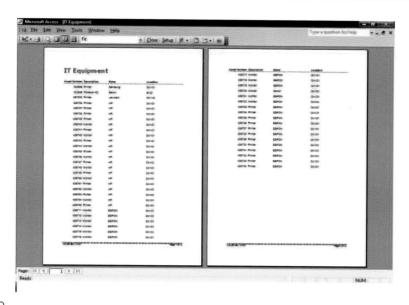

Figure 4.30

Task A2.4.2

1 Create a new report based on the **Printers sorted** query.
2 Choose your own styles and layout.
3 Save and print the report as **Printers sorted**.
4 Save and close the database.

Mini Assignment

You have been asked to assist the IT Manager of the Parkview Academy with creating a relational database. The Academy has purchased a number of different games to help make lessons more interactive and you have been asked to record the hire of different games, the users and uses of the games which can be loaned to students. Only those students who have achieved three gold stars per week for good behaviour are allowed to borrow games.

You will create one table of student details. A list of student details is provided below.

1 Create a new folder and name this **Games**.
2 Create a new database using the fieldnames and details given in Figure 4.30.
3 Enter the details from Figure 4.30 above into the database.
4 Check that all details have been entered correctly.
5 Create a query to find all students who live in Leeds. Produce a report to show all students who live in Leeds.
6 Create a query to find all those students who are allowed to borrow games this week. Sort the students into alphabetical order of surname.
7 Produce a report to show the results.
8 Close the database and file.

FIRST NAME	SURNAME	ADDRESS 1	TOWN	POSTCODE	DRAW?
Rebecca	Ferguson	7 Queens Drive	Bristol	BS19 0DN	Y
Charlotte	Robinson	17 Clive Road	Cardiff	CR11 6FV	N
Lindsey	Tait	13 Sunderland Road	Chester	CB14 2NT	Y
Georgia	Short	12 Council Avenue	Chester	CB15 5XN	Y
Vicky	Elliot	5 Canterbury Road	Dundee	DL16 9RD	Y
Lindsey	McCabe	10 Willowbank Road	Shrewsbury	ST12 5NP	N
Casey	Banks	18 Academy Road	Shrewsbury	ST13 5NT	N
Gabby	Blake	19 Walkworth Avenue	Shrewsbury	ST13 5RR	Y
Tracy	Chambers	20 Rothbury Road	Shrewsbury	ST14 3JN	N
Kelly	Barnes	2 Bath Homes	Shrewsbury	DL12 1JF	Y
Lisa	Hetherington	8 The Mansion	Shrewsbury	DL13 0JH	N
Laura	Johnson	9 St James Road	Shrewsbury	DL16 6XN	Y
Kimberley	Watson	14 Chester Road	Leeds	LS13 5HF	N
Samantha	Taylor	15 Shrewsbury Street	Leeds	LS13 6PL	N
Kerry	Turnbull	16 Rotary Way	Leeds	LS20 5NT	Y
Claire	Bowden	3 Kings Road	Leeds	LS21 1FF	N
Angela	McKenna	1 The Grove	Liverpool	LS15 8RT	Y
Kayleigh	Reed	11 The Denes	Manchester	MS13 2RF	Y
Charni	Cornwall	5 Richmond Road	York	YO03 7NZ	N
Danielle	Brown	4 Barrasford Road	York	YO21 2FW	N

Level 2

This unit is all about creating and modifying a single table, non-relational database and using tools and techniques to extract data. You will develop knowledge and skills relating to entering familiar and unfamiliar data, retrieving information by creating queries and producing reports by setting up menus or shortcuts. More complex reports may be about sales activities, order details or project management.

By working through the **Overview**, **Worked Examples**, **Tasks** and **Consolidations** in this chapter, you will demonstrate the skills required for Database Software Level 2.

ELEMENT The competent person will…	PERFORMANCE CRITERIA To demonstrate this competence they can…	KNOWLEDGE To demonstrate this competence they will also …
DB:B1 Create and modify non-relational database tables	B1.3 Create and modify database tables using a range of field types B1.5 Respond appropriately to problems with database tables B1.6 Use database tools and techniques to ensure data integrity is maintained	B1.1 Identify the components of a database B1.2 Describe the field characteristics for the data required B1.4 Describe ways to maintain data integrity
DB:B2 Enter, edit and organise structured information in a database	B2.1 Create forms to enter, edit and organise data in a database B2.2 Select and use appropriate tools and techniques to format data entry forms B2.3 Check data entry meets needs, using IT tools and making corrections as necessary B2.4 Respond appropriately to data entry errors	
DB:B3 Use database software tools to run queries and produce reports	B3.1 Create and run database queries using multiple criteria to display or amend selected data B3.2 Plan and produce database reports from a single-table non-relational database B3.3 Select and use appropriate tools and techniques to format database reports B3.4 Check reports meet needs, using IT tools and making corrections as necessary	

Step-by-step examples are provided as a demonstration of what you need to do. These demonstrations are based on Microsoft Access® 2003. Review the **Overview** in each section and then watch the demonstrations in the **Worked Example** before commencing any **Tasks**.

If you are familiar with the topic covered, move onto the **Tasks** in this chapter.

Consolidation exercises are provided throughout the chapter for extra practice.

B1 Create and modify non-relational database tables

B1.1 Identify the components of a database

Sometimes you might be given a database and be required to enter and update data and run queries and reports. As you have not designed or created this database, it is sometimes more difficult until you are familiar with the database to enter and amend the data. This may mean that you have to familiarise yourself with the database by opening and viewing tables, queries, forms and reports before entering any data.

In this section, you will have the opportunity to create a database and manipulate an existing database.

Before you start to create your database in Microsoft Access® 2003, you should consider the design of any tables and queries first. This design can be drawn by hand or created on the computer – however, make sure that you carefully plan the database so that it works effectively. Planning is crucial in deciding what you want in your database and what information you need to get out. If you do not plan the database before starting to key in the information, you may have to spend a considerable amount of time later sorting it out.

Databases contain tables, forms, queries and reports.

In a database, a table holds the information in a basic format. Each record (row) in a database table consists of a number of fields (columns). A field is a column and a record is a row in a table. Fields in a database are where information is stored, for example, using a cars database you may have a field 'manufacturer' and a different field 'colour'. Each field may have different characteristics or formats and therefore different fields can be represented differently, for instance as text, numbers, currency, and so on.

See the example below, which shows a basic table and its field properties:

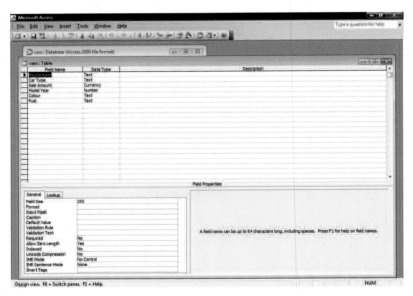

Figure 4.31

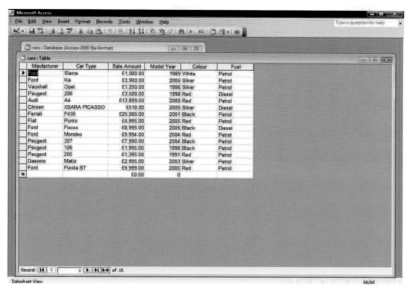

Figure 4.32

A form is a more 'user-friendly' way of entering the data into the database. The form is created and linked to a table and provides a graphical interface for being able to see and enter the data.

An example form is shown below:

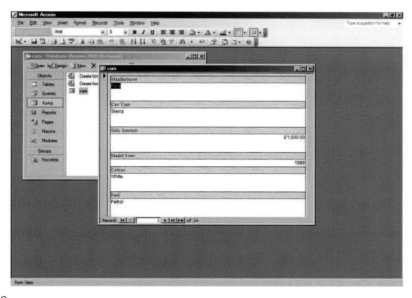

Figure 4.33

A query is the action you perform if you want to extract or find specific data from the database. Imagine if a customer came into a car showroom and asked to see all red Ford cars. The salesperson could run a query on the database which would then show all red Ford cars.

Data extracted from the database after running such a query is shown in Figure 4.34.

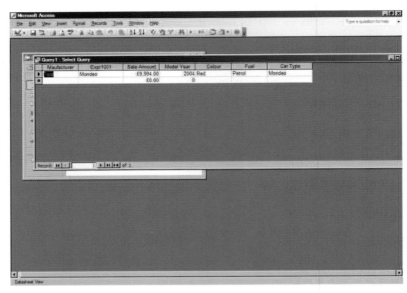

Figure 4.34

A report allows you to display and print your data in a professional way. Microsoft Access® contains a number of different report templates that you can use to adapt the way your report is produced. A report can be produced from either a table or query. You can change the page orientation of a report, change the font style and size and add images to produce a corporate report.

An example report is shown below:

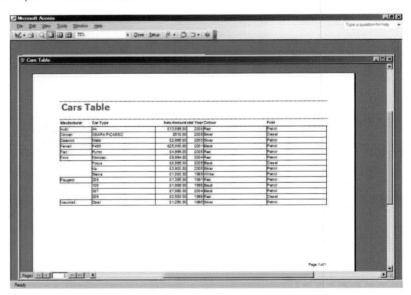

Figure 4.35

For the purpose of this unit, you will create and edit databases. You have been asked to create a single table database to record the computer equipment that is stored in different classrooms. The design plan should consider the different field names to be used in the database and different field types. Any field names that are created should be appropriate. For example, for surname you might want to use the fieldname LastName. It is good practice not to have any spaces between words in a field.

B1.2 Describe the field characteristics for the data required

When a database is created, different fields have different characteristics set. For example, if you are entering a date into a database, you need to set a date/time field using the design view in the table. Otherwise, when you come to query your data in the table you will be unable to extract the data effectively as Microsoft Access® will not see this as a date type field but a text field (which is the default) and will be unable to retrieve the data correctly.

The following is a list of field characteristics (data types) which can be set in Microsoft Access®:

- Text – this allows text and numeric data to be entered in a field.

- Numeric – this allows only numeric text to be entered, e.g. 123.

- Currency – this formats the data to currency, e.g. £1.20.

- Date/time – this formats the data to date and time, e.g. 21 March 2009.

- AutoNumber – this allocates an auto number to a field, e.g. 1, 2, 3 (usually primary key).

- Yes/No – this allows Yes or No to be entered, e.g. √.

- Lookup Wizard – this allows multiple values to be entered into a field so that the user can select from a number of options later (like a drop-down list).

Once fields have been set, the field size can also be changed. A text field usually defaults to 255 characters but you may need to enter data where the field size is not large enough. The LastName field below has been set to a maximum of nine characters:

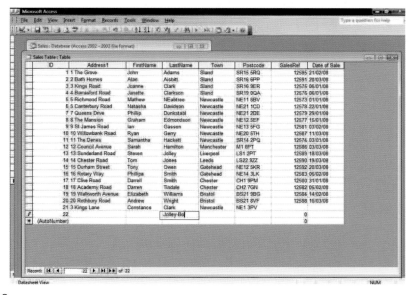

Figure 4.36

In this case Microsoft Access® will not allow you to enter any more than nine characters into this field. To change the field size, click on **Design** and click in the **LastName** field and change the field size from 9 to 20.

B1.4 Describe ways to maintain data integrity

In a database, data integrity must be maintained. Basically, this means correctness of data and keeping the data secure. If data integrity is not maintained, queries will be of no use to the end user as the information may have been incorrectly entered. One way of maintaining data integrity is by introducing a primary key.

Primary key

A primary key is a unique reference number; for example, if you are a shop owner who sells curtain poles, each customer will have a unique reference number and each order will have a unique reference number. If customers and orders had the same number, you would be unable to track customers and orders efficiently and provide good customer service. A primary key is one attribute (column) in a relational (table).

Using a library database scenario as an example, if we know the ISBN number of a book then we also know the author and title of the book. The ISBN number is the unique number in this case. The first table could be created as follows:

Book					
ISBN	**AUTHOR**	**TITLE**	**PUBLICATION DATE**	**STOCK NO**	**CATEGORY**

You will have the opportunity to create a primary key. However, you are more likely to use a primary key in a relational database; for example, one that contains more than one table rather than a single non-relational table, as this allows data to be linked by unique reference numbers.

Accuracy

When data is entered into a table or form, you need to proofread it very carefully to ensure that you have copied the data correctly. You could also ask one of your colleagues to check your accuracy until you are confident in what you are doing. If data is not accurate, you will get inaccurate results.

Consistency

Data should be entered consistently, for example, all the same words should start with a capital letter and should use the same format.

Effect of malicious or accidental alteration

Data can be maliciously or accidentally altered and this can destroy the validity of the data held in the database. To prevent this, data should be kept secure – this could be achieved by adding passwords or allowing different levels of permitted access to the data. For example, a user may only get 'read' access where another may be given 'read and write' access. Data should be backed up regularly so that if something does go wrong, data can be retrieved quickly. Validation can also help by keeping data secure by checking the entry and processing of data.

Validation

Validation of data within a database simply means that the data is checked to ensure that the data entered makes sense to the computer. For example, you could check that age has been entered as a number instead of as words. The following are examples of data validation checks:

Presence check	Checks that field has not been left blank
Type check	E.g. checks that age is entered as a number
Length check	E.g. checks that any surname entered is no more than 12 characters in length
Range check	Checks that any entered value falls within a range, e.g. £0–£1250
Format check	Checks that a particular format has been entered, e.g. TS1 3DF
Check digit	Checks that the last digit at end of string is a check digit, e.g. ISBN number

You can create validation rules and messages to specify data input into specific fields. When data is entered into a database field and violates the validation rule, you can display validation text with a message for the user.

For example, if you tried to enter 'Master' into a field with a validation rule of 'Mr' or 'Mrs', you would probably see the following message:

Rule: Enter only 'Mr' Or 'Mrs'

Message text: Invalid entry

An input mask allows you to restrict the data entry into certain fields. For example, you might want to ensure that you obtain the correct telephone number for someone and therefore you might set an input mask so that the user has to enter 10 numbers (4 for the area code and 6 for the number). In database tables/queries, input masks are used in fields to control the values that may be entered.

Worked Example B1.4

You have been asked by the Parkview Academy to record the details of computer equipment kept in different computer rooms at the Academy. All of the equipment is replaced every three years. The database needs to record the dates that the equipment was obtained, the date it is next to be checked, a brief description of the equipment and the room in which the equipment is held.

A plan has been drawn up as an example to show how the database could be created (see Figure 4.37).

Examples of input masks from Microsoft.com

INPUT MASK DEFINITION	EXAMPLES OF VALUES
(000) 000-0000	(206) 555-0248
(999) 999-9999!	(206) 555-0248 ( ) 555-0248
(000) AAA-AAAA	(206) 555-TELE
#999	-20 2000
>L????L?000L0	GREENGR339M3 MAY R 452B7
>L0L 0L0	T2F 8M4
00000-9999	98115- 98115-3007
>L<?????????????	Maria Pierre
ISBN 0-&&&&&&&&&-0	ISBN 1-55615-507-7 ISBN 0-13-964262-5
>LL00000-0000	DB51392-0493

PARKVIEW ACADEMY

COMPUTER EQUIPMENT DATABASE

Single table flat file database

FIELD NAME	FIELD TYPE
Assest_Number	Number
Date_Bought	Date
Description	Text
Make	Text
Location	Text
Date of last check	Date

Figure 4.37

Now it's your turn to have a go.

Task B1.4

You have been asked to create a database to hold the car sales for Cambridge Road Cars. You have been provided with the following data and you must decide on appropriate field names and field types and draw up a design plan, which can be used when the database is created. Ensure that the plan you design shows appropriate field names and field types – identify these on your plan:

Ford	Sierra	£1,000.00	1989	White	Petrol
Ford	Ka	£3,900.00	2005	Silver	Petrol
Vauxhall	Opel	£1,250.00	1996	Silver	Petrol
Peugeot	206	£3,500.00	1998	Red	Diesel
Audi	A4	£13,899.00	2000	Red	Petrol
Citroen	Xsara Picasso	£5,150.00	2005	Silver	Diesel
Ferrari	F430	£25,000.00	2001	Black	Petrol
Fiat	Punto	£4,995.00	2005	Red	Petrol
Ford	Focus	£8,995.00	2005	Black	Diesel
Ford	Mondeo	£9,994.00	2004	Red	Petrol
Peugeot	307	£7,990.00	2004	Black	Petrol
Peugeot	106	£1,995.00	1998	Black	Petrol
Peugeot	205	£1,395.00	1991	Red	Petrol
Daewoo	Matiz	£2,995.00	2003	Silver	Petrol
Ford	Fiesta ST	£9,999.00	2005	Red	Petrol

B1.3 Create and modify database tables using a range of field types

Once you have designed your database, you will need to create the database and include at least one table using the field names and field types you have included in your design plan. You will now watch a demonstration to see how a database can be created from the design plan.

4.11 Demonstration

Worked Example B1.3.1

The demonstration below creates a database using the field names and field types shown in the plan in Figure 4.37.

1 Load Microsoft Access®.

2 Click **New**.
3 Select **Blank Database**.

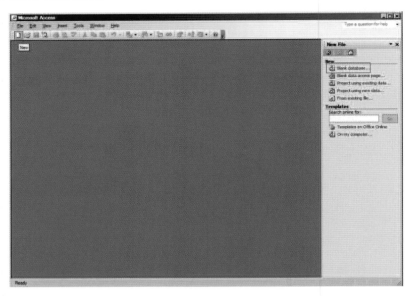

Figure 4.38

4 Choose a suitable location folder in which to save the file.
5 Enter the filename **Equipment** and click **Create**. A new blank database has been created.
6 Click **New**.
7 Click **Design View** and click **OK**.
8 Enter the field names as shown in your design plan.
9 Enter the field data types as shown in your design plan.
10 Save and close the table and database.

Once you have set the field types and sizes, you are then in a position to enter input masks and validation rules.

Task B1.3.1

1   Using the cars design plan that was drawn up in Task B1.4, create a new database using the filename **Cars**.
2   Create a new table and name it **Stock**.
3   Enter the field names as shown on your design plan.
4   Enter the following data as shown below.
5   Save and close the database and table.

Cars					
MANUFACTURER	**CAR TYPE**	**SALE AMOUNT**	**MODEL YEAR**	**COLOUR**	**FUEL**
Ford	Sierra	1000	1989	White	Petrol
Ford	Ka	3900	2005	Silver	Petrol
Vauxhall	Opel	1250	1996	Silver	Petrol
Peugeot	206	3500	1998	Red	Diesel

Watch the demonstration to see how this works.

4.12 | Demonstration

Worked Example B1.3.2

1 Open the **Equipment** database and the IT Equipment table in **Design View**.
2 Create an input mask in the Location field so that only room numbers with two letters and three numbers can be entered into this field.
1 Click on the **Location** field row.
2 Click on the **Input mask** row.
3 Type in: **>LL000;;_**

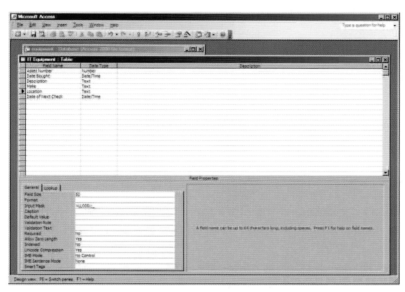

Figure 4.39

4 Save and close the table.
5 Try out the input mask by entering data into the Location field to check that the input mask works – for example, enter **C123**. You should get an error message saying that this does not conform to the input mask.
6 Create a validation rule for the Location field so that the only data can be entered is CM131 or CM101.
7 Open the table in Design View and key in the following validation information:

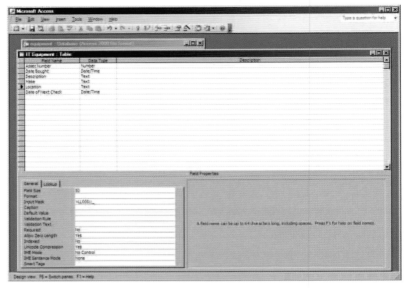

Figure 4.40

8 Check that the validation rule works correctly by entering the data **E120**.
9 Save and close the tables and database.

Task B1.3.2

1 Open the **Cars** database and the **Stock** table.
2 Create an input mask on the Model Year field, which only allows four numeric characters to be entered.

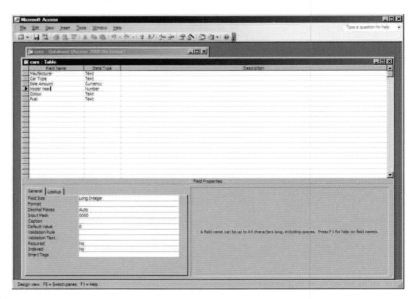

Figure 4.41

3 Save and close the table.
4 Create a validation rule for the Fuel field to be Petrol or Diesel only.

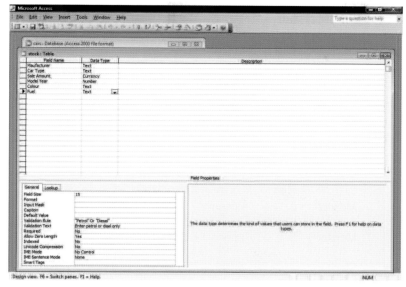

Figure 4.42

5 Check that the validation rule works by entering a new record with fuel as **LPG**.
You should get an error message.

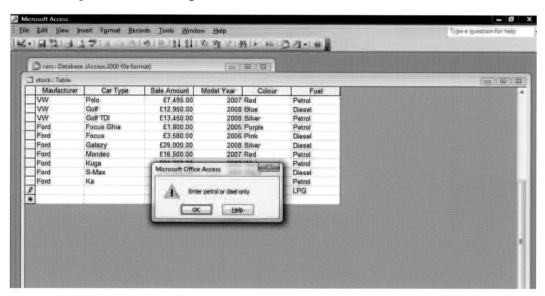

Figure 4.43

6 Save and close the table and database.

Worked Example B1.3.3

1 Open the **IT Equipment** database and the **IT Equipment** table.
2 Enter the first five records only as shown on pages 170–171.

IT Equipment					
ASSET NUMBER	**DATE BOUGHT**	**DESCRIPTION**	**MAKE**	**LOCATION**	**DATE OF LAST CHECK**
123455	21/06/2007	Portable HD	Belkin	E120	18/09/2007
436740	09/02/2007	Monitor	Epson	CM101	09/05/2007
436742	22/01/2007	Monitor	Epson	CM101	21/04/2007
436745	28/06/2007	Printer	Epson	CM101	
436711	19/06/2007	Monitor	Epson	CM131	16/09/2007
436712	18/06/2007	Monitor	Epson	CM131	15/09/2007
436713	08/07/2007	Monitor	Epson	CM131	05/10/2007
436714	04/03/2007	Monitor	Epson	CM131	01/06/2007
436715	05/03/2007	Monitor	Epson	CM131	02/06/2007
436717	15/02/2007	Monitor	Epson	CM131	15/05/2007
436718	20/07/2007	Monitor	Epson	CM131	17/10/2007
436719	21/07/2007	Monitor	Epson	CM131	18/10/2007
436720	22/07/2007	Monitor	Epson	CM131	
436721	12/10/2007	Monitor	Epson	CM131	09/01/2008
436723	07/06/2007	Printer	Epson	CM131	04/09/2007
436724	06/06/2007	Printer	Epson	CM131	03/09/2007
436725	26/06/2007	Printer	Epson	CM131	
436726	20/02/2007	Printer	Epson	CM131	20/05/2007
436727	21/02/2007	Printer	Epson	CM131	21/05/2007
436729	03/02/2007	Printer	Epson	CM131	03/05/2007
436730	08/07/2007	Printer	Epson	CM131	05/10/2007
436731	09/07/2007	Printer	Epson	CM131	06/10/2007
436732	10/07/2007	Printer	Epson	CM131	
436733	30/09/2007	Printer	Epson	CM131	28/12/2007
436734	28/05/2007	Printer	Epson	CM131	25/08/2007
436736	26/05/2007	Printer	HP	CM101	23/08/2007

IT Equipment					
ASSET NUMBER	DATE BOUGHT	DESCRIPTION	MAKE	LOCATION	DATE OF LAST CHECK
436737	25/05/2007	Printer	HP	CM101	22/08/2007
436738	14/06/2007	Monitor	HP	CM101	11/09/2007
436739	08/02/2007	Printer	HP	CM101	
436741	10/02/2007	Printer	HP	CM101	10/05/2007
436743	26/06/2007	Printer	HP	CM101	23/09/2007
436744	27/06/2007	Monitor	HP	CM101	24/09/2007
436746	18/09/2007	Monitor	HP	CM101	16/12/2007
436747	16/05/2007	Printer	HP	CM101	13/08/2007
436748	21/06/2007	Monitor	HP	CM101	18/09/2007
436749	19/06/2007	Printer	HP	CM101	16/09/2007
436750	18/06/2007	Monitor	HP	CM101	
436751	08/07/2007	Printer	HP	CM101	05/10/2007
436752	04/03/2007	Monitor	HP	CM101	01/06/2007
436753	05/03/2007	Printer	HP	CM101	02/06/2007
436754	06/03/2007	Monitor	HP	CM101	03/06/2007
436755	15/02/2007	Printer	HP	CM101	15/05/2007
436716	06/03/2007	Monitor	HP	CM131	
436722	09/06/2007	Monitor	HP	CM131	06/09/2007
436728	22/02/2007	Printer	HP	CM131	22/05/2007

3 Instead of keying in all the data you can import a datafile into Microsoft Access®.
4 Click on **File** → **Get External Data** → **Import** → **Next** → Tick **First Row Contains Field Names** → **Next** → **In an Existing Table** → **IT Equipment** → **Next** → **Finish**.
5 Save and close the table, using the name **IT Equipment**.

Now you have a go.

Task B1.3.3

1 Open the **Cars** database.
2 Import the datafile **cars.csv** to the **Cars** database.

3   Click on **File** → **Get External Data** → **Import** → **Next** → Tick **First Row Contains Field Names** → **Next** → **In an Existing Table** → **Stock** → **Next** → **Finish**.

4   Save and close the table using the name **Cars**.

Now that you have created your table and imported the data you must check that the data types are appropriate and that field sizes are set correctly.

Watch the demonstration to see how this is done.

4.13   Demonstration

> **Worked Example B1.3.4**

1   Open the **Equipment** database, click **IT equipment** table → **Design View** and check field characteristics.

2   Set the following field types in the table as indicated below:

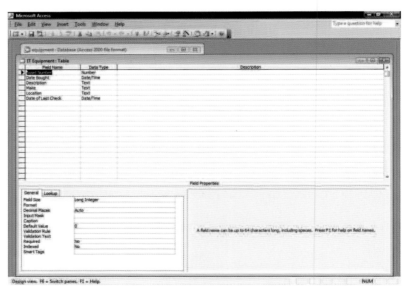

Figure 4.44

3   Set the following field sizes:

Date bought	short date
Description	40
Make	15
Date of last check	short date

4   Save and close the **IT equipment** table.

> **Task B1.3.4**

1   Open the **Cars** database and open the **Stock** table in **Design View**.

2   Check that you have the following field types:

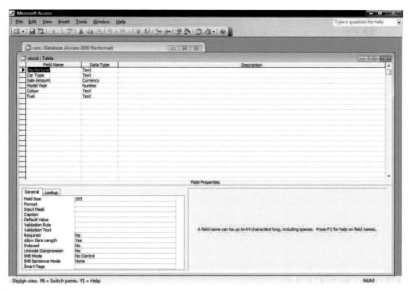

Figure 4.45

3 Set the following field sizes:

Manufacturer	50
Car type	40
Sale amount	currency, 2 decimal places
Colour	40
Fuel	15

4 Save and close the **Stock** table and **Cars** database.

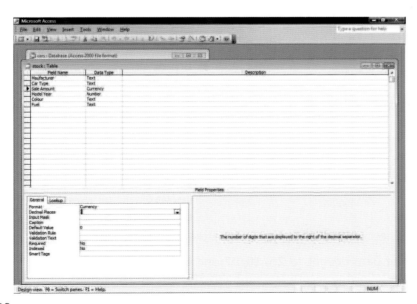

Figure 4.46

Consolidation

1 Design and create a new database to hold details of books held at the Parkview Academy Library.

2   You have been supplied with the data on pages 175–8 to help you create suitable file names and field types (this data is also available at www.hodderplus.co.uk/itq as **library.csv** so it can be imported if you prefer):

1   Set appropriate field types.
2   Set a primary key.
3   Set an input mask on the DBR number field so that it only allows four numeric values to be entered.
4   Set a validation rule for the Title so that only Mr, Mrs, Ms and Dr can be entered.
5   Save and close the library table and database.

Once you have created your database, you might decide that incorrect field characteristics have been set. For example, a telephone number field must be set as a text field otherwise the first '0' at the start of a telephone number will not be shown. You might also decide that the field lengths have been set incorrectly. Make sure that you check before you make any changes because if you make the wrong changes, the data that is already held in the database tables may be lost.

Watch the demonstration to see how this works.

4.14 Demonstration

Worked Example B1.3.5

1   Open the **Equipment** database and the **IT equipment** table.
2   Scroll to the bottom of the table to the next available blank row and add the following new record accurately:

IT equipment					
ASSET NUMBER	**DATE BOUGHT**	**DESCRIPTION**	**MAKE**	**LOCATION**	**DATE OF NEXT CHECK**
436765	02/01/2008	Printer	Epson	CM131	02/01/2008

1   Find the following record with an AssetNumber of 436476 and amend it as shown below:

IT equipment					
ASSET NUMBER	**DATE BOUGHT**	**DESCRIPTION**	**MAKE**	**LOCATION**	**DATE OF NEXT CHECK**
436746	25/10/07	Monitor	HP	CM131	16/12/2007

Note: The easiest way of doing this is by clicking on **Edit, Find**.

2   Change the Date Bought to **25/10/07** and the Location to **CM131**.
3   Delete the following record by highlighting the record and pressing the **Delete** key on the keyboard:

IT equipment					
ASSET NUMBER	**DATE BOUGHT**	**DESCRIPTION**	**MAKE**	**LOCATION**	**DATE OF NEXT CHECK**
123455	21/06/2007	Portable HD	Belkin	E120	18/09/2007

4   Check that you have made the amendments correctly.
5   Close the table and database.

Library table

ID	TITLE	FIRST NAME	SURNAME	DB NUMBER	EPDR	BOOK 1	AUTHOR 1	DATE OUT 1	RETURNED 1	BOOK 2	AUTHOR 2	DATE OUT 2	RETURNED 2
1	Mr	Alex	Brydges	123	25/10/2007	The Hobbit	J.R.R Tolkien	23/06/2007	25/07/2007				
2	Mr	Amy	Baker	107	18/08/2007	Elfstones of Shannara	Terry Brooks	13/06/2007	15/07/2007				
3	Mr	Andrea	Barclay	289	06/09/2007	The Straken	Terry Brooks	02/07/2007	04/08/2007				
4	Mr	Andrew	O'Neill	156	13/07/2007	Ellenois	Robert Stratford	09/06/2007	11/07/2007				
5	Mr	Andrew	Richards	219	11/09/2007	The Guv'nor	Lenny Mclean	01/07/2007	03/08/2007				
6	Mr	Ben	Parkinson	133	21/09/2007	Redeemed	Sarah Eastleigh	03/07/2007	05/08/2007				
7	Mr	Benjamin	Smith	178	05/08/2007	Edge of Time	Roger Smith	29/05/2007	11/07/2007				
8	Ms	Bobby	Simmons	102	27/11/2007	Premonition	Amy White	06/06/2007	08/07/2007				
9	Mr	Caroline	Atkinson	214	23/08/2007	Among the Rest	Trevor Mason	10/07/2007	12/08/2007				
10	Ms	Chris	Kent	288	16/10/2007	The Magicians Guild	Daniel Lee	27/05/2007					
11	Ms	Daniel	Mercer	154	30/08/2007	Bloodfire	Terry Brooks	03/06/2007	05/07/2007				
12	Mr	Dean	Wright	106	19/12/2007	Touching the Void	Joe Simpson	12/06/2007	15/07/2007				
13	Mr	Dwayne	Law	269	21/11/2007	Recall	Robert Orion	19/06/2007	21/07/2007				
14	Ms	Elyssa	Forester	199	19/08/2007	The Summer Love	Mark Hughes	25/05/2007	01/07/2007				

Library table

ID	TITLE	FIRST NAME	SURNAME	DB NUMBER	EPDR	BOOK 1	AUTHOR 1	DATE OUT 1	RETURNED 1	BOOK 2	AUTHOR 2	DATE OUT 2	RETURNED 2
15	Mr	Frank	Stevens	212	30/11/2007	The Two Towers	J.R.R Tolkien	02/07/2007	05/08/2007				
16	Mr	Harold	Ramsey	122	15/12/2007	Remaining Soldiers	Richard Hughes	04/06/2007	05/07/2007				
17	Mrs	Harry	Parker	124	09/11/2007	The Witches Broom	Ruth Barb	05/07/2007	07/08/2007				
18	Mr	James	Keerson	342	23/10/2007	Forever Young	Christopher Teech	09/08/2007					
19	Mr	Jason	Feerton	294	29/11/2007	Happy Days	Barbara Franch	21/08/2007	29/09/2007				
20	Mrs	Jason	Smith	324	14/01/2008	Along the Line	Graham Mitchell	23/09/2007	18/10/2007				
21	Ms	John	Humpton	111	13/04/2008	Girls Talk	Rachel Danson	29/05/2007	12/06/2007				
22	Mr	Julie	Hart	367	19/01/2008	Silver Talon	Richard Feist	30/08/2007	29/09/2007				
23	Mr	Kenny	Meecham	144	24/05/2008	Bloodline	Mary Jones	03/09/2007	04/10/2007				
24	Mr	Kevin	Dean	432	12/01/2008	Gravel Pit	Harold Warren	12/05/2007	18/06/2007				
25	Ms	Kevin	May	465	13/11/2007	Herald of Times	Melissa Long	16/06/2007					
26	Mr	Leanne	Graham	399	24/10/2007	Demons and Ghouls	Frank Reed	13/07/2007	12/08/2007				
27	Mr	Leanne	Sampson	455	15/11/2007	Groundhogs	Liam Harsk	15/05/2007	11/06/2007				
28	Mr	Liam	Costilek	376	12/04/2008	Blown Away	Keeley Gamble	03/08/2007	07/09/2007				

Library table

ID	TITLE	FIRST NAME	SURNAME	DB NUMBER	EPDR	BOOK 1	AUTHOR 1	DATE OUT 1	RETURNED 1	BOOK 2	AUTHOR 2	DATE OUT 2	RETURNED 2
29	Ms	Liam	Groom	286	15/06/2008	Stirlings Men	David Stirling	04/08/2007	04/09/2007				
30	Mr	Michael	Yuill	1079	22/03/2008	Mind Tricks	Derren Brown	17/10/2007	03/11/2007				
31	Ms	Patrick	Morrisey	565	04/09/2008	Handling Lives	Susan Impton	23/09/2007	19/10/2007				
32	Mr	Rachel	Wilkinson	333	13/03/2008	Aggressor	Andy Mcnab	19/08/2007	23/09/2007				
33	Mr	Rachel	Hope	431	19/11/2007	Backdraft	Harry Moorson	12/05/2007					
34	Mr	Richard	West	334	27/12/2007	Narcotics	Richard Wilson	07/08/2007	03/09/2007				
35	Mr	Ricky	Cowley	355	11/11/2007	Bravo Two Zero	Andy Mcnab	23/07/2007	19/08/2007				
36	Mr	Robert	Andrews	376	14/11/2007	Silverthorn	Richard Feist	05/08/2007	01/09/2007				
37	Ms	Robert	Baker	531	23/10/2007	Trackers	Kevin Bantren	04/09/2007	07/10/2007				
38	Mr	Robert	Jole	566	19/10/2007	Heroes	Harrison Mealey	23/05/2007	29/06/2007				
39	Mr	Roger	Grand	146	14/11/2007	Reality Strikes	Jonathan Cosack	12/06/2007	23/07/2007				
40	Mr	Ronald	Harrison	311	01/02/2008	Tempest	Susan Anston	25/08/2007	13/09/2007				
41	Mr	Ronald	Stevens	599	03/05/2008	Killing Ground	Daniel Creek	24/06/2007	07/07/2007				
42	Mr	Roxanne	Peters	577	06/01/2008	Breakdown	Henny Tress	01/07/2007	03/08/2007				

Library table

ID	TITLE	FIRST NAME	SURNAME	DB NUMBER	EPDR	BOOK 1	AUTHOR 1	DATE OUT 1	RETURNED 1	BOOK 2	AUTHOR 2	DATE OUT 2	RETURNED 2
43	Mr	Sarah	Kuston	381	05/11/2007	Come Again	Sarah Eve	06/08/2007	27/08/2007				
44	Mr	Sarah	Harold	360	03/12/2007	Vector	Nina Franklin	24/09/2007	13/10/2007				
45	Ms	Sarah	Simpson	412	13/10/2007	Freedom	Darren Neek	13/05/2007	14/06/2007				
46	Mr	Tony	Serenson	563	24/12/2007	The Game	John Bicky	13/06/2007					
47	Mr	Tony	Thompson	628	13/09/2007	Immediate Action	Andy Mcnab	23/05/2007	16/06/2007				
48	Mr	Warren	Johnson	616	23/01/2008	Harvest Winter	Jonathan Major	30/06/2007	11/07/2007				
49	Ms	Warren	French	678	19/06/2008	Ready for Life	Rachel Watts	19/08/2007	23/09/2007				
50	Mr	William	Grant	782	11/10/2007	Carry On Up	Lindsay Cooke	25/06/2007	29/08/2007				

Now it's your turn.

Task B1.3.5
---

1 Open the **Cars** database and the **Stock** table.
2 Add the following new record to the cars database:

Cars					
MANUFACTURER	**CAR TYPE**	**SALE AMOUNT**	**MODEL YEAR**	**COLOUR**	**FUEL**
Vauxhall	Corsa	£1,250.00	2002	Silver	Petrol

3 Amend the following record in the **Cars** database:

Cars					
MANUFACTURER	**CAR TYPE**	**SALE AMOUNT**	**MODEL YEAR**	**COLOUR**	**FUEL**
Fiat	Punto	£4,995.00	2008	Black	Petrol

4 Change the model year to **2009** and the colour to **White**.
5 Check that you have made the amendments correctly.
6 Save and close the table and database.

B1.5 **Respond appropriately to problems with database tables**

B1.6 **Use database tools and techniques to ensure data integrity is maintained**

Data can be checked by proofreading, by using a spell checker, the validation tools or help.

Now watch the demonstration to see how this works.

4.15 *Demonstration*

Worked Example B1.5
---

1 Open the **Equipment** database and the **IT equipment** table.
2 Run a spell check to check the data in the table.
3 Ensure all company names are correct.
4 Save and close the database and table.

Now it's your turn.

Task 1.5
---

1 Open the **Cars** database and the **Stock** table.
2 Run a spell check on the table.
3 Save and close the table.

B2 Enter, edit and organise structured information in a database

B2.1 Create forms to enter, edit and organise data in a database

A data entry form can be used to enter details into a database in a more user-friendly way instead of directly into a table. The form can include combo boxes (drop-down lists) to make the data selection easier. These also reduce data entry error and the forms can be customised.

Watch the demonstration to see how this works.

4.16 | Demonstration

Worked Example B2.1.1

1   Open the **Equipment** database and click on the **Forms** tab.
2   Click **New → Form Wizard**. Select the **IT equipment** table from which the form is to be created. Click **OK**.

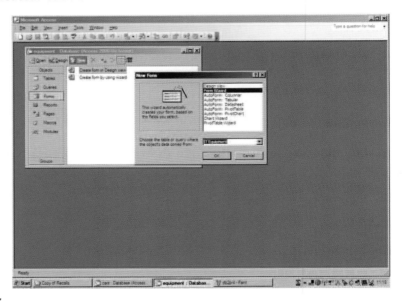

Figure 4.47

3   Select all the fields to be displayed in the form by clicking on the double-headed arrow.
4   Click on **Next** and select the layout type (e.g. justified).
5   Click on **Next** and select the background (e.g. ricepaper).
6   Click on **Next** and add a title for the form **IT equipment**. Click **Finish**.
4   See the form displayed.

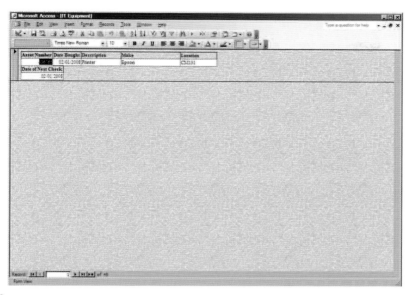

Figure 4.48

5 Save and close the form.

Creating a combo box

A combo box is a drop-down box that allows you to select data from a list rather than typing it in.

> **Worked Example B2.1.2**

1 Open the **IT equipment** form in **Design View**. Create a drop-down box by selecting the **Combo Box** icon from the Toolbox.

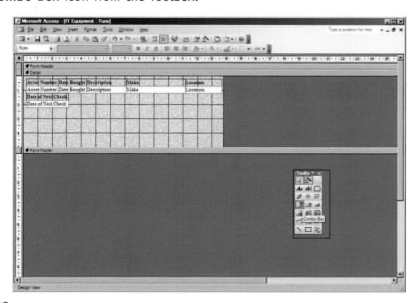

Figure 4.49

2 Draw the shape of your box onto your form. Select **I will type in the values I want**.
3 Click **Next** → **Combo Box Wizard**. Type in the information to be stored in the combo box (e.g. Printer, Monitor).

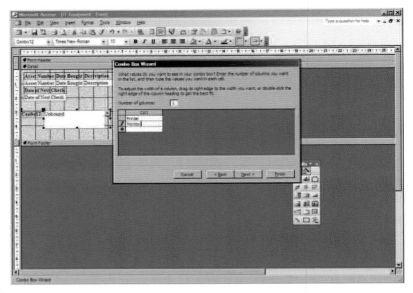

Figure 4.50

1 Click **Next**. Store the values in the Description field
2 Click **Next** and add the label name **Description1**. Click **Finish**.
3 View the form in **Design View** and delete the existing Description field by selecting the box and pressing **Delete** on the keyboard.
3 Save the form as **IT Equipment**.

Now it's your turn.

Task B2.1.2

1 Open the **Cars** database and the **Stock** table.
2 Create a new form based on the **Stock** table.
3 Include all fields.
4 Create a combo box for the manufacturer field and use the following details:

Audi
Citroen
Daewoo
Ferrari
Fiat
Ford
Peugeot
Vauxhall
VW
Seat

5 Check that the form works by creating the following new record. Use the combo box to select the manufacturer:

Stock					
MANUFACTURER	CAR TYPE	SALE AMOUNT	MODEL YEAR	COLOUR	FUEL
Seat	Ibiza	8750	2008	Sporting Green	Petrol

6 Save and close the form and the database.

B2.2 Select and use appropriate tools and techniques to format data entry forms

Worked Example B2.2

1 Using the **IT Equipment** database, open the form in **Design View**.
2 Change the font to **Arial 12**.
3 Increase the size of each box to ensure that all data is shown in full (annotate – form 2).
4 Fill the answer boxes with pale green.
5 Preview the form to make sure it looks professional.
6 Make any other amendments that you feel are appropriate.
7 Save and close the form and database.

Task B2.2

1 Using the **Cars** database, open the form in **Design View**.
2 Change the font to **Verdana 12**.
3 Increase the size of each box to ensure that all data is shown in full (annotate – form 2).
4 Fill the boxes with orange.
5 Preview the form to make sure that it looks professional.
6 Make any other amendments that you feel are appropriate.
7 Save and close the form and database.

B2.3 Check data entry meets needs, using IT tools and making corrections as necessary

Locate and amend record

As with data entry into the database table, any data entered into the form must be checked for accuracy, consistency, completeness, validity and spell checked for errors.

It is easy to find records in a form.

Worked Example B2.3

1 Open the **Equipment** database.
2 Open the form.
3 Click **Edit** → **Find** → **436740**.
4 Change date last checked to **09/05/08**.

Another way to find a form is to use a wildcard or search operator.

4   Click **Edit** → **Find** → **H***. Select record **436728** by clicking **Find Next** and **Change to Monitor**.
5   Check that the validation works by clicking **Edit** → **Find** → **436738**. Change the equipment to **laptop** – you should get an error message.
6   Save and close the forms.

Over to you.

Task B2.3

1   Open the **Cars** database and the **Stock** form.
2   Find the **KA** car form. Change the model year to **2007**.
3   Find **Altea*** – two records should be displayed.
4   Change **Petrol** to **LPG** in one of the records and check that the validation rule still works.
5   Open the **Cars** database and run through each form and check that each record is 100 per cent correct.
6   Save and close the database.

B2.4   Respond appropriately to data entry errors

Now that the cars database has all the data entered, before you move onto the next section of querying the data, you should check all the data.

Worked Example B2.4

1   Open the **IT equipment** table in **Design View** and check the field sizes, data types, validation checks and error messages to make sure these are correct.
2   Open the form and check that all data is displayed in full and that the field sizes are appropriate.
3   Check that that the combo boxes work.
4   Check that the validation rules and input masks work.
5   Save and close the form and database.

Task B2.4

1   Open the **Cars** database and **Stock** table in **Design View** and check the field sizes, data types, validation checks and error messages to make sure these are correct.
2   Check that all data is displayed in full and that the field sizes are appropriate in the form.
3   Check that the combo boxes work.
4   Check that the validation rules and input masks work.
5   Save and close the form and database.

B3 Use database software tools to run queries and produce reports

B3.1 Create and run database queries using multiple criteria to display or amend selected data

Simple queries

Simple queries can be created within the database to search for and find specific results that match a given criteria, for example you might want to search for all red cars in a database. Microsoft Access® then returns the results showing all the red cars.

Multiple queries can be created to find more than one item within a database – you could search for 'Ford' and 'red' to return the results showing all red Ford cars. However, you can also use multiple criteria in the same field, for example 'Ford' and 'BMW' and Microsoft Access® will return the results showing all Ford and BMW cars.

Complex queries (not, between, and)

Complex queries look at more than one field. They are made up of two or more simple queries joined together by logical operators, such as AND, OR and NOT; for example 'Ford' and 'BMW'.

The table below shows the logical operators that can be used in Microsoft Access®.

NOT	WHERE NOT (Author = Jones)
	This will search for all records where the author is 'not' Jones.
AND	WHERE Author = Jones AND Date = 1999
	This will search for all records where the author is 'Jones' AND had a book published in '1999'.
OR	WHERE Author = Jones OR Date = 1999
	This will search for all records where the author is 'Jones' OR had a book published in '1999'.

Example range operators to be used in queries

The table below shows the range operators that can be used in Microsoft Access®:

OPERATORS	DESCRIPTION
>	Greater than
<	Less than
>=	Greater than or equal to
<=	Less than or equal to
<>	Not equal to

Wildcard or Like Queries

The asterisk (*), per cent sign (%), question mark (?), underscore (_), number sign (#), exclamation mark (!), hyphen (-) and brackets ([ ]) are wildcard characters. These can be used in queries and expressions to include all records, file names or other items that begin with specific characters or match a certain pattern.

Queries from linked tables

Both simple and complex criteria can be used in single or linked tables. More than one table can be added to the query design and then data selected from both tables.

View the demonstration of running a query to see how this works.

4.17 | *Demonstration*

Now you will have the chance to run queries that use more than one criterion.

Watch the demonstration to see how this is done.

4.18 | *Demonstration*

Worked Example B3.1

1 Open the **Equipment** database.
2 Click on **Queries** → **New** → **Design View** → **OK** → **Add**.
3 **Close** after adding the **IT Equipment** table.
4 Transfer all fields from the **IT Equipment** table into the query design.
5 Search for Make **HP** equipment in Location **CM101**.
6 Run the query.

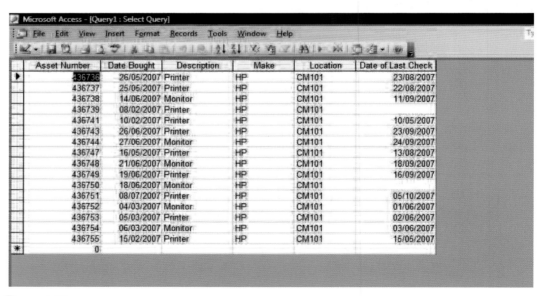

Figure 4.51

7 Save and close the query as **HP**.
8 Create a new query and search for **printer**, between 01/01/2007 and 30/06/2007. Save and close the query as **Printer**.
9 Sort the data into ascending order of **Make**.
10 Close the database.

An alternative way to create a query is to run a Filter. To create a filter:

1 Open the **IT Equipment** table → click on the **Field Name Make** in the database table.
2 Click on the **Filter** icon.

3 Click on the **Field name** drop-down arrow and choose **HP** and click on the **Filter** icon

4 Your results will be shown.

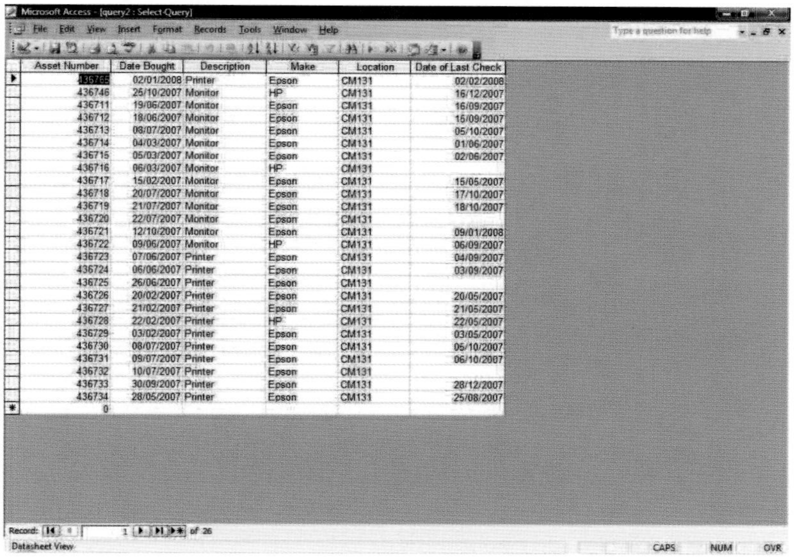

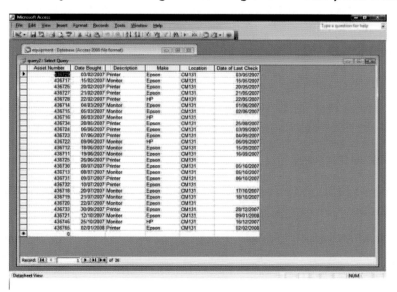

Figure 4.52

1 Create a further query which searches for HP or Epson equipment in room CM131.

2 Sort alphabetically with **Date Bought Ascending** and **IT Description Descending**.

Figure 4.53

3 Save and close the query as **CM131**.

Now it's your turn to have a go.

Task B3.1

1 Using the **Cars** database run the following queries:

a   Create a new query which searches for cars where the model year is after 2001 and the colour is red.

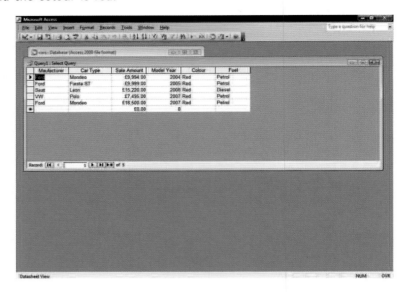

Figure 4.54

b   Save and close the query as **Red Cars**.
c   Create a new query to search for red or black cars where the fuel is petrol.
d   Add an alphanumeric sort.
f   Save and close the query as **Petrol Cars**.

Consolidation

Create the following new queries using the **Library** database:

1   Search for books that are on loan in June 2007 and where the author is Brooks.
2   Save and close the query.
3   Search for all books that have not been returned, in the **Date Returned 1** field.
4   Save and close the query.

B3.2   Plan and produce database reports from a single-table non-relational database

Microsoft Access® allows you to create a variety of reports to display the information from your tables and/or queries more effectively. The reports that you produce should include a range of standard templates. Reports can be customised by adding background or by changing the font styles/sizes.

Using menus, wizards, shortcuts, selected fields, selected records

Worked Example B3.2

1   Open the **Equipment** database.
2   Click on **Reports** → **New** → **Report Wizard**.
3   Select the query **CM131** → **OK**.
4   Slect all the fields to be displayed in the report by clicking on the double-headed arrow → **Next** → **Group by Date Bought by Month** → **Next**. Do not sort at this point.

5   Select **Block** layout and **Portrait** orientation → **Next** → choose **Casual**.
6   Add a title **Equipment** in **Room CM131** → **Finish**.

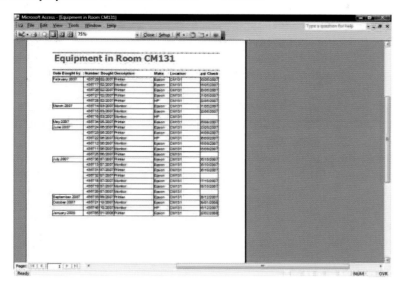

Figure 4.55

Your completed report will now be displayed.

Note: Some of the fields are not wide enough and the data is not shown in full – we will amend this in a later exercise.

Sort in reports

Data can be sorted in reports. However, if you use the sort when using the Report Wizard, then the sorted fields are automatically displayed as the first field in the database report. To avoid this happening, open the report in Design View and click on the sorting and grouping icon. Manually select the fields to be sorted in either ascending or descending order.

B3.3   Select and use appropriate tools and techniques to format database reports

Creating a customised report

Worked Example B3.3

1   Using **Equipment in Room CM131** report, click on **Design** and change to **Design View**.
2   To add a background colour to a section, right click on an area within the design, for example **Details** → **3**.
3   Choose a fill colour to change the background colour.
4   To change the font style/size, select the text boxes and then change the font style/size.
5   Add a background image. Click on **Insert** → **Picture** and select your image.
6   To change the page setup, click on **File** → **Page Setup**.
7   Save and preview the report.

Now it's your turn to have a go.

> ### Task B3.3
>
> 1 Using the **Cars** database, create a new report based on the **Red Cars** query.
> 2 Do not include the Model Year field.
> 3 Group the report by Manufacturer.
> 4 Once the report has been created, sort the **Sale Amount** into ascending order.
> 5 Once you have created the report, customise it by:
>   a Adding a background colour to rows. Colour can only be added to sections/controls in a database report.
>   b Click on the row and go to Design View. Click on a row in the margin, choose fill colour and select pale blue.
>   c Ensure that all data is shown in full.
>   d Add your name as a header/footer by drawing a text box in the page header or footer area of the report.
>   e Change the orientation of the report to **Landscape**.
>   f Change the margins so that they are 4cm all the way round.
>   g Remove the page number from the report.
>   h Add the date and time to the footer of the report.
>   i Save and close the report.

Format data in a database report

Once your reports have been created, you need to ensure that all data is shown in full and that none of the fields have been truncated 'or cut short'.

The **Equipment** report created in Task 2 has truncated data and the fields must be expanded to show the data in full.

> **B3.4** Check reports meet needs, using IT tools and making corrections as necessary

> ### Worked Example B3.4.1

Using the **Equipment** database and the **Equipment in Room CM131** report:

1 Change the page layout to **Landscape** if this has not already been changed.
2 Make the following fields larger:
   a **Asset Number**
   b **Date Bought**
   c **Date of Next Check**.
3 Check that all data is shown in full.
4 Change the orientation of the report.
5 Change the margins.
7 Add the date to the header area of the report.
8 Add your name to the footer area of the report.
9 Save and close the report.

Now it's your turn to have a go.

> **Task B3.4.1**

Using the **Cars** database and the **Red Cars** report:

1 Check through all the reports and change any fields so that they are wide enough to show all data in full.
2 Save and close the report.

> **Consolidation**

1 Open the **Library** database.
2 Create a report on the **June 2007** query – do not display the ID or fields which contain no data.
3 Format the report.
4 Ensure all data is shown in full.
5 Save and print one copy of the report.
6 Create a customised report based on the **Outstanding books** query. Only include the names, date of loan and book title so that this information can be forwarded to the borrower.
7 Choose an appropriate format.
8 Ensure that all data is shown in full.
9 Save and print the report.
10 Close the database.

Database reports: Using menus or shortcuts

One way to improve efficiency can be by creating a shortcut by creating a form.

> **Worked Example B3.4.2**

You may have to run a report from a menu that has already been created. Open the **IT Equipment** database shown on the CD and access the reports. This database has had a form created with several macros which you can run by clicking on the appropriate button.

1 Open the **IT equipment** database.
2 Access the **IT equipment** form by clicking on the button – this should open the form.
3 Close the form.
4 Click on the **Room CM131** report by clicking on the button – this should open and print the report.
5 Close the database.

Mini Assignment

In this Mini Assignment, you will practise all the skills you have learned throughout this chapter.

The Mini Assignment is based around the estate agency database. Your manager has given you the following instructions and you are required to complete these tasks.

Create a new folder to store your work for this assignment and then produce evidence to meet the unit requirements.

In this task, you will practise everything you have learned.

1 Create a new folder and name this **Agency** database.
2 Create a new database named **estateagency.mdb** and create a new **Property** table.
3 The data has been provided in the file **estateagency.csv** and this can be imported into Microsoft Access® by selecting **File** → **Get External Data** → **Import**.
4 Follow the steps in the wizard and the data for your database will be imported.
5 Create a **Property** form that will allow you to enter data more easily into the database.
6 Carry out a spell check. Ignore all Addresses and Areas as these have been checked and are correct.
7 Save and close all tables and forms.
8 Run the following queries:
   a Search for all properties with a Date Listed later than 21/6/07, using all fields. Save and close the query.
   b Search for all properties with an Asking Price of more than £150,000. Save and close the query.
   c Create a new query and sort Date Listed into Ascending order. Save and close the query.
   d Search for all properties with an Asking Price of between £150,000 and £180,000 and within the Knowlsley area. Save and close the query.
   e Search for all properties with four or five bedrooms. Save and close the query.
9 Create the following reports:
   a Create a report based on the **Date Listed Sorted** query. Show all fields and ensure that all data is shown in full. Customise the report by changing the background colour.
   b Create a report based on the **Asking Price > £150,000** query. Show only the Date Listed, Asking Price, Bedrooms, Street and House Number fields. Customise the report by changing the font styles/sizes of the report.
10 Save and close all queries and reports.
11 Save and close the database.
12 Close Microsoft Access®

5

Spreadsheet Software

This unit will develop your knowledge and skills relating to producing, presenting and checking straightforward spreadsheets. You will have the opportunity to use a range of tools to enter, manipulate, format and output data for different purposes. You will use formula and functions, for example sum, divide and multiply. The spreadsheet you will use will have a pre-determined structure.

By working through the **Overview, Worked Examples, Tasks** and **Consolidations** in this chapter, you will demonstrate the skills required for Spreadsheet Software Level 1.

ELEMENT The competent person will...	PERFORMANCE CRITERIA To demonstrate this competence they can...	KNOWLEDGE To demonstrate this competence they will also...
SS:A1 Use a spreadsheet to enter, edit and organise numerical and other data	A1.2 Enter and edit numerical and other data accurately A1.3 Store and retrieve spreadsheet files effectively, in line with local guidelines and conventions where available	A1.1 Identify what numerical and other information is needed and how the spreadsheet should be structured to meet needs
SS:A2 Use appropriate formulas and tools to summarise and display spreadsheet information	A2.2 Use functions and formulas to meet calculation requirements A2.3 Use spreadsheet tools and techniques to summarise and display information	A2.1 Identify how to summarise and display the required information
SS:A3 Select and use appropriate tools and techniques to present spreadsheet information effectively	A3.1 Select and use appropriate tools and techniques to format spreadsheet cells, rows and columns A3.3 Select and use appropriate tools and techniques to generate, develop and format charts and graphs A3.4 Select and use appropriate page layout to present and print spreadsheet information A3.5 Check information meets needs, using spreadsheet tools and making corrections as necessary	A3.2 Identify which chart or graph type to use to display information

Step-by-step examples are provided as a demonstration of what to do. These demonstrations are based on Microsoft Excel® 2003. Review the **Overview** in each section and then watch the demonstrations in the **Worked Examples** before commencing any **Tasks**.

Once you are familiar with the topic covered, move onto the **Tasks** in this chapter.

Consolidation exercises are provided throughout the chapter for extra practice.

Throughout the **Worked Example** sections, the demonstrations relate to charting the income of different departments. The **Tasks** relate to costing a course.

There are **Consolidation** exercises throughout this chapter relating to cafe sales. A Mini Assignment is included at the end of the chapter, which can be used for additional practice only.

A1 Use a spreadsheet to enter, edit and organise numerical and other data

What is a spreadsheet?

A spreadsheet is a software program that allows you to enter data in columns and rows and perform different calculations. Spreadsheets are useful in helping to make predictions into profit, loss and sales but they can be used for many different subjects as they can organise information easily and neatly.

When you open Microsoft Excel®, you will see the screen as shown below:

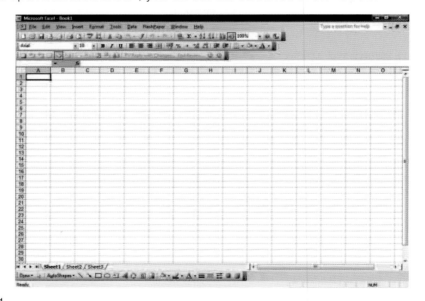

Figure 5.1

Spreadsheet components include cells, rows, columns, tabs, pages, charts, ranges, workbooks, worksheets, structure, design and layout.

A1.1 Identify what numerical and other information is needed and how the spreadsheet should be structured to meet needs

When designing and creating a spreadsheet, you need to decide what information to include. It is easier to plan your spreadsheet before you start entering data. At Level 1 spreadsheets will include:

- numbers

- charts

- graphs

- text.

Numbers

A spreadsheet will contain different types or formats of numbers that can be used in a variety of calculations. Numbers can be formatted as shown below:

NUMBER FORMAT	EXAMPLE
Number	1
	1.20 (with 2 decimal places)
Currency	£1.20
Date	14 March 2010

Charts

In Microsoft Excel®, a chart is a visual representation of numerical data. There are different types of charts that can be used to display information, for example histogram, bar chart and pie chart.

A histogram shows the quantity of points within grouped data (e.g. ages).

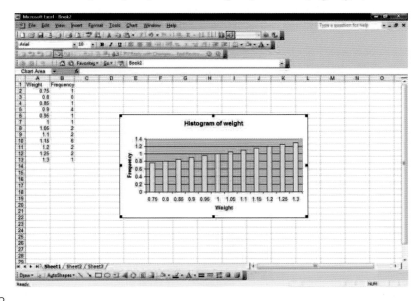

Figure 5.2

A bar chart uses bars to show frequencies of data.

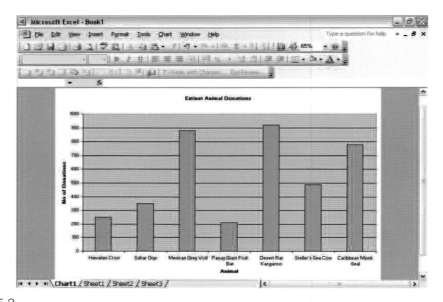

Figure 5.3

A pie chart shows percentage values as a slice of a pie.

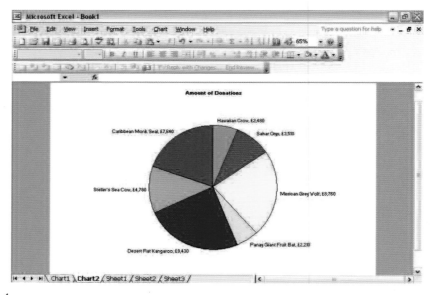

Figure 5.4

Graphs

A graph shows a visual representation of numerical data, but it shows the relationship between two or more numbers, for example x and y axis numerical data. The x axis could be ages and the y axis could be maths scores.

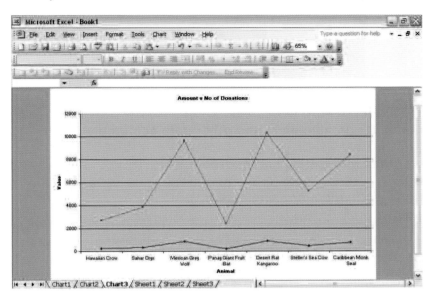

Figure 5.5

Text

Text can be entered into rows and columns to label the data, and describe column headings.

Before you start keying data into a Microsfot Excel® spreadsheet, you should think carefully about the design. It could be that you decide to draw a design sketch so that it covers all the requirements. It is easier to get it right in the beginning rather than having to make amendments as you work through the spreadsheet.

Watch the demonstration to see how this is done.

 **5.1 Demonstration**

> **Worked Example A1.1**

In the task below is a design plan for the **Income** spreadsheet. The user has been asked to create a spreadsheet for some new training courses. This has been drawn based on the information required to chart the income of various departments.

Over to you.

> **Task A1.1**

You have been asked to create a spreadsheet for some new training courses. You have been provided with the information below to help you create your spreadsheet.

The spreadsheet will calculate the total cost of each course and the cost to be charged for each delegate.

COURSE	HIRE OF ROOM	REFRESHMENTS	PHOTOCOPYING	TUTOR
Admin	650	125	35	240
ICT for beginners	450		35	200
ICT Level 2	450		35	200
Interviewing skills	600	125	35	300
Time management	500	125	35	300

A1.2 Enter and edit numerical and other data accurately

A1.2.1 Enter data into existing spreadsheet

A1.2.2 Insert information into single cells

You have been provided with a spreadsheet which will allow you to calculate the income for various departments. The spreadsheet includes the column headings you will now enter the data into. Consider – is there anything about the design here you would change?

Watch the demonstration to see how this is done.

5.2 Demonstration

Worked Example A1.2.1

1 Click on the **Start** button and click **Microsoft Excel**.
2 Open the spreadsheet **shop1.xls**.
3 Key in the following data – the first column has already been created for you.

CATEGORY	STOCK LEVEL	NUMBER SOLD	LEFT IN STOCK	RETAIL AMOUNT	SALE PRICE	REORDER
Chocolate bars	10	21		£0.35		
Ready salted crisps	15	13		£0.29		
Chews	8	8		£0.18		
Salt and vinegar crisps	15	9		£0.29		
Cheese and onion crisps	13	8		£0.29		
Prawn cocktail crisps	12	7		£0.29		
Mints	5	6		£0.37		
Chewing gum	5	6		£0.24		
Cereal bars	8	8		£0.54		
Low cal chocolate bars	12	11		£0.43		

CATEGORY	STOCK LEVEL	NUMBER SOLD	LEFT IN STOCK	RETAIL AMOUNT	SALE PRICE	REORDER
Juice	15	18		£0.55		
Fizzy drinks	15	17		£0.65		
Hot drinks	15	13		£0.76		

4   Click on the **Save** button and save the file keeping the same filename.
5   Close the spreadsheet.

Task A1.2.1

1   Open **Microsoft Excel**® and find the spreadsheet **courses.xls.**
2   Open the spreadsheet.
3   Key in the following data – the first column has already been completed for you.

COURSE	HIRE OF ROOM	REFRESHMENTS	PHOTOCOPYING	TUTOR
Admin	650	125	35	240
ICT for beginners	450		35	200
ICT Level 2	450		35	200
Interviewing skills	600	125	35	300
Time management	500	125	35	300

4   Save and close the spreadsheet file.

A1.2.3 Edit cell contents

Once you have entered data into a spreadsheet, you should check carefully that you have input it correctly. The following changes need to be made to the spreadsheet.

Watch the demonstration to see how this is done.

5.3   *Demonstration*

Worked Example A1.2.3

1   Open the spreadsheet **shop1.xls**
2   The following changes need to be made to the spreadsheet:

Delete the following row:

Chews	8	8		£0.18		

Amend the following row by changing the Stock Level to 8 and Retail Amount to £0.34:

CATEGORY	STOCK LEVEL	NUMBER SOLD	LEFT IN STOCK	RETAIL AMOUNT	SALE PRICE	REORDER
Chewing gum	5	6		£0.24		

1   Save the spreadsheet as **shopamend.xls.**
2   Close the spreadsheet.

Task A1.2.3

1   Open the **courses.xls** spreadsheet.
2   Carry out the following amendments:

Add a new row at the bottom of the spreadsheet:

COURSE	HIRE OF ROOM	REFRESHMENTS	PHOTOCOPYING FEE	TUTOR
Spreadsheet Level 1	300		35	250

Amend the following row so that the hire of room is £500 and not £600:

Interviewing skills	600 (change to 500)	125	35	300

3   Save the spreadsheet as **coursesamend.xls** and close the file.

A1.2.4 Replicate data

In a spreadsheet, data can be replicated (this is another name for copy). This can be text, dates or formulas. For example, instead of typing in dates you can type in the first date and then replicate it. For example, you can type in 01/01/10 and then replicate this in the column so that you don't have to type in the consecutive dates. These will be shown automatically as 02/01/10, and so on.

A1.2.5 Find and replace

Microsoft Excel® has a feature that allows you to find and replace data quickly. Find and replace lets you find all instances of a word or phrase that already exists in the spreadsheet and automatically replaces this with the alternative you suggest. For example, you could search for 'pupils' and replace all instances of this with 'candidates'.

A1.2.6 Add and delete rows and columns

When you have first created your spreadsheet, you will probably need to add or delete rows and columns in the spreadsheet. New rows and columns can also be added to the existing data.

Watch the demonstration to see how this is done.

5.4   Demonstration

Worked Example A1.2.6

1   Open the spreadsheet **shopamend.xls.**
2   Carry out a find and replace – click on **Edit → Replace.**

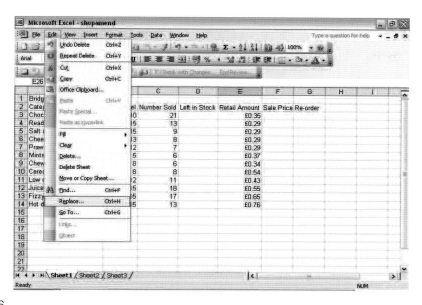

Figure 5.6

3 Enter the data as shown below in the **Find what** and **Replace with** boxes as shown below.

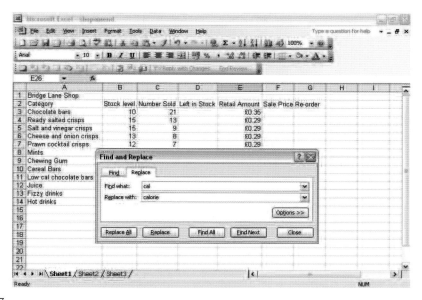

Figure 5.7

4 Click **Replace All** → **Close**.
5 Check that the data has been changed in row 11.
6 Add the following row of data as row 8. Click in row 8, → right click and choose **Insert**.

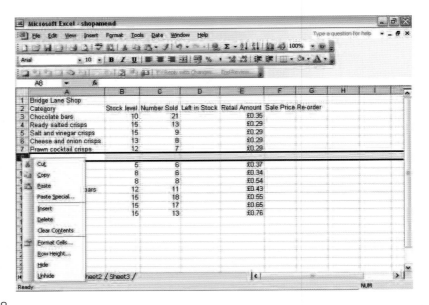

Figure 5.8

Key in the following data:

CATEGORY	STOCK LEVEL	NUMBER SOLD	LEFT IN STOCK	RETAIL AMOUNT	SALE PRICE	REORDER
Apples	9	3		£0.15		

7   Delete the column **Reorder**. Highlight this column by clicking in the G column at the top of the column.

8   Click **Edit → Delete**. The column will now have been deleted.

8   Save the spreadsheet as **sales** and close it.

Task A1.2.6

1   Open the spreadsheet **courseamend.xls**.

2   Replicate the photocopying fee into the row below. Select cell D7 and move your mouse to the bottom right corner so that the mouse changes to a cross.

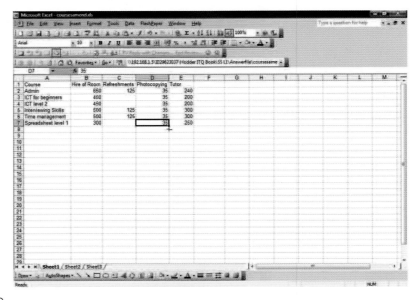

Figure 5.9

3   Drag and drop the cell into row D8.
4   Add the following data to row D8:

Appraisee training	500	125		300

5   Carry out a find and replace. Find **Admin** and replace it with **Administration**.
6   Save the spreadsheet as **training.xls** and close the spreadsheet.

A1.3   Store and retrieve spreadsheet files effectively, in line with local guidelines and conventions where available

Once you have created your spreadsheet you will need to save it. There are various options available to you – you can save the file as it is or save it with a different name by using the Save As option. You will also need to know where you have saved the file so you can find and open it again later. In previous exercises we have used Save and Save As so we can progress with the exercises.

Watch the demonstration to see how this is done.

5.5   *Demonstration*

Worked Example A1.3

1   Open the **sales.xls** spreadsheet and click **File → Save**. This saves the file with the same filename.
2   Create a new folder in the **My documents** folder and name this **TuckShop**.
3   The **sales.xls** spreadsheet should still be open. Now save this as **Revenue** in the **Tuck Shop** folder.
4   Click **File → Save As** and type in the file name **revenue.xls**, ensuring you are in the Tuckshop folder. Click **Save**.

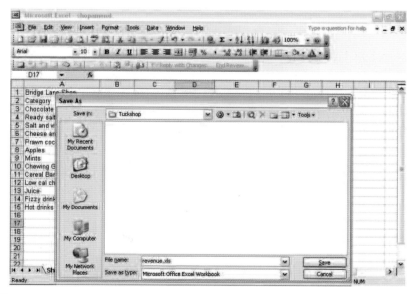

Figure 5.10

4   Click on **File → Close**.

Consolidation

AniVets have launched a new vet service in the community and they have asked you to create a spreadsheet that will record the expenditure items for them to run the business.

You have been provided with the file **vets.xls**, which shows the first set of data. You will need to key in, amend and save the spreadsheet as you go through it.

1 Open the **vets.xls** file and key in the data for Quarter 1 to Quarter 4.

| AniVets | | | | | |
EXPENDITURE	QUARTER 1	QUARTER 2	QUARTER 3	QUARTER 4	TOTAL
Advertising and Marketing	£789.00	£850.00	£750.00	£300.00	
Gas and Electricity	£650.00	£650.00	£650.00	£650.00	
Maintenance	£500.00	£250.00	£300.00	£100.00	
Rates	£1,169.00	£1,169.00	£1,169.00	£1,169.00	
Rent	£2,500.00	£2,500.00	£2,500.00	£2,500.00	
Tax	£1,250.00	£1,250.00	£1,250.00	£1,250.00	
Vet Products	£12,500.00	£12,500.00	£9,230.00	£12,500.00	
Wages	£5,500.00	£5,500.00	£5,500.00	£5,500.00	
Water	£85.00	£85.00	£85.00	£85.00	
2009 Total Expenditure					

1 It has been noticed that the Vet Products for Quarter 3 should be £12,500 – please amend this row.
2 The following row has been omitted – please add this as row 1:

Admin	£1,100.00	£1,110.00	£1,100.00	£1,100.00

3 Carry out a search and replace **wages** with **salaries**.
4 Create a new folder and name this **AniVets**.
5 Save the spreadsheet as **vets1.xls** in the **AniVets** folder.
6 Close the spreadsheet.

A2 Use appropriate formulas and tools to summarise and display spreadsheet information

Once all the data has been entered into the spreadsheet, you can now use the information to calculate totals and summarise the information.

You can create the following formulas within Microsoft Excel® to calculate a variety of different sums:

+   This allows you to add one or more numbers together.
−   This allows you to subtract one or more numbers.
*   This allows you to multiply numbers together.
/   This allows you to divide numbers.

Watch the demonstration to see how this is done.

5.6   *Demonstration*

> Worked Example A2.1

1   Open the spreadsheet **sales.xls** from the My Documents folder.
2   Sort the category column into alphabetical order (A–Z). Highlight the data in the spreadsheet and click on **Data** → **Sort**. Ensure that it shows category (ascending).

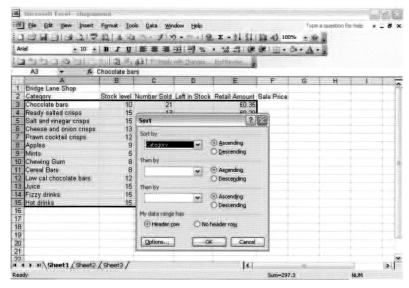

Figure 5.11

Click **OK** so that the category column is shown in ascending alphabetical order.

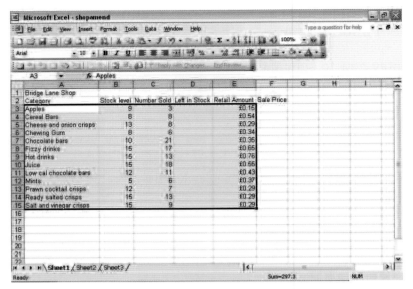

Figure 5.12

3 Find the **Sale Price** column heading in cell F2 and change this to **Sales**.
4 Calculate the sales by multiplying the Number Sold by Retail Amount.

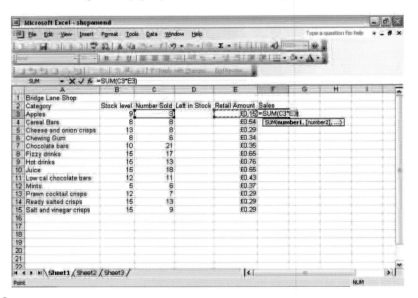

Figure 5.13

5 Replicate the Sales by dragging so that the total is shown in cells F3:F15.
6 Save the spreadsheet keeping the same name, **sales.xls**, and close the file.

Task A2.1

1 Open the spreadsheet **training.xls**.
2 Sort the data in the Tutor column into ascending order.
3 In cell F1 add the sub-title **Total**.
4 Calculate the Total for each course by adding together cells B2:E2. Type in each cell **=sum(** and then select cells B2:E2, close the bracket and click **Enter**.
5 Replicate the total for the other courses.
6 Save the file as **training1.xls** and close the spreadsheet.

A2.2   Use functions and formulas to meet calculation requirements

A2.3   Use spreadsheet tools and techniques to summarise and display information

Microsoft Excel® has many formulas and functions that can be used to calculate different sums. A formula is generally a sum that uses mathematical operators, e.g. +, –, *, /. A function is generally average, min, max, and so on.

Watch the demonstration to see how this is done.

5.7   Demonstration

> **Worked Example A2.2**

1   Open the spreadsheet **sales.xls** and carry out the following calculations.
2   In cell D3 calculate the Left in Stock by taking the Number Sold from the Stock level.
3   Replicate this formula.
4   The owners of the shop are looking at whether or not to increase their retail amount. Add a new column called **10% Increase** in cell G2.
5   In cell G3, calculate the 3 per cent increase by multiplying the Retail amount by 10 per cent.

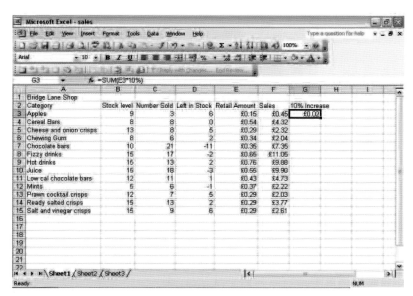

Figure 5.14

6   Replicate these formulas for the other products in this category.
7   Close and save the spreadsheet as **sales.xls**.

> **Task A2.2**

1   Open the **training1.xls** spreadsheet.
2   In cell G1, add the subheading **Per Delegate**.

3   Calculate the per delegate fee by dividing the total by 12 (max number of delegates on a course).

4   In row A10, type in **Total Course** and in cell F10, calculate the Total Course by adding together all the Total costs per course. As all the cells are together, you can click on the **Autosum** button to calculate this.

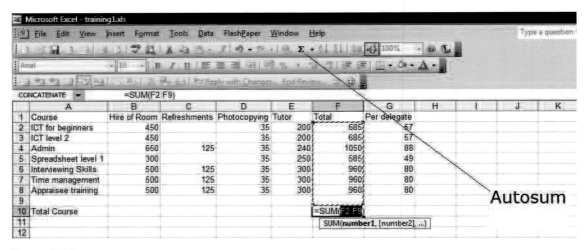

Figure 5.15

5   In cell A12, type in **Average Tutor Fee** and in cell E12, calculate the average fee. Click on the **Insert Function** button.

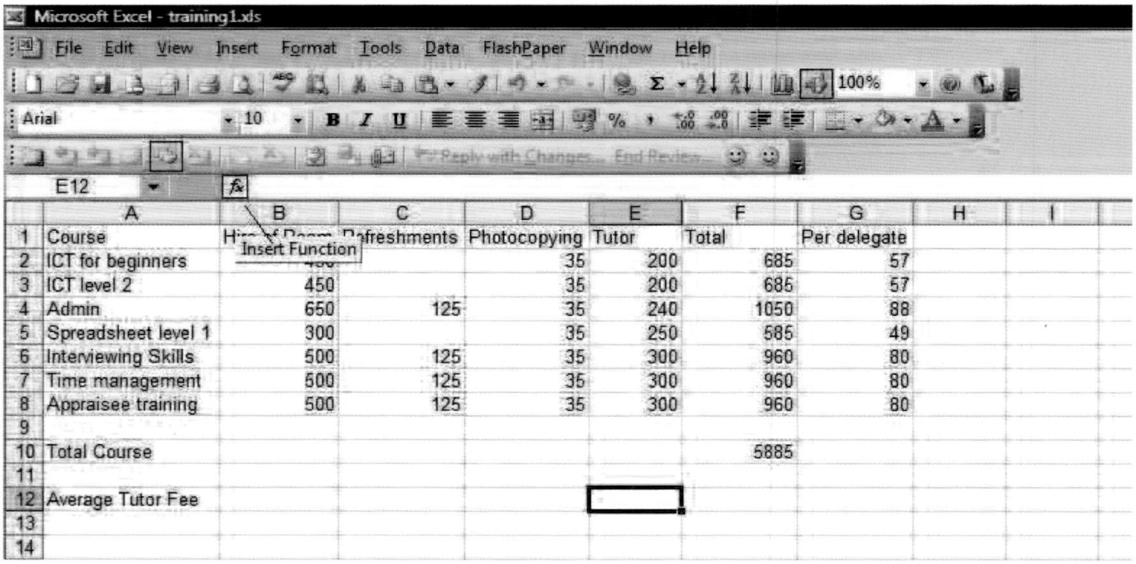

Figure 5.16

6   Type in the Search for a function box **Average** and click **OK**. In the Number 1 box, ensure that it is shown as E2:E11 and click **OK**.

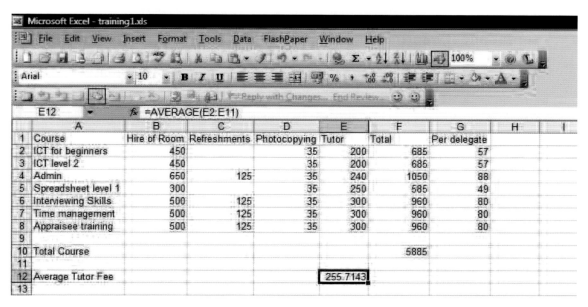

Figure 5.17

Consolidation

1 Open the **vets.xls** spreadsheet and calculate the Total for Quarters 1, 2, 3 and 4.
2 Calculate the Total Expenditure for 2009.
3 In row A17, add in **Average Monthly Expenditure** (dividing the Total Expenditure by 12 months).
4 Save the file as **vets1.xls** and close the file.

Suggested answer:

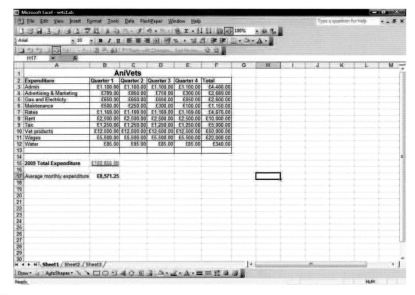

Figure 5.18

A3 Select and use appropriate tools and techniques to present spreadsheet information effectively

A3.1 Select and use appropriate tools and techniques to format spreadsheet cells and rows and columns

Data in a spreadsheet can be formatted by changing the number style and text style. Colours can be changed and borders can be added to make the spreadsheet look more professional.

Watch the demonstration to see how this is done.

5.8 | *Demonstration*

> **Worked Example A3.1**

1 Open the spreadsheet **sales.xls**.
2 Amend the Retail Amount, Sales and 10% Increase so that they are Currency and show two decimal places. Click on **Format** → **Cells** → choose **Currency** and **Decimal places: 2**.

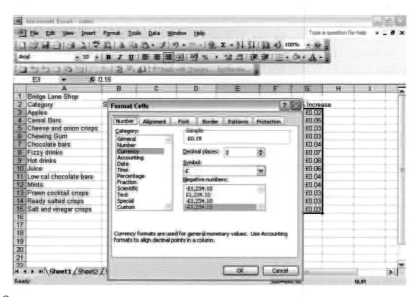

Figure 5.19

3 Format the Left in Stock column data so that this is shown as **Number**, and Negative Numbers as **Red**.

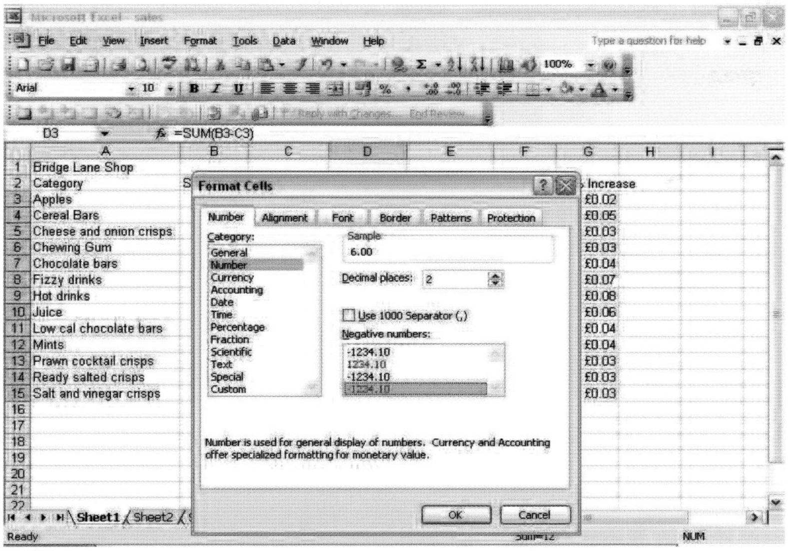

Figure 5.20

4 Highlight all the data in the spreadsheet and change the font to Arial, bold and font size 11.
5 Some of the data will be truncated (not shown in full). You now need to increase the cells so that all data is shown in full. Take the mouse between columns A and B until you get a cross mouse button and double click. Column A will now be wide enough to display all data in full.
6 Repeat this for the remaining columns in the spreadsheet.

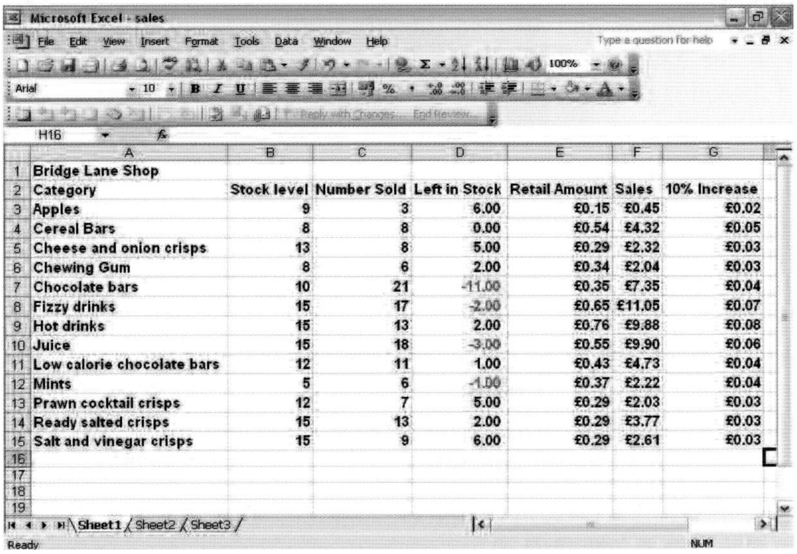

	A	B	C	D	E	F	G
1	Bridge Lane Shop						
2	Category	Stock level	Number Sold	Left in Stock	Retail Amount	Sales	10% Increase
3	Apples	9	3	6.00	£0.15	£0.45	£0.02
4	Cereal Bars	8	8	0.00	£0.54	£4.32	£0.05
5	Cheese and onion crisps	13	8	5.00	£0.29	£2.32	£0.03
6	Chewing Gum	8	6	2.00	£0.34	£2.04	£0.03
7	Chocolate bars	10	21	-11.00	£0.35	£7.35	£0.04
8	Fizzy drinks	15	17	-2.00	£0.65	£11.05	£0.07
9	Hot drinks	15	13	2.00	£0.76	£9.88	£0.08
10	Juice	15	18	-3.00	£0.55	£9.90	£0.06
11	Low calorie chocolate bars	12	11	1.00	£0.43	£4.73	£0.04
12	Mints	5	6	-1.00	£0.37	£2.22	£0.04
13	Prawn cocktail crisps	12	7	5.00	£0.29	£2.03	£0.03
14	Ready salted crisps	15	13	2.00	£0.29	£3.77	£0.03
15	Salt and vinegar crisps	15	9	6.00	£0.29	£2.61	£0.03

Figure 5.21

7 Highlight all the data in the spreadsheet and click on the borders icon and select **All borders**.
8 Highlight cells A1:G1, which contain the Title Bridge Lane Shop, and centre this over the column by clicking on the **Merge and Center** button.

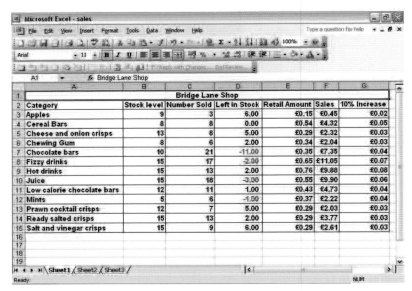

Figure 5.22

9 Save the file as **monthlysales.xls**.
10 Close the spreadsheet.

Task A3.1

1 Open the spreadsheet **training1.xls**.
2 Format the Hire of Room, Refreshments, Photocopying, Tutor, Total and Delegate fields so that they are Currency and show two decimal places.
3 Change the Total Course and Average Tutor Fee to two decimal places.
4 Highlight all the data in the spreadsheet and change the font to Verdana size 11.
5 Check and amend the data so that it is all shown in full.
6 Highlight all the data in the spreadsheet and click on the borders icon and select **All borders**.
7 Insert a new row and type in a heading **Parkview Course** and merge and centre this over columns A:G.
8 Save the file as **trainingsales.xls**.
9 Close the spreadsheet.

A3.2 Identify which chart or graph type to use to display information

A3.3 Select and use appropriate tools and techniques to generate, develop and format charts and graphs

Different types of graphs and charts can be created to display data. Earlier in this chapter we looked at different types of charts. You will now create a pie, bar and line graph.

Watch the demonstration to see how this is done.

 **5.9** *Demonstration*

Worked Example A3.3.1

1 Open the **monthlysales.xls** spreadsheet.
2 Create a pie chart which shows the category and stock level.
3 Highlight the Category and Stock Level Columns in the spreadsheet.
4 Click on **Chart Wizard**.

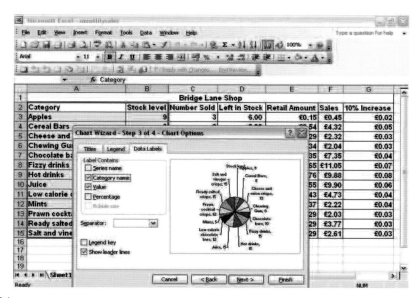

Figure 5.23

5 Choose **Pie** → **Next** → **Next** → **Chart Title** → type in **Stock Level**.
6 Click on the **Legend** tab and remove the 'tick' from the **Show legend** box.
7 Click on the **Data Labels** tab and put a tick in the **Value** and **Category Name** boxes.

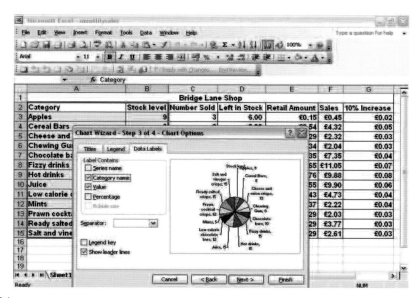

Figure 5.24

  8 Click **Next** → **Place chart: As new sheet** and choose **Chart 1** → **Finish**.
  9 Chart is now displayed.
10 Save the spreadsheet and leave it open for the next exercise.

Watch the demonstration to see how this is done

5.10   *Demonstration* _____

Worked Example A3.3.2

1   Open the **monthlysales.xls** spreadsheet.
2   Click on **Sheet1** so that the data table is shown.
3   Highlight the Category, Stock Level and Number Sold columns and click on the **Chart Wizard** → **Column** (although this is a column chart in Microsoft Excel®, we would normally call this a bar chart) → **Next** → **Next**.
4   Click on the **Titles** tab and key in the **Total Sales v Stock**. In the X axis, type in **Products** and in the Y axis type in **Number** → **Next** → **Place chart: As new sheet** → **Finish**.
5   Save the spreadsheet and leave it open for the next exercise.

Watch the demonstration to see how this is done

5.11   *Demonstration* _____

Worked Example A3.3.3

1   Open the **monthlysales.xls** spreadsheet.
2   Click on **Sheet 1** so that the data is shown. Plot the Category and Sales as a single line chart. In this exercise, we will need to select data which is non-adjacent.
3   Highlight the Category column and then hold down the Ctrl Key on the Keyboard and highlight the Number Sold column.
4   Click **Chart Wizard** → **Line** → **Next** → **Next** → **Total Sales** → X axis **Category** → Y axis **Number** → **Next** → **As new sheet** → **Finish**.

Task A3.3.1

1 Open the **trainingsales.xls** spreadsheet.
2 Create a pie chart which plots the Course and Hire of Room.
3 Enter the Chart Title: **% Room Hire**.
4 Remove the legend.
5 In Data labels, show the Category Name and Percentage.
6 Display the chart as a new sheet and click **Finish**.

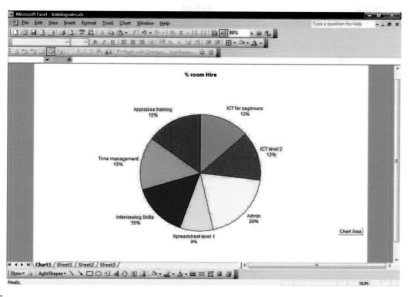

Figure 5.25

7 Create a bar chart that plots the Hire of Room, Refreshments, Photocopying and Tutor against each course.

8 Add the title: **Course Costs**.

9 Add the X axis label: **Course**.

10 Add the Y axis label: **£**.

11 Ensure that the legend is shown.

12 Create the chart as a new sheet.

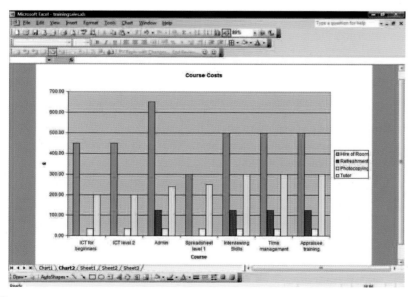

Figure 5.26

13 Create a line graph to plot the course against the total cost.

14 Add the Title **Total Course Costs**.

15 Add the X axis label: **Course**.

16 Add the Y axis label: **Value**.

17 Remove the legend.

18 Create as a new sheet.

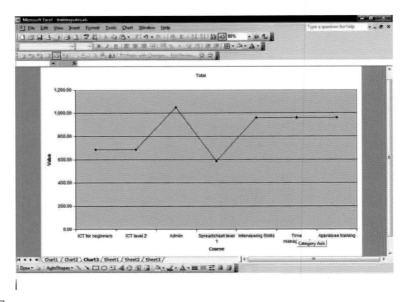

Figure 5.27

19 Save and close the spreadsheet.

| A3.4 | Select and use appropriate page layout to present and print spreadsheet information |

Before you print out your spreadsheet, make sure that the data is formatted correctly and fits to the page correctly so that the data looks professionally produced.

Pages can have portrait or landscape orientation.

Watch the demonstration to see how this is done.

5.12 | **Demonstration**

| Worked Example A3.4.1 |

1 Open the **monthlysales.xls** spreadsheet.
2 Click on the **Print Preview** button on the toolbar and you will see that the spreadsheet is split over two pages.

Figure 5.28

3 Click **Close**.
4 Click on **File** → **Page Setup** → **Change**. Change the page orientation to **Landscape** and click **Print**.
5 Preview to check that the data is now all shown on one page.

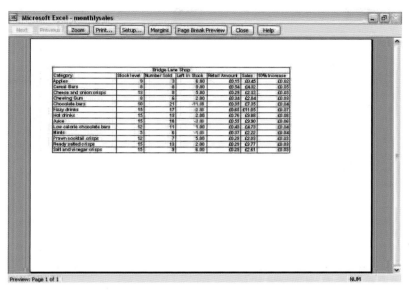

Figure 5.29

6 Click **Setup** whilst in **Print Preview** and you can also change the paper size. However, the default is shown as A4 and it is unlikely that you will want to change this.

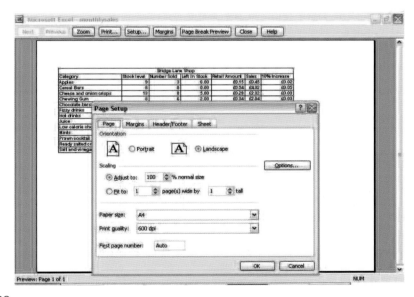

Figure 5.30

7 Click on the **Header/Footer** tab and you can add your name and page numbers. Click on **Customer Header** and in the left-hand section type in your name. Click **OK**.
8 Click on **Customer Footer** and in the right-hand section, click on the **Insert Page Number** icon.

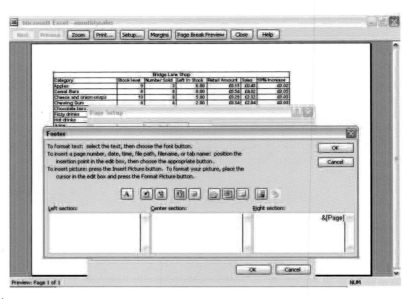

Figure 5.31

9 Click **OK**. Click **OK** again and you will now see your name in the header and page number in the bottom right of the spreadsheet.
10 The date can also be added. Click on **Setup** → **Customer Header**. In the right-hand section, click on the **Date Icon** → **OK**→ **OK**.
11 Close Print Preview.
12 Save the spreadsheet as **monthlyprint.xls**.
13 Close the file.

Watch the demonstration to see how this is done.

5.13 | Demonstration

Task A3.4.1

1 Open the **trainingsales.xls** spreadsheet.
2 Click on the **Print Preview** button on the toolbar and you will see that the spreadsheet is split over two pages.
3 Click **Close**.
4 Change the page orientation to Landscape and click **Print Preview** to check that the data is now all shown on one page.
5 Click on the **Header/Footer** tab and can add your name as a header in the left section. Add the date field in the right-hand section of the header.
6 Click on **Customer Footer** and in the right-hand section, click on the **Insert Page Number** icon.
7 Save the spreadsheet as **trainingprint.xls**.
8 Close the file.

A3.5 Check information meets needs using spreadsheet tools and making corrections as necessary

Before you print out your spreadsheet, check that all the data is correct and that the printout will be fit for purpose.

Watch the demonstration to see how this is done.

🖱 5.14 | Demonstration

Worked Example A3.5

1   Open the **monthlyprint.xls** spreadsheet.
2   Check through the formulas and check that these are correct.
3   Check that all the data is shown in full in Print Preview.
4   Check each of the charts are correctly labelled and will be displayed correctly when printed out.
5   Once you have carried out all the checks, print out the spreadsheet table by clicking on the print icon.
6   Print out each of the charts.
7   Save and close the spreadsheet.

Task A3.5

1   Open the **trainingprint.xls** spreadsheet.
2   Check through the formulas and check that these are correct.
3   Check that all the data is shown in full in Print Preview.
4   Check that each of the charts is correctly labelled and will be displayed correctly when printed out.
5   Once you have carried out all the checks, print out the spreadsheet table by clicking on the print icon.
6   Print out each of the charts.
7   Save and close the spreadsheet.

Consolidation

1   Open the **vets1.xls** spreadsheet.
2   Create a pie chart that plots the Expenditure against Quarter 1.
3   Insert the title **Quarter 1 Expenditure**.
4   Do not show the legend.
5   Show the Category name and percentage.
6   Show as a new sheet.
7   Create a bar chart that plots all four Quarters of expenditure.
8   Enter the chart title **Yearly Expenditure**.
9   Enter the X axis title **Items**.
10   Enter the Y axis title **Value**.
11   Display as a new work sheet.
12   Change the page setup to Landscape.
13   Add your name and the page number as a header.
14   Save the spreadsheet as **vetsfinal.xls**.
15   Check the spreadsheet. Print out the table file and print out each chart.
16   Close the file.

Mini Assignment

In this Mini Assignment, you will practise all the skills you have learned throughout this chapter.

The Mini Assignment is based around a school trip. Your manager has given you the following instructions and you are required to complete these tasks.

Create a new folder to store your work for this assignment and then produce evidence to meet the unit requirements.

1 Open Microsoft Excel® and create a new spreadsheet as shown below.
2 Save the spreadsheet as **trip.xls**.
3 Insert a blank row and in cell A9 enter the subheading **Total**.
4 Calculate the total for each trip.
5 Replicate this for each trip.
6 Calculate the cost of each trip per child – there will be a maximum of 16 children.
7 Format the cells so that all monetary amounts are shown as currency with two decimal places.
8 Change the font to Verdana 11 throughout the spreadsheet.
9 Change the column widths to ensure that all data is shown in full.
10 Add a thick box border around all the data.
11 Centre and merge the heading **School Trip.**
12 Embolden the column headings in B2:E2.
13 Embolden **Total** and **Cost per Child**.
14 Change the colour of the text Cost per Child to red.
15 Create a bar chart to plot the trip costs for each of the three options.
16 Enter the chart title **Cost of School Trips**.
17 Enter the X axis title **Costs** and in the Y axis enter **£**.
18 Show as a new sheet.
19 Create a pie chart to plot the three options against the totals. (Remember you will need to hold down the CTRL key on the keyboard to select row 2 and row 9.)
20 Enter the Title **Options**.
21 Show the legend and data labels value.
22 Show the pie chart as a new sheet.
23 Shade the Title Row by clicking on the **Fill Colour** button.
24 Set the page orientation to Portrait.
25 Add your name, date and page number to the header/footer.
26 Check all the calculations and page setups so that all details are shown in full.
27 Print out the spreadsheet and charts.
28 Save and close the spreadsheet.

School trip	OPTION 1	OPTION 2	OPTION 3
Transport	250	275	221
Staffing cover costs	300	300	300
Cost of entertainment	1000	650	500
Insurance costs	300	300	300
Refreshments	125	125	125
Cost per child			

Level 2

This unit will develop your knowledge and skills relating to creating, presenting and checking spreadsheets. You will have the opportunity to use a range of tools to enter, manipulate, format and output data for a range of different purposes. You will use a variety of mathematical formulas and functions. The spreadsheet will be set up and developed by you.

By working through the **Overview**, **Worked Examples**, **Tasks** and **Consolidations** in this chapter, you will demonstrate the skills required for Spreadsheet Software Level 2:

ELEMENT The competent person will...	PERFORMANCE CRITERIA To demonstrate this competence they can...	KNOWLEDGE To demonstrate this competence they will also...
SS:B1 Use a spreadsheet to enter, edit and organise numerical and other information	B1.2 Enter and edit numerical and other data accurately B1.3 Combine and link data across worksheets B1.4 Store and retrieve spreadsheet files effectively, in line with local guidelines and conventions where available	B1.1 Identify what numerical and other information is needed in the spreadsheet and how it should be structured
SS:B2 Select and use appropriate formulas and data analysis tools to meet requirements	B2.2 Select and use a range of appropriate functions and formulas to meet calculation requirements B2.3 Use a range of tools and techniques to analyse and manipulate data to meet requirements	B2.1 Identify what tools and techniques to use to analyse and manipulate data to meet requirements
SS:B3 Select and use tools and techniques to present and format spreadsheet information	B3.2 Select and use appropriate tools and techniques to format spreadsheet cells, rows, columns and worksheets B3.3 Select and format an appropriate chart or graph type to display selected information B3.4 Select and use appropriate page layout to present and print spreadsheet information B3.5 Check information meets needs, using spreadsheet tools and making corrections as necessary B3.7 Respond appropriately to any problems with spreadsheets	B3.1 Plan how to present and format spreadsheet information effectively to meet needs B3.6 Describe how to find errors in formulas

Step-by step examples are provided as a demonstration of what to do. These demonstrations are based on Microsoft Excel® 2003. Review the **Overview** in each section and then watch the demonstrations in the **Worked Examples** before commencing any **Tasks**.

Once you are familiar with the topic covered, move onto the **Tasks** in this chapter.

Throughout the **Worked Example** sections, the demonstrations relate to the income and expenditure of a computer games online seller. The **Tasks** relate to Escape Travel.

There are **Consolidation** exercises throughout this chapter which relate to a CD/video stock control. A Mini Assignment is included at the end of the chapter and this can be used for practice only.

B1 Use a spreadsheet to enter, edit and organise numerical and other information

B1.1   Identify what numerical and other information is needed in the spreadsheet and how it should be structured

A spreadsheet is a software program that allows you to enter data into columns and rows and perform calculations. Spreadsheets are useful in helping to make predictions of profit, loss and sales but they can also be used for many different subjects as the information they hold can be organised easily and neatly.

When you open Microsoft Excel®, you will see the screen as shown below:

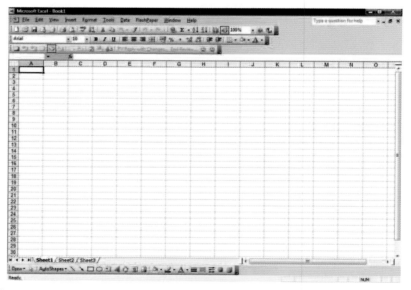

Figure 5.32

A spreadsheet typically contains cells, rows, columns, tabs, pages, charts, ranges, workbooks, worksheets, structure, design and layout.

A cell is part of a column or row and it is where individual data is entered – this usually contains text, numbers or dates. To move between cells, press the TAB key on the keyboard.

A row is horizontal and a column is vertical. Data can be entered into columns and rows. Each row and column is labelled in Microsoft Excel® – columns as letters and rows as numbers. These labels can be printed out when the spreadsheet is printed out – see the example in Figure 5.33.

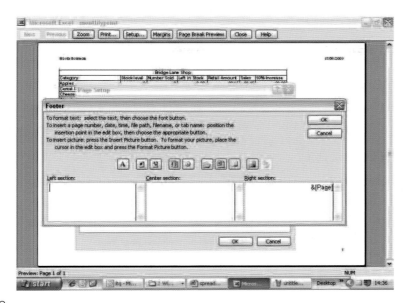

Figure 5.33

Each spreadsheet file (or workbook) can contain a number of worksheets. At Level two, worksheets will be linked together to perform more complex calculations – at the bottom of each workbook, 'tabs' show which worksheet is active.

Within Microsoft Excel®, you can use a range of different graphs and charts to display numerical data. These are discussed later in the chapter in more detail.

Before you start entering any data into a spreadsheet, you need to think about the design and structure of the spreadsheet.

B1.2 Enter and edit spreadsheet data accurately

When designing and creating a spreadsheet, you need to decide what information to include. It is easier to plan your spreadsheet before you start entering data. A Level 2 spreadsheet will include:

■ numbers

■ charts/graphs

■ text

■ absolute and relative cell references

■ functions and formulas.

B1.2.1 Numbers

A spreadsheet will contain different types of numbers that can be used in a variety of calculations.

B1.2.2 Charts

In Microsoft Excel®, a chart is a visual representation of numerical data. There are different types of charts, for example, histogram, bar chart and pie chart are all available in a spreadsheet.

B1.2.3 Text

Text can be entered into rows and columns to label data, add column headings or titles.

B1.2.4 Absolute and relative cell references

Absolute and relative cell references are used in calculations in a spreadsheet. A relative cell reference is displayed in the spreadsheet formulas as A4 and when it is replicated down a column, it becomes A5, A6, and A7. Figure 5.34 shows the sum as a relative cell reference, for example = SUM (B2:B6).

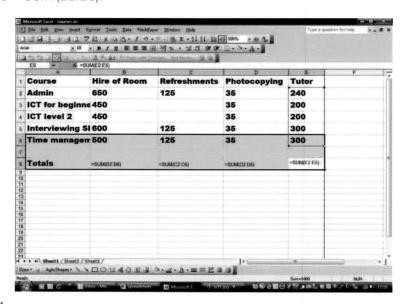

Figure 5.34

An absolute cell is displayed in the spreadsheet formulae as A4 and the '$' makes both the column and row reference within the cell absolute (i.e. it does not change) when it is replicated. However, you can make either the column or the row absolute. The formula in the VAT column uses an absolute cell reference.

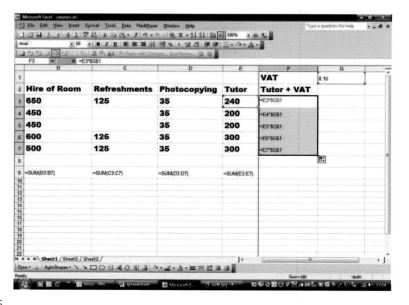

Figure 5.35

Before you start keying anything into a Microsoft Excel® spreadsheet, you should think carefully about the design. It is good to draw a design sketch so that it covers all the requirements of the spreadsheet at the beginning rather than having to make amendments later on.

The computer games shop spreadsheet needs to calculate the quarterly hire charges and to find out how many games have been hired over the quarter. The owner also needs to know about the income and will need to present some of the data graphically. At Level 2, different worksheets will be used.

The design plan should consider different calculations that could be used, charts and graphs and at least two worksheets, which link cells together and include:

- the layout of the spreadsheet

- user requirements for the spreadsheet

- different cell formats (currency, date/time, text, decimal places)

- formulas to be used

- different functions

- charts to be used.

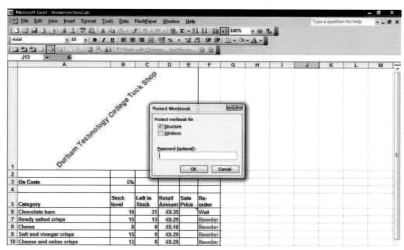

Figure 5.36

B1.2.5 Creating a spreadsheet

Now that you have designed the spreadsheet, you can create it.

See how this is done.

 **5.15** | **Demonstration**

> **Worked Example B1.2.5**

1   You have been asked to create a spreadsheet that records the ingoings and outgoings for an online computer games hire shop. You have been provided with the information on the following page to help you create your design.

Problemsolving4U Games Hire Charges First Quarter

Hire Charge	Charge							
A	3.5							
B	2.95							
C	2.75							

Game	Jan	Feb	Mar	Rate	Total Hired	Hire Charge	No in Stock	Restock?
1966 – Year Of Glory	9	12	8	A			25	
1-to-1	0	2	1	B			5	
2D Action Games	18	20	16	A			50	
2D Games	1	0	2	B			5	
3D Games	6	9	4	A			20	
Action & Adventure Games	2	4	5	B			15	
Arcade Games	16	18	23	B			50	
Avengers	2	0	5	B			10	
Bingo Games	13	11	15	A			40	
Bingo Number Games	2	4	5	B			15	
Board Games	0	2	1	A			5	
Escape Travel	3	0	1	B			5	
Brain Teasers Games	7	6	9	A			25	
Car Chases	7	6	9	A			25	
Card Games	18	21	17	A			60	
Cheats Games	5	4	8	A			20	
Arcade-type Games	10	13	11	B			30	
Dungeons of the Deep	14	10	17	B			45	
Dice Games	2	0	5	B			10	

Game	Jan	Feb	Mar	Rate	Total Hired	Hire Charge	No in Stock	Restock?
Diving	4	7	3	A			10	
Educational Games	17	20	14	A			50	
Fort	1	2	1	B			5	
English 4 U	11	9	12	A			35	
English Kings	3	2	4	B			10	
Football 2008	17	20	14	A			50	
Gaming Tools & Utilities	3	2	4	B			10	
Grand Auto Theft	11	9	12	A			35	
Keep Fit	1	0	2	B			5	
Maths 4 U	3	2	4	B			10	
Memory Games	13	12	14	A			40	
OO7	18	20	16	B			50	
Problem Solving	13	12	14	A			40	
Racer 2	13	11	15	A			35	
Revenge 2	16	18	23	B			50	
Ring Today	3	0	1	B			5	
Sim Sons	1	2	1	B			5	
Skateboarding	4	7	3	A			15	
Tetris	9	12	8	A			25	
Wii Talk		9	4	A			15	

3   Enter the data you have been provided with and save the spreadsheet as **games.xls**.
4   Close the spreadsheet.

B1.3 Combine and link data across worksheets

Microsoft Excel® allows you to link data across worksheets. In the computer games spreadsheet, there will be an overall summary sheet at the front which will summarise the sales and income for each quarter. As we have not done any calculations in our spreadsheet yet, we will use another spreadsheet to demonstrate how data can be combined and linked across worksheets. You will be able to have a go at this as the computer games spreadsheet is developed.

Watch the demonstration to see how this is done.

5.16 | Demonstration

> **Worked Example B1.3**
>
> 1 Open the spreadsheet **budget1.xls** from the **My documents** folder.
> 2 You will find that this spreadsheet includes three worksheets – one tab is named Overall Summary, one is Academic Departments and one is Admin Depts.
> 3 Calculations have been carried out to show the expenditure for the Academic Departments and the Admin Departments – a linked calculation will now be calculated to the overall summary sheet.
> 4 Click in cell B6 and type in **=sum(**. Now click in cell C17 in the Academic Departments worksheet and click on the **+** and click in cell C15 in the Admin Departments worksheet – click **Enter** to close the sum.
> 5 The overall summary worksheet should now show the overall summary total of £622,300.
> 6 Save the spreadsheet as **budget2.xls** and close the spreadsheet.

B1.4 Store and retrieve spreadsheet files effectively, in line with local guidelines and conventions where available

Once you have created your spreadsheet, you will need to save it. There are various options available to you when you come to save the file. You can save the file as it is, save it with a different file name by using the Save As option, or save it in a different file format. You will also need to know where you have saved the file so you can find and open it again later. In the previous exercises, we have used Save and Save As so that we can progress with the exercises.

Watch the demonstration to see how this is done.

5.17 | Demonstration

> **Worked Example B1.4**
>
> 1 Open the file **budget1.xls**.
> 2 Save As **budgetsave.xls**.
> 3 Close.

B1.4.1 Non-specific formats

When using spreadsheet files, you might sometimes receive a file to open which has been saved in a non-specific format (e.g. CSV). CSV stands for comma-separated values and this is a non-specific software format so it can be opened with different software. In a row, fields (or columns) are separated by commas when the file is saved as a CSV file. CSV files are sometimes used when importing data into a database or when sending files to other users who may not have the latest versions of spreadsheet software so that files can be opened easily. You can open or save an existing file in CSV format. A CSV file contains no formatting, so if you save a formatted spreadsheet as a CSV file, it will lose all the formatting.

You can use a spreadsheet template when creating and updating spreadsheets that are used regularly. These hold text styles and data formats, which can be protected and cannot be changed when a spreadsheet is created.

Watch the demonstration to see how this is done.

5.18 | *Demonstration*

> **Worked Example B1.4.1**

1 Open the spreadsheet **totals.csv.**
2 Click on **File → Open → change files of type → all files.**

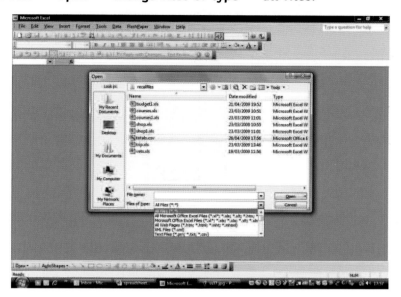

Figure 5.37

3 Open the file and you will see that it has no formatting options saved and that it only contains one workbook.
4 Save the file as **amendments.xls** and close the file.

Now it's your turn to have a go.

> **Task B1.4.1**

1 Open the spreadsheet **vets.csv.**
2 Add bold to the column headings.
3 Save the file as **amendments.xls** and close the file.

B2 Select and use appropriate formulas and data analysis tools to meet requirements

In this section, you will learn about different formulas and tools available in Microsoft Excel® that allow you to carry out a variety of calculations. You will calculate using the computer games and college spreadsheets.

B2.1 Identify which tools and techniques to use to analyse and manipulate data to meet requirements

One of the first things you need to do is identify the calculations that are required in your spreadsheet. Ideally, this should be completed at the design stage. Go back to the design plan and see the calculations that it suggested you use.

B2.1.1 Sub-totals and totals

A sub-total is a total of numbers – usually groups of data added together so that an overall total can be calculated. For example, the screen print below shows sub-totals being calculated for each month and an overall sales total:

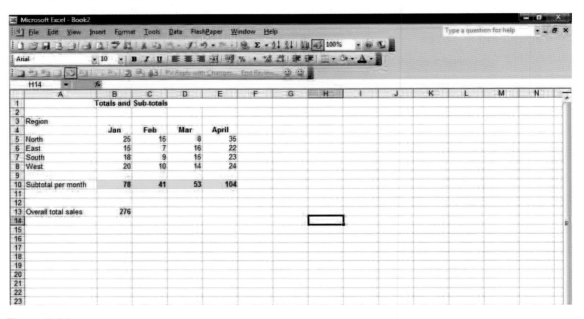

Figure 5.38

B2.1.2 Sorting and display order

Another way to display data is to sort it into different orders. For example, if we look at the games spreadsheet, the games are currently in ascending alphabetical order of Game Name. However, this could be changed so that the Hire Charge Rate is sorted alphabetically. For example:

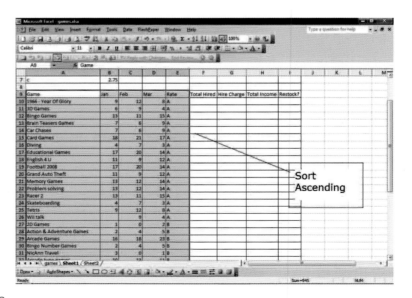

Figure 5.39

B2.1.3 Filter rows and columns

B2.1.4 Judgement of when and how to use these methods

Filtering data is like running a query in a database. A filter looks at a range of data within the worksheet to check that it meets a certain criteria, e.g. crisps or 20p. It is important to plan when and how you will sort and filter data so that it is relevant and realistic. Microsoft Excel® will show only the records that meet the given criteria and the remaining data in the worksheet will remain hidden. Data can be filtered using:

- auto filter – filters the data using simple criteria, e.g. crisps

- advanced filter – filters the data using more complex criteria, e.g. crisps and 20p.

> **Worked Example B2.1.4**

1 Open the **games_answer.xls** spreadsheet.
2 To filter the data, highlight the data from the subheading Game to the end of the spreadsheet and then click on **Data → Filter → Auto filter.**
 A small arrow is then shown next to each subheading. Click on the arrow in the Restock column and make your selection to be used in the filter, for example, **Restock.**

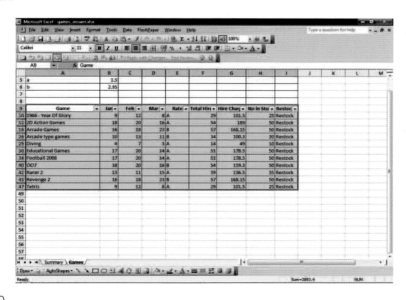

Figure 5.40

3 Remove the filter by clicking on **Restock** column and change this to **All.**
4 To create an advanced filter, click **Data → Filter → Advanced Filter.**
5 Click in the **Number in Stock** column → **Custom → is greater than → 25 → OK.**

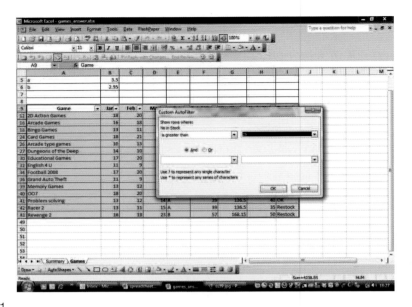

Figure 5.41

Task B2.1.4

1 Open the spreadsheet **shop.xls**.
2 Create a customised filter that will allow you to filter the Retail Amount so that it is more than £0.30. The suggested answer should be:

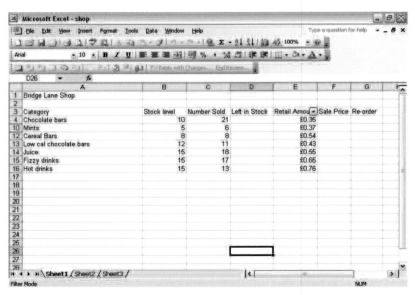

Figure 5.42

3 Save the file as **shop_filter.xls**
4 Close the file.

B2.2   Select and use a range of appropriate functions and formulas to meet calculation requirements

B2.3   Use a range of tools and techniques to analyse and manipulate data to meet requirements

Looking back at the design plan, you will now use the calculations that you planned in the spreadsheet. This will be to calculate the stock levels and income from the hire of computer games. There are a variety of different formulas and functions that can be used in a spreadsheet and some of these are shown below.

B2.3.1 Arithmetic and statistical functions

The following arithmetic and statistical functions may be used in the spreadsheet.

- Sum: this adds up a range of cells.

Tip: To add cells in a continuous row or column, use the Autosum button on the toolbar (e.g. A1:A6). If data is not in a continuous row or column, then use the =sum formula.

- Average: this calculates an average across a number of cells, for example =average (A1:B3).

- Max: this returns the Maximum value over a range of cells, for example =MAX(B1:C10).

- Min: this returns the Minimum value over a range of cells, for example =MIN(B1:C10).

- Median: this returns the median or the number in the middle of a set of numbers, for example =Median(B1:C10).

- Mode: this returns the mode or the most frequently occurring, or repetitive, value in a range of data, for example =MODE(B1:C10).

- Count: counts numbers or dates, for example =count(B1:C10).

Tip: If you wish to count the number of text items in a range of cells, use the function =counta(B1:C10).

- Countif: counts the number of cells that meet a specific criteria, e.g. counts the number of items that need to be re-ordered, e.g. =COUNTIF(B6:B18, 10).

B2.3.2 Financial

The PMT function allows you to work out the loan costs over a set period of time using the following arguments:

- PMT (rate, nper, pv).

B2.3.3 Conditional and logical functions

- IF: returns one value if a condition you specify evaluates to TRUE and another value if it evaluates to FALSE. Use IF to conduct conditional tests on values and formulas. For example, in the tuck shop spreadsheet you may wish to use an IF to see whether any products need to be re-ordered.

- Nested IF: a nested IF can include AND, IF or OR within the IF statement.

B2.3.4 Lookup

A lookup function allows you to look up values in a table of data and use these in calculations. An example is shown below:

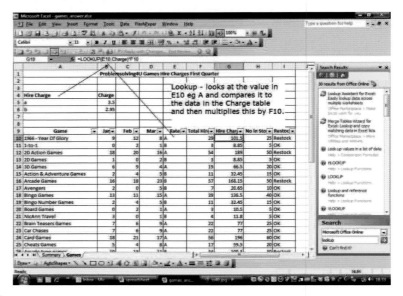

Figure 5.43

Worked Example B2.3.4

1 Open the spreadsheet **games.xls** and carry out the following calculations:
  a Calculate the total hired by adding together Jan, Feb and Mar.
  b Calculate the Hire Charge by using a lookup function and then multiplying this by the Total Hired.
  c Calculate an IF Function to work out whether any of the computer games need to be restocked.
  d Go to the summary sheet and create a linked formulas that calculates the total computer games hired in January, then February and then March.
  e Calculate an overall quarterly total on this spreadsheet.
2 Save the spreadsheet as **games_function.xls** and close the spreadsheet.

Task B2.3.4

1 Open the **travel.xls** spreadsheet.
2 Carry out the following calculations:
  a Calculate the Total Cost by using a lookup function.
3 Carry out the following calculations on the summary sheet:
  a Calculate the Total Income using the Total Cost column on the main spreadsheet.
  b Calculate the Total number of holidays sold.
  c Use a Countif to calculate the Busy Periods.
  d Use a Max function to calculate the maximum takings in one month.
4 Save and close the spreadsheet as **travel234.xls**.

Consolidation

1 Open the **consol_DVD.xls** spreadsheet.

2   Carry out the following calculations on the income worksheet:
   a   Calculate the Stock Balance by using the Stock In and Stock Out columns.
   b   Calculate the Stock Value by using a lookup function, absolute cell reference and calculations – you will need to use the Warehouse Price multiplied by the Stock Balance, a lookup using the Warehouse Code and add this to the Insurance cost as an absolute cell reference.
   c   Use an IF statement to calculate the reorder – show Yes or No.
3   Carry out the following calculations on the summary worksheet:
   a   Use a Count function to calculate the CDs and videos.
   b   Use a sum to calculate the Stock In and Stock Out for the CDs and Videos.
4   Save the spreadsheet as **consol_dvd_B234.xls**.
5   Close the file.

B3 Select and use tools and techniques to present and format spreadsheet information

B3.1   Plan how to present and format spreadsheet information effectively to meet needs

B3.2   Select and use appropriate tools and techniques to format spreadsheet cells, rows, columns and worksheets

Now that the spreadsheet has been created, you can format these to make them look professional and business like, and cells can be formatted as follows:

NUMBER FORMAT	EXAMPLE
Number	1 1.20 (with two decimal places)
Currency	£1.20
Date	14 March 2010
Percentage	%

B3.2.1 Font and alignment

Within a spreadsheet, the font style and size can be changed as can the way the text is aligned. The following table shows some different examples of fonts and styles of alignment.

FONT STYLE AND SIZE	ALIGNMENT
Arial, 12	Centre
Verdana, 14	Left
Times New Roman, 11	Right
Comic Sans, 14	Justified text is where both the left and right margin text is justified (i.e. it starts and ends in the same place).

B3.2.2 Shading and borders

Within a spreadsheet, borders and shading can be added to different cells. It is a good idea to apply different borders around different sections within the spreadsheet so that different types of cells can be emphasised, for example, a border around text cells, a different border around number cells and then an overarching thick border around all active cells. See the example below, which shows different cell borders and shading:

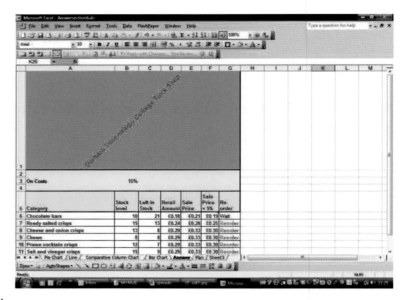

Figure 5.44

B3.2.3 Wrap text

Text in cells can be 'wrapped' or displayed on more than one line. If you look at Figure 5.44, you will see that in row five of the spreadsheet the column headings have been wrapped.

B3.2.4 Format row and columns including height and width

You will need to ensure that all the data in your spreadsheet is shown in full and to do this you will need to adjust row height/column width. Sometimes when you key data directly into Microsoft Excel®, it is not always fully shown. To ensure that data is shown in full you need to adjust the row height/column width. If you view the spreadsheet above, you will see that both rows and columns have been amended to display the information effectively.

Tip: if you see #### in your cells, this means that you have data in a column that needs to be widened.

A heading, for example, can be merged and centred across a number of cells to make it stand out or to ensure that the data is shown in full. If you look at Figure 5.44, you will see that the title Durham Technology College Tuck Shop has been merged and centred across the other rows of data in the spreadsheet.

B3.2.5 Hide and freeze

Sometimes you might want to hide rows or columns or even freeze them to enable easier viewing of the spreadsheet. If a row or column is hidden, it is not shown in the spreadsheet. Usually in a large spreadsheet, you would freeze the column headings. This would allow you to easily move up and down the spreadsheet while still viewing the column headings.

Watch how this is done.

 **5.19** | **Demonstration**

B3.2.6 Help for the user

Within the spreadsheet, you may need to include help for the user so that when they are using the spreadsheet they can operate it easily. Help can be in the form of:

■ cell comments

■ an input message (drop-down list)

■ validation

■ conditional formatting

■ protecting a worksheet.

Cell Comments

A comment is a note that you attach to a particular cell in a spreadsheet and can be used to provide feedback to users or as a reminder for yourself.

To add a comment:

Select the cell where the comment is to be shown, click **Insert** → **Comment** and add the text into the comment box.

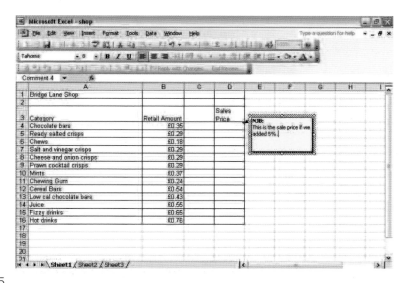

Figure 5.45

Validation

Validation within the spreadsheet allows you to restrict the input of data into specific cells, for example, only allow decimal numbers to be entered into a cost column.

To set the validation, click **Data** → **Validation** and then select **Allow Decimal**. This selects a minimum and maximum amount, for example 0.01 and 9.99.

Input messages

An input message allows you to show a message to the user when they are using the spreadsheet. If they enter some data incorrectly, for example, you can advise that they can only enter decimal numbers of between 0.01 and 9.99 into these cells.

Click **Data** → **Validation** and then the Input Message tab. Make sure the **Show input message when cell is selected check** box is selected, and then fill in the title and text for the message.

Figure 5.46

Conditional Formatting

Conditional formatting allows you to change the format of specific cells within a worksheet if they meet set criteria. For example, you might want to show cells in red if the stock falls below a certain number but show them in green if they are above a particular stock level.

To apply conditional formatting:

Click on **Format** → **Conditional Formatting**. Set the criteria and then click on **Format**. Change the cell colour to red.

Protecting a workbook

To protect a workbook:

Click on **Tools** → **Protection** → **Protect Workbook.** Then enter the password to protect the workbook.

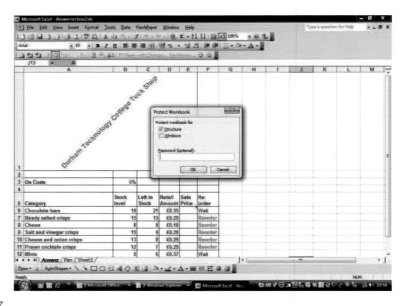

Figure 5.47

See how the formatting is applied to the computer games spreadsheet.

5.20 | Demonstration

Worked Example B3.2.1

1 Open the **games.xls** spreadsheet and carry out the following formatting tasks.
   a Format the title so that it is merged and centred across columns A–I.
   b Format all of the subheadings so that they are bold and centred.
   c Wrap the text in the column headings onto two lines.
   d Add borders around all the cells in the spreadsheet.
   e Shade the Hire Charge and Charge column data.
   f Freeze the subheading columns.
   g Apply conditional formatting to the If statement in the Restock column.
2 Save and close the file.

Task B3.2.1

1 Use the **travel.xls** spreadsheet and add the following formatting options:
   a Change the font style and size.
   b Change the alignment.
   c Shade some of the text.
   d Add borders.
   e Wrap text.
   f Change the column widths and heights to ensure that all data is shown in full.
   g Free column panes.
2 Save and close the spreadsheet.

B3.3 Select and format an appropriate chart or graph type to display selected information

A graph/chart is a visual representation of numerical data but it shows the relationship between two or more variables, for example, X and Y axis numerical data.

A variety of charts can be created in Microsoft Excel®. The following charts are the most common:

■ pie chart

■ line graph

■ column/bar chart/histogram

■ comparative bar/line graph

■ area

■ XY scatter

■ stock

■ radar

■ doughnut

■ surface.

A histogram shows the quantity of points within various numeric ranges.

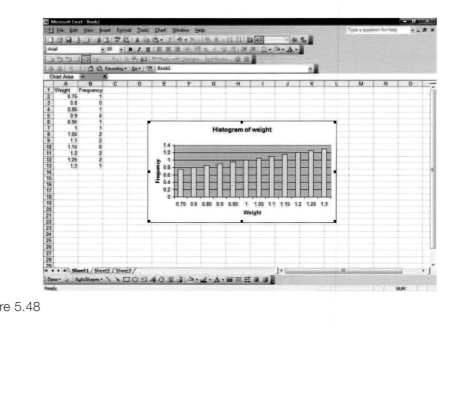

Figure 5.48

A bar chart uses bars to show frequencies.

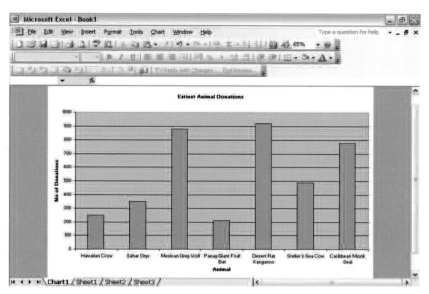

Figure 5.49

A pie chart shows percentage values as a slice of a pie.

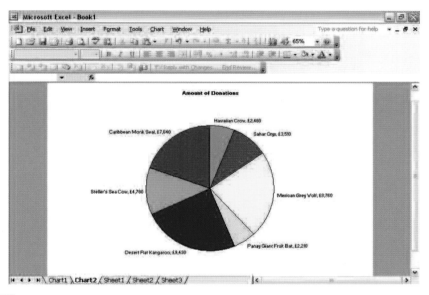

Figure 5.50

Line graph

A line graph is used to plot independent and dependent variables, for example, to show the frequency of data.

An example line graph is shown in Figure 5.52.

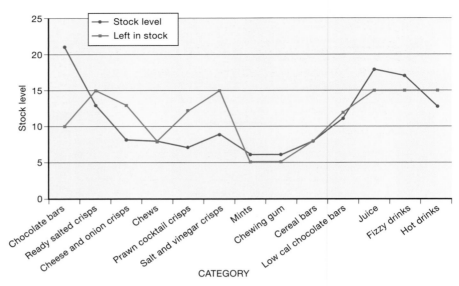

Figure 5.51

Comparative column/bar chart

A column/bar chart displays data in different categories or groups.

An example is shown below:

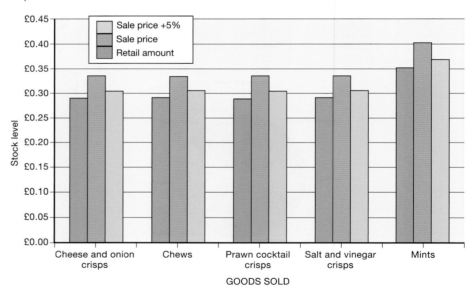

Figure 5.52

Area

An area chart shows the trend of values over time. For example, the following area chart shows sales over a number of years for different regions in the UK.

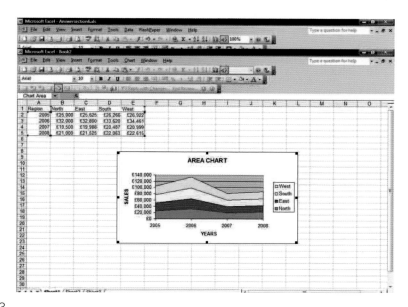

Figure 5.53

XY scatter

XY (scatter) charts show the relationships between values two values – the XY scatter below plots the width against the length.

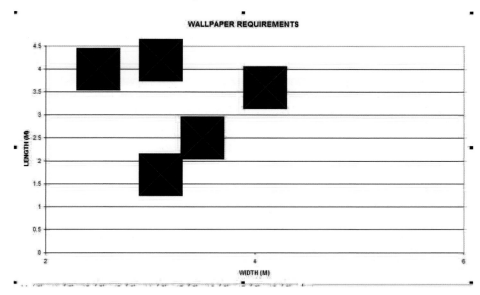

Figure 5.54

Stock

A stock chart is sometimes used to track share price or stock price data. See the example in Figure 5.56.

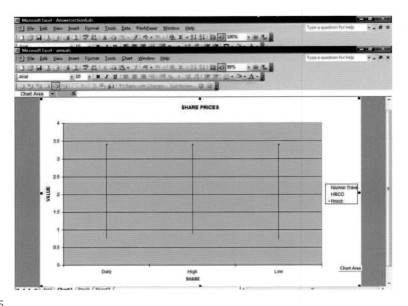

Figure 5.55

Radar

A radar chart compares the total values and displays the changes in values to a centre point.

Doughnut

A doughnut chart is similar to a pie chart; however, where a pie chart can only contain one data series, a doughnut can show more than one data series.

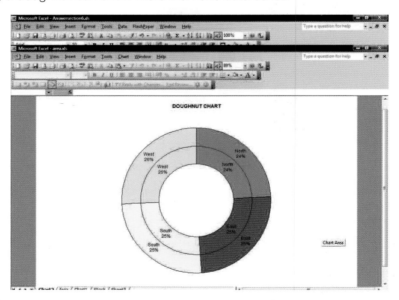

Figure 5.56

Surface

A surface chart is useful when you want to find combinations between two sets of data. This chart can show trends in values as a continuous curve.

Continuous and discrete data

Continuous data is data that can be measured on a scale, for example, money, time and temperature.

Discrete data is data where units of measure cannot be split into smaller units. For example, there is nothing between 1 and 2 DVDs.

B3.4 Select and use appropriate page layout to present and print spreadsheet information

As you are creating your charts, you need to add suitable titles, axes, labels, and so on.

See how this is done.

5.21 Demonstration

Worked Example B3.4.1

1 Open the computer **games.xls** spreadsheet.
2 Create a comparative bar chart to plot the computer games that have been hired during January, February and March.
3 Highlight the data to be used in the chart. Click the **Chart Wizard** icon, select the column chart type, then check that the data is displayed correctly in the preview window.
4 Enter the appropriate title and labels, click **Legend** to have the legend displayed on or off, and then display the chart on a new sheet.
5 Save and close the spreadsheet.

Task 3.4.1

1 Open the **travel.xls** spreadsheet.
2 Create a pie chart to show the number of rooms booked in each month.
3 Add suitable title and labels.
4 Create a line graph to show the Total Cost against the months.
5 Add suitable titles and labels.
6 Save and close the spreadsheet.

Consolidation

1 Open the **consol_dvd_b234.xls** spreadsheet.
2 Format the spreadsheet so that you have used different fonts, alignment, borders, shading, column widths and conditional formatting.
3 Create an XY scatter graph to compare the Stock In against the Stock Out.
4 Add appropriate titles and labels.
5 Create a bar chart that graphs the stock Balance for CDs only.
6 Add appropriate titles and labels.
7 Create a comparative bar chart that graphs the Stock Movement in and out.
8 Add appropriate titles and labels.
9 Save and close the spreadsheet as **consol_dvd_graphs.xls**.

Once you have created your spreadsheet, you can then set the page to change the orientation and margins so that all the information is correctly printed on the page.

B3.4.1 Size

The size of the paper that the spreadsheet or graph can be printed on can be changed. It is usual that spreadsheets are printed on A4 paper. However, sometimes you might want to print onto A3. Ensure that you have an A3 printer before you change the setup.

B3.4.2 Orientation

Spreadsheets can be printed in either portrait or landscape orientation. Portrait means that the pages are taller and thinner whereas with landscape they are shorter and wider. You should always check the printouts in print preview before you start to ensure that the spreadsheet is not inappropriately over two pages.

B3.4.3 Margins

Margins can be increased or decreased so that the spreadsheet is displayed correctly on the page.

B3.4.4 Header and footer page numbers, date and time

Headers and footers are helpful in a spreadsheet to show page numbers, dates, times and also the author's details and filename locations.

B3.4.5 Page breaks

Appropriate page breaks should be set so that the data is displayed accurately on the pages. This can be done by clicking **Insert** and then **Page Break**.

Worked Example B3.4.1

1 Open the **games.xls** spreadsheet.
2 Change the orientation to landscape for the main spreadsheet and change the margins to 2.5 cm all round.
3 Select **Print Preview** to check where the page breaks fall.
4 Instead of changing page breaks, choose **File → Page Setup → Fit to one page**.
5 Add your name as a header and insert today's date, using a date field in the footer.
6 Save and close the spreadsheet.

Task 3.4.1

1 Open the **travel.xls** spreadsheet.
2 Check the page layout and change the page orientation and margins so that the spreadsheet will be printed out appropriately.
3 Add suitable headers and footers.
4 Save and close the spreadsheet.

B3.5 Check information meets needs, using spreadsheet tools and making corrections as necessary

Now that the spreadsheet is completed, check the accuracy of the numbers by proofreading and check that the results that have been presented make sense. The suitability of graphs and charts also needs to be checked. For example, you would not use a pie chart to plot two sets of data. This would be better plotted as an XY scatter chart. The formulas can be checked and the spreadsheet can be viewed and printed out. Before printing the spreadsheet, check the page layout and formatting options so that it will be displayed correctly when you print it.

B3.6 Describe how to find errors in spreadsheet formulas

B3.7 Respond appropriately to any problems with spreadsheets

B3.7.1 Using help

Microsoft Excel® has some excellent help information available within the program. Most of the information is now located on Microsoft's website but you can visit the help pages to find information if you have any problems. Microsoft's own website also has tutorials, which are helpful if you are struggling with a certain topic.

Watch how this is done.

🖱 5.22 | *Demonstration*

B3.7.2 Sorting out errors in formulas

Before you complete your spreadsheet, check that the formulas presented are correct. Have a quick look and check that everything makes sense. You could even check on a calculator that the sums are correct.

B3.7.3 Circular references

A circular reference message is sometimes displayed when formulas have been incorrectly created. Usually a circular reference refers back to its own cell. For example, in the screen print below, cell B49 is the cell where the answer will be displayed. However, this has been included in the sum function and therefore the circular reference message is displayed. You could correct this by amending the sum function.

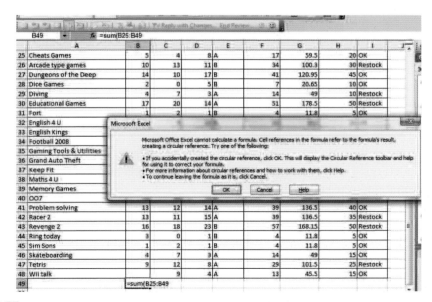

Figure 5.57

Mini Assignment

In this Mini Assignment, you will practise all the skills you have learned throughout this chapter.

The Mini Assignment is based around a minimart. Your manager has given you the following instructions and you are required to complete these tasks.

1 Create a new folder to store your work for this assignment and then produce evidence to meet the unit requirements.
2 Open Microsoft Excel® and open the spreadsheet **minimart.xls**.
3 Save the spreadsheet as **sales.xls**.
4 Format the spreadsheet so that it includes:
   - font style and size
   - alignment
   - wrapped text
   - merged and centred data
   - formatting of numbers.
5 Change to column/row widths/heights.
6 Calculate the Total by using a lookup function. You will need to add together the Balance B/f and the Sales and take this away by multiplying the Sales by the lookup data.
7 Calculate the Interest Charge by multiplying the Balance b/f by the Interest Charge on the summary worksheet.
8 Calculate the Balance by deducting the Interest Charge from the Total.
9 Use an If statement to show the order status as either 'hold on further orders' or 'OK'.
10 Go the summary sheet and calculate the:
   - average sales
   - number of restaurants
   - total monthly sales
   - outstanding balances.
11 Create the following graphs/charts:
   - Create a pie chart to show the Sales for each restaurant – use appropriate titles and labels.
   - Create an XY scatter to plot the Sales against Total. Use appropriate titles and labels.
12 Check the pagination, page layout and margins of the spreadsheet.
13 Add suitable headers and footers.
14 Check the spreadsheet thoroughly.
15 Print out a copy of the spreadsheet, each of the graphs and the spreadsheet showing the formulas.
16 Save and close the spreadsheet.

6

Presentation Software

This unit will develop the knowledge and skills relating to the production of simple presentations, such as text-based or diagram-based slides shows and lecture notes.

By working through the **Overview**, **Worked Examples**, **Tasks** and the **Consolidations** in this chapter, you will demonstrate the skills required for Presentation Software Level 1:

ELEMENT The competent person will...	PERFORMANCE CRITERIA To demonstrate this competence they can...	KNOWLEDGE To demonstrate this competence they will also...
PS:A1 Input and combine text and other information within presentation slides	A1.2 Select and use different slide layouts as appropriate for different types of information A1.3 Enter information into presentation slides so that it is ready for editing and formatting A1.5 Combine information of different forms or from different sources for presentations A1.6 Store and retrieve presentation files effectively, in line with local guidelines and conventions where available	A1.1 Identify what types of information are required for the presentation A1.4 Identify any constraints which may affect the presentation
PS:A2 Use presentation software tools to structure, edit and format slides	A2.2 Select and use an appropriate template to structure slides A2.3 Select and use appropriate techniques to edit slides A2.4 Select and use appropriate techniques to format slides	A2.1 Identify what slide structure to use
PS:A3 Prepare slides for presentation to meet needs	A3.2 Prepare slides for presentation A3.3 Check presentation meets needs, using IT tools and making corrections as necessary	A3.1 Identify how to present slides to meet needs and communicate effectively

Step-by-step examples are provided as a demonstration of what to do. These demonstrations are based on Microsoft PowerPoint® 2003 and are produced for each **Worked Example** task.

Review the overview in each section and then watch the demonstration in the **Worked Example** before commencing any tasks.

Once you are familiar with the topic covered, move onto the **Tasks** section of this chapter.

Consolidation exercises are provided throughout the chapter for extra practice.

Throughout the **Worked Examples** and **Tasks** sections, you will be working on a theme of creating presentations for a publishing company, as requested by various organisations and people.

In the **Consolidation** sections, you will produce a document for the publishing company above.

For the **Mini Assignment** you will be working on the theme of creating presentations for Escape Travel, a holiday company.

A1 Input and combine text and other information within presentation slides

A1.1 Identify what types of information are required for the presentation

Microsoft PowerPoint® is graphics presentation software, used to show audiences information. The software includes word processing, drawing, graphing and presentation tools.

When you create a presentation, it is made up of a series of slides. The slides you create can be presented electronically over a computer system, the internet or as overhead transparencies. In addition to slides, you can print audience handouts, outlines, and speaker's notes.

You can import what you have created using other Microsoft products, such as Word® and Excel®, into any of your slides. This can be useful if you have created a graph in Microsoft Excel® that you wish to present on a slide – you do not need to re-create the graph; you simply copy and paste the graph onto your slide. You can also include graphics, images and sound files.

A1.2 Select and use different slide layouts as appropriate for different types of information

Opening Microsoft PowerPoint®

On opening Microsoft PowerPoint®, your screen will display a standard slide layout in Title Slide format. You can change this if it is not the slide format you wish to use.

Choosing a layout

The following screen appears:

Figure 6.1

You can choose the slide layout suitable for the text and layout you are to present by selecting **Format → Slide Layout.** Here you can choose from many different slide layouts (see Figure 6.2.).

Viewing your presentation

Using the toolbar at the bottom of your screen, choose the icon that looks like a block of four squares:

Figure 6.3

| A1.3 | Enter information into presentation slides so that it is ready for editing and formatting |

Inserting text

There are specific areas on a slide for text, as shown in Figure 6.4.

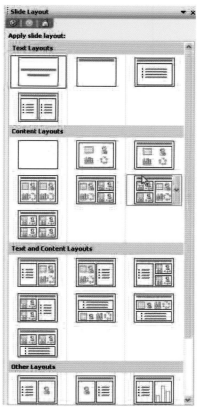

Figure 6.2

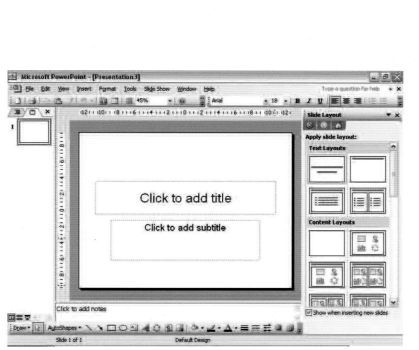

Figure 6.4

In Figure 6.4, the slide layout is Title Slide. This allows you to place a main heading and a subheading on the slide. Other layouts and the general layout are as shown in Figure 6.5.

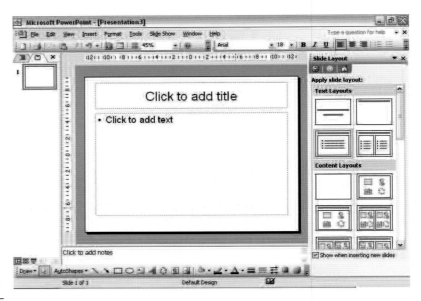

Figure 6.5

The above layout allows you to place a heading and bulleted items on the slide and is the one generally used for presentations of just text items.

A1.4   Identify any constraints which may affect the presentation

When you create any presentation or document, there are several constraints such as content, copyright law, acknowledgement of sources, avoiding plagiarism, equality and diversity and local guidelines.

Content

Check before you start: do you have all the information? Is there anything missing? Do you need to check the content with anyone before you finalise the presentation? Consider these questions before delivering your presentation.

Copyright law

It is very important when creating any kind of presentation that you don't download and use music/image files without the owner's permission. Most images/sound files that can be downloaded from the internet are subject to copyright and it is imperative that you either contact the owner and obtain their permission to use the text/music/image or don't use them at all.

Acknowledgement of sources

If you do use text/images/sound from other sources, obtain permission before you use them and acknowledge the source. There are various ways of doing this but most commonly you would add the author's name and date of publication in the text, for example, Bowman and Jones (2009). At the end of the presentation, there should be a bibliography which shows the full names of the author, title of the publication, date it was published and author details. For example:

Bibliography

Bowman, N.J. and Jones, A.C., 2009, *Succeed in iTQ: Levels 1 and 2*, Hodder Education.

Plagiarism

Plagiarism is becoming a growing concern as text can be 'copied' and 'pasted' from the internet into documents without any source information or referencing and it can be passed off as someone's own work. Some academic institutions now use software that allows them to scan documents produced by students and check them to make sure that any assignments submitted are the student's own work and not plagiarised from somewhere else.

It is very important that you do not copy and paste any text and pass it off as your own.

Equality and diversity

Make sure when creating your presentations that you consider equality and diversity legislation and that your presentation is not biased, unsuitable and can be read/seen by everyone. For example, you need to consider your audience and ensure that any text/images you display are not inappropriate and do not cause any offence.

Think about the font style, colours and text size that you use to make sure that the presention can be easily read by all.

Local guidelines

Find out what the local guidelines are when producing presentations. For example, if your organisation has a house style or master slide, you may have to use colours, fonts and styles that have been pre-set.

A.1.5 Combine information of different forms or from different sources for presentations

Adding clip art to your presentation

Using clip art is one way to add graphics to a presentation without having to create each graphic yourself. When the Clip Art gallery is displayed, point and click to select a graphic and then click on Insert. Your graphic will be inserted.

Any image included can be resized. Initially the image will appear in the centre of your slide at a default size, and you usually need to move and resize it.

Watch the demonstration to see how this is done.

6.1 Demonstration

Worked Example A1.5

1 Open Microsoft PowerPoint®.
  A new slide will have appeared. This is the Title Slide.
2 Add the following text in the first box:
  WELCOME TO OUR NEWEST CLUB THE HEADQUARTERS
3 Add your name to the second box.
4 Insert a picture that represents a club scene.
  Select **Insert → Picture → Clipart**. On the right side of your screen will appear a dialog box. Key in **celebration** under Search for. Click on **Go**.
5 When you find a picture you wish to insert double click on the image and it will insert. You may need to resize the image if it is too large or small.
6 Right click on the image. Select **Format Picture → Size → Height**. Change this to **5 cm** and move your image to a desired location on your slide.
7 To insert a new slide, select **Insert → New Slide** or you can use key combination **Ctrl+M**.

The slide that opens next is the default slide for text and bulleted lists.

8 On this slide, key in the following in the top box:
MEMBERSHIP

9 In the rest of the box below the main box, key in the following:
Free 1-year membership to first 120 guests
Free drinks until 10:30 pm

10 Insert a new slide and add the following text:
THEME NIGHTS
60s and 70s night – music from the 60s and 70s will be played all evening – clothes to match
Rock night – only rock and roll on this evening – clothes to match

11 Insert a new slide this time. Use the template for Title and Content.

Figure 6.6

12 Add the following text as the title: **Membership charges**

13 Select the icon on the slide that looks like a table and the following should appear:

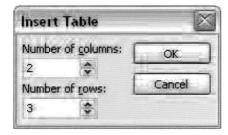

Figure 6.7

14 Select **2** columns and **3** rows. Click **OK**.
Key in the following:

General admission	£15
Themed nights	£20
Special occasions	£25

15 Insert a new slide again. Use the template for Title and Content and add the following text as the title: **Come and join our opening event**.

16 Select the icon on the slide that looks like a graphical picture of a person and the following should appear: In the box **Search text**, key in **club** → select **Go** and select a suitable image. Click on the image and click **OK**. The image should appear on your slide.

17 Resize the image with your mouse, by clicking on the outer edge of the image and dragging your mouse to either reduce the size or increase it.

18 Save your presentation. Select **File** → **Save As**. Locate the area where you are going to save your work and give your presentation the name **Headquarters**.

Now it's your turn to have a go.

Figure 6.8

Task A1.5

1 Create a new presentation.
2 There is no title slide to this presentation – start with Title and bullet list and enter the following text:

Slide 1

Marsden

■ **Gateway to the West**
■ **For centuries, a Pennine crossing place**

Slide 2

What to visit

■ **Mechanics' Hall**
■ **Old Stocks, Towngate**
■ **St Bartholomew's Church**
■ **Snail Horn Bridge**
■ **Tunnel End**
■ **Umpteen Pubs!**

Slide 3

Huddersfield Narrow Canal

■ **Visit the Countryside Centre at Tunnel End**
■ **Walk along the towpath and have a cup of tea**
■ **You can go through England's longest and highest tunnel in a glass-topped boat**

Slide 4

Visitors

Add an image of people.

If you can find an image of a canal barge, add this also.

3 Save your presentation as **Marsden**.

A1.6 Store and retrieve presentation files effectively, in line with local guidelines and conventions where available

Once you create a presentation, you should save it using sensible filenames and in places which make it easy to retrieve later on.

Files can be created, saved, named, opened, saved with a different name, printed, closed and found.

Saving

As with any Microsoft Windows® document, save your work using **File → Save As** and choose where you wish to save to and give the document a filename.

Naming

When naming files, you should consider using sensible filenames to help you find the file later. Good practice would suggest short filenames of about seven characters without any spaces or punctuation.

Saving with a different name

Sometimes you might decide to save the file with a different filename – this could be as 'version2', or something completely different.

Printing

There are different print options. These range from:

■ single slide per page

■ handouts – multiple slides per page (2–6)

■ notes pages – printouts with speaker's notes and a miniature of the slide

■ outline view – just the text – showing no images or objects.

Watch the demonstration below to see how this is done.

6.2 Demonstration

Worked Example A1.6

1 Create a new presentation.
2 There is no title slide to this presentation – start with Title and bullet list and enter the following text:

Slide 1:

Ideal Villa Holidays

■ **We only offer exclusive villas**

- All privately owned
- Many 'out of the way' secluded places

Slide 2:

Welcome to our villas

- **Our range is extensive**
- **From one twin bedroom to sleeping 16**
- **All with private swimming pools**

Slide 3:

Resorts and locations

- **Lanzarote**
- **Majorca**
- **Ibiza**
- **Portugal**
- **Cyprus**

1 Insert an image of a villa on one slide of your choice.
2 Create a new slide 4 and add a table to a slide giving prices of the villas as shown below:
3 Save the file as **Villa 2**.

Slide 4

Example costs of villas in Cyprus

Villa name	Charge per week summer
Cynthia	£1200
Sea View	£800
Sunset	£1000
Sea Caves	£750

Task A1.6

1 Create a new presentation.
2 Start with a Title slide and enter the following text:

Slide 1:

San Francisco

The city with everything!

'Let's go to San Francisco ...'

Insert a picture that represents San Francisco. This could be from the results of a search on "bay" in the Clip Art library.

Slide 2:

Sites you can't miss

- **Golden Gate Bridge and Park**
- **Fisherman's Wharf**
- **Chinatown**
- **Nob Hill**
- **Alcatraz**
- **Union Square**

Slide 3:

Restaurants

Shop until you drop

- **Go to Union Square for famous names**
- **Try the Napa Valley Winery Exchange too**

Slide 4:

Weather

Insert a picture that represents sunny weather.

Slide 5:

San Francisco Bay

- **Spend a day on a boat and go around the Bay, stopping at Sausalito for lunch**

Insert a picture showing either a boat or people eating.

3   Save your presentation as **SanFran** and close the file.

A2 Use presentation software tools to structure, edit and format slides

A2.1   Identify what slide structure to use

A2.2   Select and use an appropriate template to structure slides

In the previous section, we used slides with different layouts. In this section, we will look at templates, designs and styles and organisational guidelines.

Templates

Microsoft PowerPoint® contains a number of design templates that can be used when creating a new presentation. Each design template has colours, backgrounds, fonts and styles already set. All you do is add the information to your presentation.

Watch the demonstration to see how this is done.

6.3   *Demonstration*

> Worked Example A2.2.1

1   Click on **File** → **New** → **Templates on my computer** → **Design templates** → **Axis template** → **OK**.
2   Add the following information to the title slide:

Learning explorers

Open Day – 22 March

2–4 pm

3   Save and close the file as **Explorers**.

Now its your turn to have a go.

Task A2.2.1

1 Create a new presentation based on the **Shimmer** design template.
2 Add the following information:

Title slide:

Welcome

Slide 2:

Opening times

Monday–Friday 8.30 am–8.30 pm

Saturday 9.00 am–3.00 pm

Sunday 12.00–2.00 pm

Slide 3:

Collections

Pre-order and collect

Have posted

Special collections

3 Save and close the file as **lib.ppt**.

Designs and styles

Slide design allows you to apply different design templates to an existing presentation.

Watch the demonstration to see how this is done.

6.4 *Demonstration*

Worked Example A2.2.2

1   Create a new presentation.
2   Click on **Format → Style Design**.
3   You have three choices: Design Templates, Colour Schemes, Animation Schemes.
4   Design templates allow you to add a design template – choose **Glass layers.pot** and apply this to your slides.

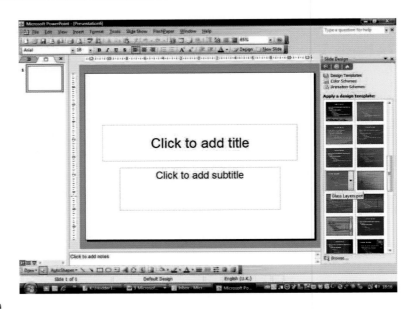

Figure 6.9

5   Add the following text:

Title Slide:

Welcome

Slide 2:

About us

- **Family owned business**
- **Three other branches in the UK**

Slide 3:

New development

- **5-acre site**
- **South of Durham city**
- **Executive houses and apartments**

6   Save the presentation as **houses**.

Now it's your turn to have a go.

Task A2.2.2

1   Create a new presentation.
2   Click on **Format → Style Design**.
3   You have three choices: Design Templates, Colour Schemes, Animation Schemes.
4   Design templates allow you to add a design template. Choose **Glass layers.pot** and apply this to your slides.

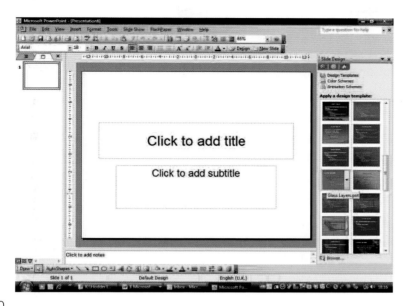

Figure 6.10

5 Add the following text:

Title Slide

New housing development

Slide 2

House prices

House prices are between:

£345,000 and £765,000

Slide 3

Release dates

Starting October 2006

Final release dates – April 2007

Slide 4

Special offers

No deposit

Part-exchange available

First six weeks only!

6 Save and close the presentation as **offers.**

Organisational guidelines

You will need to find out what your organisational guidelines are for creating presentations. Do they follow a house style? If so, where do you get a copy from and what does it look like?

Presentations that have been saved can be opened and edited, just like any other text-based document.

It could be that you are asked to place shapes and lines on a slide. This is easily achieved using the drawing toolbar, just like using this in Microsoft Word®.

A2.3 Select and use appropriate techniques to edit slides

In this section you will edit slides by using drag and drop, find, replace, undo/redo, size, crop and position objects, wrap text, add lines and simple shapes.

To edit text, highlight the text with your mouse or key combinations, then use the DELETE key or the BACKSPACE key on the keyboard.

To highlight text with mouse: click, hold down the mouse button and drag the mouse pointer over the text, then release the mouse button and the text is highlighted.

To highlight using the keyboard: with your cursor at the beginning of the text using the key combination SHIFT and right arrow – this will select a character at a time or you can use CTRL and right arrow to select a word at a time.

Once you have deleted the text, you can then key in the new text.

If the text has been highlighted, you do not need to hit the DELETE or BACKSPACE key, but key in the text and this action will automatically delete the highlighted text.

Watch the demonstration to see how to edit text.

6.5 Demonstration

Worked Example A2.3.1

1. Open the presentation **develop.ppt**.
2. Go to slide 4 and cut the text **Location and Facilities** and paste it as the title on this slide.
3. Copy slide 1 and paste this as a new last slide.
4. Save the presentation as **devamend.ppt**.
5. Close the file.

Now it's your turn to have a go.

Task A2.3.1

1. Open the presentation **hols.ppt**.
2. On slide 2 cut the text **Go to Union Square for famous names Try the Napa Valley Winery Exchange too** and paste it onto slide 3.
3. Cut the slide **Weather**.
4. Save and close the file **hols1.ppt**.

Adding simple lines and shapes

Watch the demonstration to see how to add lines and simple shapes.

6.6 Demonstration

Worked Example A2.3.2

1. Open the presentation **Sans**.
2. You have been asked to add some graphics to the first slide.
3. If the drawing toolbar is not open at the bottom of your screen, select **View → Toolbars → Drawing**.

4   On the first slide, using **AutoShapes**, add some stars. Click on **Stars and Banners**. Choose a star shape and your mouse pointer will become a cross **+.** Using your mouse, place the cross where you wish to draw a star (don't worry if it is not in the correct place, you can always place it correctly afterwards). Click the left button, hold it down and draw out a star shape.

5   When you release the mouse button, your star shape will be on the slide. It may have a filled colour. You can use the other toolbar options to change these features. The Paint pot on the Drawing toolbar gives fill colours.

Figure 6.11

1   Save the file as **Sans2**.

Now it's your turn to have a go.

Task A2.3.2

1   Open a blank presentation.
2   On the first slide of your choice, using the drawing toolbar options, create some shapes using colours, lines, fill options and arrows.
3   Save your slide as **practice**.

A2.4   Select and use appropriate techniques to format slides

With any text you have placed on a slide, you can change the following:

■ alignment

■ colour

■ size

■ fonts

■ line spacing

■ bullet symbol

■ numbers

■ background.

You can make changes to other items on your slides:

■ change the background colour

■ add an image to the background

■ change the colours of objects on your slides.

Watch the demonstration to see how this is done.

6.7   *Demonstration*

Worked Example A2.4.1

1   Open the file **Villa**.
2   On Slide 1, make the following changes:
    Highlight the heading and change the font size to a larger font.
    Change the font so that it is bold and italic.
    Change the alignment of the heading to be right-aligned.

3   On Slide 3 make the following changes:
Highlight the bullets as you are going to change the bullet symbol.
Select **Format** → **Bullets and Numbering** → choose one style → click **OK**.

4   On Slide 4 change the text in the table:
Highlight the text in the table and change the font size.
Change the font so that it is italic.
Change the colour of the text.

5   Add a new slide and add the following:
Contact details
Josie Smith
01484 021 001
This last text should not be displayed with bullets.

6   Highlight the bullets. You are going to remove the bullet symbol. Select **Format** →
Bullets and Numbering → choose **None** → click **OK**.

7   Save as **Villa**.

Add a background

Worked Example A2.4.2

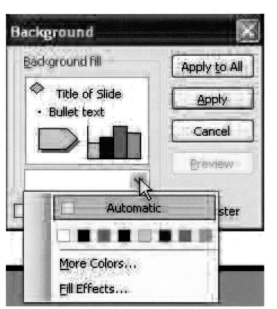

Figure 6.12

1   Open the file **stars**.
You are going to change the background colour to make the slides more interesting.

2   Select **Format** → **Background**. Choose the box with the drop-down arrow. Click on the arrow.

3   You can select a colour from the boxes shown or choose **More Colours**. Once you have chosen your colour, select **Apply All**. This will apply the same colour to all your slides in your presentation.
You are going to add an image that will appear on each slide.

4   Select **View** → **Master** → **Slide Master**. You are now on the background of the whole presentation. Don't worry that you have no text here. This is the template, not an actual slide.

5   Select **Insert** → **Clip Art**. Choose from the **Holiday** section. Resize the image to make it small and place it in the bottom right of the slide.

6   You have a dialog box open, which you need to close to get back to your presentation. Click on **Close Master View**. Your image should now be on each slide.
NOTE: if you do not have the above dialog box, then click on the Slide Sorter View at the bottom left of your screen.

7   Save as **stars3**.

Now it's your turn to have a go.

Task A2.4.1

1   Open the file **stars**.

2   On the second slide, there are four bulleted items – you are going to change the line spacing of these items.

3   Highlight the bullet items. Select **Format** → **Line Spacing** → select **1.5** → click **OK**.

4 Change the bullets to numbers. Select the bullet items. Select **Format** → **Bullets and Numbering**. Select the **Numbered** tab → choose a number format → click **OK**.

5 Add a background colour of pale green.

6 Save as **stars2**.

Consolidation

1 Create a new presentation.

2 Set up a background colour of pale blue.

3 Add an image to the Master Slide background. Place this image in the bottom left corner. Close the Master Slide View.

4 On the first slide (which should be a title slide), add the heading **Many special offers**.

5 Add your name in the second box on the first slide.

6 Add a new slide. Add the text **Come and buy today**. This text should be a different colour to the first slide. Align this text to the right of the slide.

7 In the bullet section of this slide, add the following:

CDs for 30p

Videos for £1

Floppy disks 10p

8 Add some pictures to this slide to suit the text. Position the images and add arrows to connect the pictures to the text.

9 Re-colour the arrows to the same colour as the heading.

10 Highlight the bullet items and change the line spacing to **1.5**.

11 Save as **Cons**.

A3 Prepare slides for presentation to meet needs

A3.1 Identify how to present slides to meet needs and communicate effectively

Microsoft PowerPoint® gives the user different options of how the slide show is presented. The options are both electronic and also paper-based. When finalising the presentation you should think about:

1   How the information is organised – is it clear? Does it follow a logical flow?

2   Is the meaning clear?

3   Is the content appropriate for the audience?

4   Do any timings need to be added?

Electronically, you can change the order of slides, hide slides you do not wish to be displayed, make customised shows and automate the slide show by adding timings and transitions. You can make the slide show more interesting by adding animations to each slide; many of these features are in Level 2.

To view the slides, you can choose from different options:

■ slides

■ outline

■ show.

As you produce your slides, you are automatically viewing in Slides view. If the pane at the left of your screen is open, you are also viewing in outline; this is just showing the text you have created, without any formatting or layout. This view does not include objects added, such as graphics. Outline view is the best way to check for spelling mistakes, whereas Slide view is best to check for layout.

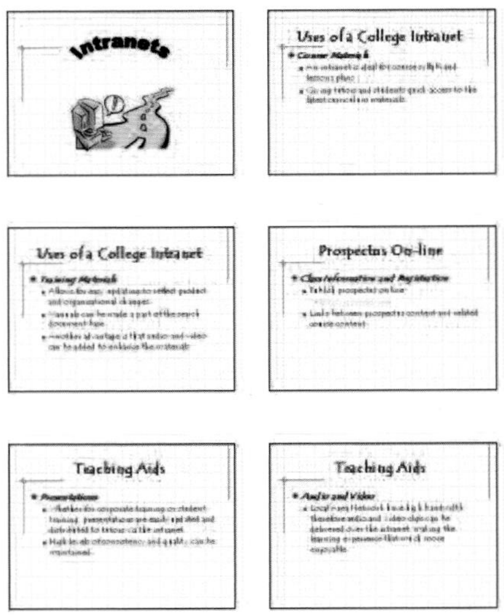

To check the slide show works and presents as you wish, it is best to view the show as it will be seen by the audience. Do this through the **View** → **Slide Show** option.

Figure 6.13

A3.2   Prepare slides for presentation

You may produce a presentation and then wish to change the order the slides present. This is a straightforward action of simply dragging the slide to the correct position and releasing it. The order of the slides is then changed.

Paper-based copies can be presented in different formats:

- slides
- handouts
- notes pages
- outline.

Slides print out one single slide per page, whereas Handouts allow you to choose how many slides appear on each page. This can be from two slides per page to nine slides per page – although nine is excessive and the audience would find it difficult to read some of the content on the slides. Generally three per page is standard and gives the audience the space to write notes. If no notes are to be taken then six per page works as the slides are exactly the same size as three per page, but there are double columns.

You can also print a paper-based version of an outline view; this can help if you are presenting the slide show as it gives you prompts of the slide content.

The best way to use a paper-based presentation as a presenter is by utilising the Notes Pages. When you create the slides, you can also create speaker's notes. When you show the presentation, these notes are not displayed, but when you print Notes Pages you get a cut–down version of the slide with notes, to aid you when delivering the presentation.

Timings can be added to the presentation, which allow you to show the slide on the screen for a specified set of time. These can be rehearsed and allow you to find out how long the presentation will last.

Watch the demonstration to see how this is done.

6.8   *Demonstration*

Worked Example A3.1

1   Open the file **intranet**. You are going to print the slide show.
2   Select **File** → **Print**.

Figure 6.14

3 Select **Print what** → **Handouts** → **Slides per page** → **3** → **OK**.

4 Check your printouts. You should see three pages printed, with all seven slides over the three pages.

5 Now you are going to print some Notes Pages for when you deliver the slide show.

6 Select **File** → **Print**.

7 Select **Print what** → **Notes Pages** → **OK**.

8 Try other print options.

9 Close the file. If prompted, do not save any changes.

Now it's your turn to have a go.

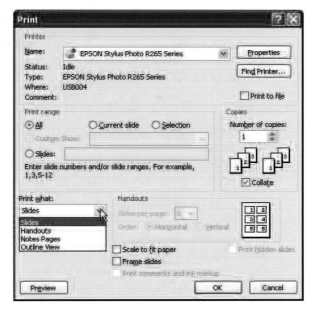

Figure 6.15

Task A3.1

1 Open the presentation **Villa**. You are going to print the slide show.

2 Select **File** → **Print**.

3 Select **Print what** → **Handouts** → **Slides per page** → **3** → **OK**. Check your printouts. You should see three pages printed with all seven slides over the three pages. Now you are going to print some Notes Pages.

4 Select **File** → **Print**.

5 Select **Print what** → choose **Notes Pages** → **OK**.

6 Try other print options.

7 Close the file. If prompted, do not save any changes.

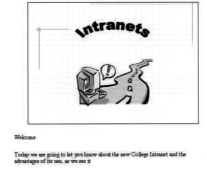

Figure 6.16

Once you have finished, you can prepare your slides for presentation. This can include re-ordering the slides, rehearsing timings and printing slides/handouts or speaker notes.

Watch the demonstration to see how this is done.

 6.9 *Demonstration*

Worked Example A3.2

1 Open the file **intranet**.
You are going to view the slide show.
2 Select **Slide Show** → **View Show**.
Transitions have been set up on this show, but not animations. You will need to click your mouse to move through the slide show.
3 Watch the show slide by slide. For each slide, think:
Does it work?
Are the slides in the correct order?
Do you need to make any changes?

The order of the slides needs changing.
Slide 7 needs moving to the slide 5 position.
4 Select **Slide Sorter View**. This is the icon at the bottom left of your screen. It looks like four squares (Figure 6.17).
5 Click on slide 7. Hold down your left mouse button. Drag the slide to the correct position. Don't worry if you get this wrong, you can always move it again. Once you have a straight line showing between slides 4 and 5, release your mouse button and slide 7 should now be slide 5.
6 Add a timing of five seconds to each slide. Select Transition to come automatically after 5 seconds.

Figure 6.17

Figure 6.18

7 Save as **intramod**.

Now it's your turn to have a go.

Task A3.2

1 Open the file **Cons** you created earlier.
2 You are going to view the slide show.
3 Select **Slide Show** → **View Show**.

You will need to click your mouse to move through the slide show.
4 Add slides so they automatically advance after 8 seconds.
5 Watch the show slide by slide. For each slide, think:
Does it work?
Are the slides in the correct order?
Do you need to make any changes?
6 Print your slide show **six** slides per page.
7 Close your file.

Consolidation

1 Open the file **Villa** you created earlier.
2 You are going to view the slide show.
3 Select **Slide Show** → **View Show**.
You will need to click your mouse to move through the slide show.
4 Watch the show slide by slide. For each slide, think:
Does it work?
Are the slides in the correct order?
Do you need to make any changes?
5 Change the order of a slide.
6 Print your slide show **four** slides per page.
7 Print your slide show as an outline view.
8 Save the changes and close your file.

A3.3 Check presentation meets needs using IT tools and making corrections as necessary

As with any document that is going to be viewed by other people, it is important that spelling mistakes are corrected.

Spellchecker

Microsoft PowerPoint® works exactly as Microsoft Word® in the use of spelling and grammar checkers.

To resize graphics

■ Click on the image to display the graphic handles (placeholders).

■ Hold the left mouse button and drag a top, bottom or middle handle to change the size.

Note: to resize without distorting the image, hold down the SHIFT key while using the mouse and only drag a corner handle.

Rotate an object

■ Click on the object to display the placeholders.

■ Click and hold the left mouse button on the green handle located above the top border – your cursor will now become a circular arrow.

■ Drag the mouse left or right to the desired rotation.

Orientation

When you view the presentation in print preview, have you chosen the correct orientation? Slides can be displayed in either portrait or landscape.

Layout

Have you chosen the correct layout? For example, have you chosen the correct slide layout for the information that has been displayed?

Slide order

Are your slides in the correct order? Do they make sense?

Text alignment

Is the text aligned consistently throughout the presentation? Is each slide consistent with the other?

Accuracy

Have you proofread and spellchecked the document to ensure that it has been produced to a professional standard?

Final checking

Before you present your presentation, it is worth checking that images, drawings, text and layout of the slides is appropriate and conveys the correct message to the audience.

Watch the demonstration to see how this is done.

6.10 Demonstration

Worked Example A3.3

1 Open the file **Intranet.**
2 Check that this presentation has no spelling errors.
3 Check the graphics are suitably placed.
4 Save as **Intranet2.**

Now it's your turn to have a go.

Task A3.3

1 Open the file **Cons.**
2 Check that this presentation has no spelling errors.
3 Check that the graphics are suitably placed.
4 Save as **Cons2.**

Mini Assignment

1 In this Mini Assignment, you will practise all the skills you have learned so far.
2 The Mini Assignment is based around the travel agency Escape Travel. Your manager has given you the following instructions and you are required to complete these, producing evidence for your portfolio.
3 You are employed as the clerical assistant for Escape Travel and produce a variety of documents to advertise the holidays.
4 Open the file **villahols**.
5 Add additional text to one slide.
6 Add further slides to the presentation – include more pictures and some drawing objects.

7 Format the text styles on the presentation to make it more interesting.
8 Change the background colour.
9 Move the image on the background to the bottom left-hand corner of the slide. Check that the image is not covering any text and resize the image if necessary.
10 Change the order of the slides.
11 View the presentation to check that it works.
12 Spell check the presentation.
13 Produce printouts – outline view and handouts.
14 Save the document.

Level 2

This unit will develop knowledge and skills relating to the production of complex presentations, such as slide shows with animation.

By working through the **Overview, Worked Examples, Tasks** and the **Consolidations** in this chapter, you will demonstrate the skills required for Presentation Software Level 2.

ELEMENT The competent person will...	PERFORMANCE CRITERIA To demonstrate this competency they can...	KNOWLEDGE To demonstrate this competency they will also...
PS:B1 Input and combine text and other information within presentation slides	B1.2 Enter text and other information using layouts appropriate to type of information B1.3 Insert charts and tables into presentation slides B1.4 Insert video or sound to enhance the presentation B1.6 Organise and combine information or different forms or from different sources for presentations B1.7 Store and retrieve presentation files effectively, in line with local guidelines and conventions where available	B1.1 Identify what types of information are required for the presentation B1.5 Identify any constraints which may affect the presentation
PS:B2 Use presentation software tools to structure, edit and format slides	B2.2 Select, change and use appropriate templates for slides B2.3 Select and use appropriate techniques to edit slides and presentations B2.4 Select and use appropriate techniques to format slides and presentations B2.6 Select and use animation and transition effects appropriately to enhance slide sequences	B2.1 Identify what slide structure and themes to use B2.3 Identify what presentation effects to use to enhance the presentation

PS:B3 Prepare slides for presentation	B3.2 Prepare slideshow for presentation	B3.1 Describe how to present slides to meet needs and communicate effectively
	B3.3 Check presentation meets needs, using IT tools and making corrections as necessary	
	B3.4 Identify and respond to any quality problems with presentations to ensure that presentations meet needs	

Step-by-step examples are provided as a demonstration of what to do. These demonstrations are based on Microsoft PowerPoint® 2003 and are produced for each **Worked Example** task.

Review the overview in each section and then watch the demonstration in the **Worked Example** before commencing any tasks.

Once you are familiar with the topic covered, move onto the **Tasks** section of this chapter.

Consolidation exercises are provided throughout the chapter for extra practice.

Throughout the **Worked Examples** and **Tasks** sections, you will be working on a theme of creating documents for a publishing company, producing documents requested by various organisations and people.

In the **Consolidation** sections, you will produce a document for the same publishing company.

For the **Mini Assignment,** you will be working on the theme of creating documents for Escape Travel, a holiday company.

B1 Input and combine text and other information within presentation slides

B1.1 Identify what types of information are required for the presentation

At Level 1, we looked at how text, numbers, images, graphics and sound files could be used in a presentation (see pages 249–71). At Level 2, video files will also be included, to enhance a presentation.

There are many tools available in presentation software. Below are some of the features that can enhance your presentation of graphics and text:

- backgrounds

- range of multimedia elements (e.g. sound, animations, etc.)

- transitions (how each slide moves from one to another – a variety of options are available)

- hyperlinks (text, images, URLs, email, document links, return to beginning or specific slide)

- user interaction – does the user need to click or use the space bar to progress through the presentation or will this be automated?

- alternate pathways (e.g. the user can select how they wish to view the presentation – this could be a menu slide at the beginning of the presentation containing each of the slides shown with links, enabling the user to look at just the areas they select)

- hide/show – a presentation that may have certain slides that would not be shown to every audience. This can be achieved by hiding slides or customising the show and saving as a customised show.

B1.2 Enter text and other information using layouts appropriate to types of information

At Level 1, on pages 247–9, different types of slide layout were shown and details of how to enter text. To revise this section, revisit these pages.

B1.3 Insert charts and tables into presentation slides

There are various different charts and tables that can be inserted, including tables, pie charts, graphs, diagrams, organisational charts and flowcharts.

Embed a chart, item or image

Charts, items or images from a different software package can be embedded in the word processed document.

One method of linking is when you have created a graph in Microsoft Excel® that you wish to embed within a presentation. This means that, once the graph is embedded into the presentation, you can double click on it and the spreadsheet program opens and the data can be amended.

If the graph is simply copied and pasted, this will not form a link. You have to instruct the computer to create a link by using **Insert → Object**, and selecting your chart.

To make any changes, double click on the graph and Microsoft Excel® will open with the graph and data ready to change. Once you have updated the spreadsheet, save in the normal way. When you go back to the presentation, right click and select **Update Link**. The data on the chart will update to the new information you have changed in the spreadsheet.

When you open the file again – let's say you want to change the Excel file data – you will get a dialog box asking whether you would like to update the link. Answer yes; this will update any data that has changed since you last opened the presentation.

Watch the demonstration to see how this is done.

Figure 6.19

🖱 Demonstration

Worked Example B1.3.1

1 Open the Microsoft Excel® file **Sales**.
2 You will embed this graph into your presentation. Copy the graph into the clipboard by right clicking on the graph and choosing **copy**.
3 Open the Microsoft PowerPoint® file **Current Sales**.
4 Place your cursor on the second slide in the text area.
5 Select **Edit → Paste Special →** select **Paste Link**.
6 Select the source **Excel Chart Object → OK**.
7 You chart should appear.
8 Save the updated file as **Current Sales1**.

Now it's your turn to have a go.

Task B1.3.1

1 Open the file **Current Sales2**.

2   Highlight the text on slide 3 (**B Daniels**) → **Insert** → **Hyperlink** → **Place in this document** → select slide 5 (**B Daniels**) from the list and click **OK**.

3   Insert a new slide as slide 6. This should be a slide type for title and content as you are going to add an image to the slide.

4   Add the text **Our prestigious award** as a title.

5   In the content area, insert the graphic **award**.
    Insert → **Picture** → **From file**. Choose your file location, select the file **award** and click **OK**.

6   Modify the size and position of the graphic to make it appear correctly on the slide.

7   Save the updated presentation as **Sales3**.

Figure 6.20

Continue working on the **Sales3** presentation.

1   Insert the graphic **award** on slide 5 **(B Daniels)**. Resize and position the graphic so that it does not overlay any text.

2   Add star shapes to slide 6 to enhance the graphic image.
    Select the drawing toolbar **AutoShapes** → **Stars and Banners** → choose a star shape. Right click on your slide and holding down your left mouse button and drag out a star shape. Add more stars.

3   Save the file as **sales4**.

You may wish to add an organisation chart to your presentation. Microsoft PowerPoint® has a function to add a standard layout, which you can add to or change.

Insert a diagram or organisation chart

Selecting the diagram or organisation chart option, you can add a structured diagram to your chart.

Different formats are available to choose from, as shown in Figure 6.20.

Watch the demonstration to see how to add a flow chart.

🖱 6.12   *Demonstration*

Worked Example B1.3.2

1   Create a new presentation and add a title slide: **House sales**.

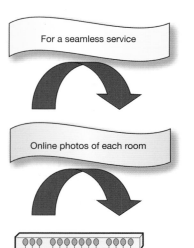

Autoshapes → Arrows → fill

2   Add a blank slide 2 and add the information in Figure 6.21 using the drawing toolbar.

3   Save and close the file as **chartsales.ppt**.

Watch the demonstration to see how to add an organisation chart.

🖱 6.13   *Demonstration*

Autoshapes → Basic shapes

Worked Example B1.3.3

1   Create a new slide and, on slide 1, key in the title **Library staffing structure**.

2   On slide 2, key in the title **Our staff** and create an organisational chart as shown in Figure 6.22.

Figure 6.21

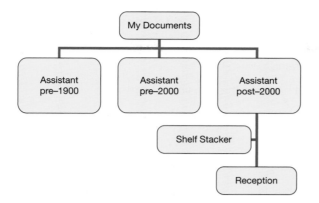

3 Format the chart choosing two different sans serif fonts and sizes for the chart and title.
4 Create a blank slide at the end.
5 Save and close the presentation using the filename **libstructure**.

Now it's your turn to have a go.

Task B1.3.3

1 Create a new presentation.
2 On slide 1, key in the title **Minimart staffing structure**.
3 On slide 2, key in the title **Revised structure**.
4 On slide 2, key in the following bullets:
   - **Area Manager**
   - **Shop Manager**
   - **Supervisor**
   - **Staff**.
5 On slide 3, create an organisational chart as shown below:

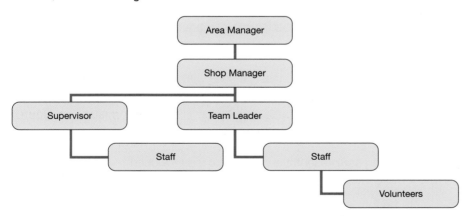

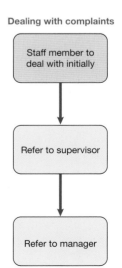

6 Format the chart using two different serif fonts and different sizes and colours for the text. Change the fill colour of the boxes to a pale yellow.
7 On slide 4, create a flowchart as shown here on the right.
8 Create a final blank slide at the end of the presentation.
9 Save and close the presentation as **ministructure**.

B1.4   Insert images, video or sound to enhance the presentation

There are many ways you can edit your presentation to make it more attractive and interesting to your audience.

Give a menu option to navigate through your slide show:

- insert object or images
- resize or position images
- rotate images or objects
- animate images or objects
- add slide numbers
- add the date.

Using the slide layout **Title and Content,** choose from the following types of content:

- table
- chart
- Clip Art
- picture
- diagram or organisation chart
- media clip.

Insert image

On a new slide, choose the option to insert a slide that has title and content.

The content you would select is either the Clip Art or Picture icon, as Microsoft PowerPoint® has several images available in the library. If you do not have these available, go to Microsoft's website and download suitable images.

Figure 6.22

Insert a media clip

On a new slide, choose the option to insert a slide with title and content.

The content you would select is Media (this looks like a video camera), as Microsoft PowerPoint® has several media clips available in the library. If you do not have these available, go to Microsoft's website and download a suitable clip.

You can also enhance your presentation when you insert a chart – you can animate the chart to make it more interesting.

The following are performed from the Slide Show menu.

Insert an animated chart

The choice to animate a chart will depend on the chart type – the best chart to animate is a bar/column chart.

You can have each bar appear one at a time.

Insert sound and video

In Microsoft PowerPoint® there are various options for adding sound and video to a presentation – sound and video files make presentations very large so you need to consider carefully when to use these before adding to your presentation.

Watch the demonstration to see how this works.

🖱 6.14 | *Demonstration*

> ### Worked Example B1.4.1

Setting up a navigation slide:

1 With your new presentation open, select **Insert** → **New slide**. To the right of your screen will appear the different types of slide you can insert into your presentation. The default is **Title**. This allows you to key in a title and a subtitle.
2 Choose **Insert** → **New slide**. You can choose a title and text slide layout. You are going to produce a navigation slide. This slide will take your audience from a menu to a specific slide.
3 On slide 2, using the numbered list, create a list of the following:
   1 Welcome
   2 Map
   3 Message
4 You need to create all your slides before you can activate this list.
   Slide 1 will actually be your introductory slide. This will be followed by the three slides above. Add the Title: **New Care Home Opens**
5 Add your name as the subheading.
   Slide 2 – this will be your menu list above.
6 On Slide 3, add the heading: **Welcome**
   Key in the following as a bulleted list:
   We are looking forward to welcoming many new guests.
   We have a wonderful facility.
   We have 15 bedrooms for short-stay clients.
7 On Slide 4, add the heading: **Map**
   Add the graphic **map.jpg** supplied.
8 On slide 5, add the heading: **Message**
   Add the following text as bullet points:
   Visiting times will be between 1 pm and 9 pm daily.
   Weekend visiting will be between 11 am and 8 pm.
9 On slide 2, which has your three-item menu, highlight the text and number **1Welcome**. Click **Insert** → **Hyperlink** → **Place in this document** → **Slide**. Choose slide 3.
10 Repeat this for each of the other two menu items and slides.
11 You have now created an alternative pathway for your viewer to use your presentation.
12 When using this method, consider that each slide should also have a hyperlink back to slide 2 to assist the viewer to return to the menu slide. You can use a graphic or text and hyperlink to slide 2.
13 Save your presentation as **home**.

Worked Example B1.4.2

1 Continue to work on your presentation **home**.
  You are now going to add slide numbers to your presentation and a background image and colour.
2 Select **Insert** → **Slide number** → tick **Footer** → tick **Slide number** → **Apply to All.**
3 Select **Format** → **Background**. From the drop-down list, select **Fill effects** → **Gradient** → **2 colour**. Choose Colour 1 and Colour 2 (do not make too dark a colour choice) from the **Shading Styles**. Click **OK** and **Apply to All.**
4 You should now see your background colour appear on all slides.
5 Save your presentation as **home2**.

Worked Example B1.4.3

Insert media, sound or video clip

1 Open the **home2** file.
2 Insert a new slide at the end of your presentation. Choose **Title, Text and Media**. Double click on the media icon and choose a media clip from the available list or insert one you have saved.
3 Insert another new slide and select **Insert** → **Movies and Sounds** → **Movie** from **Clip Organiser**. Insert a movie from the Clip Art gallery.
4 Insert another new slide and select **Insert** → **Movies and Sounds** → **Sounds** from **Clip Organiser**. Insert a sound from the Clip Art gallery.
5 Save and close the file as **home3**.

Worked Example B1.4.4

Animate a chart

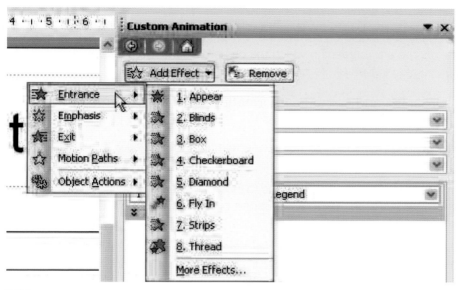

Figure 6.23

1 Open the presentation **diagram**.
2 On slide 2, there is a graph. Select this and then select **Slide Show** → **Custom animation**. To the right of your screen, a new dialog window opens. Select **Add Effect** → **Entrance** → **Effect**. In the animation task pane, select the animation effect from the list. Select the drop-down arrow → **Effect options** → **Chart animations** → **Group chart**. Here you can choose to animate by series, categories, or elements of either series or categories.
3 Save your presentation as **diagram2**.

Now it's your turn to have a go.

Task B1.4.4

1 Open the file **liblinks**.
2 Insert a slide number on each slide.
3 Add a gradient, two-colour background to all slides.
4 Insert a media clip on slide 2.
5 Insert a sound clip on slide 3.
6 Insert a movieclip on slide 5.
7 Animate the chart on slide 4.
8 Change the background colour.
9 Save and close the file as **amend2.ppt**.

B1.5   Identify any constraints which may affect the presentation

At Level 1, we looked at content, copyright law, acknowledgement of sources, plagiarism, equal opportunities and local guidelines. Refresh your memory by looking back at pages 252–3.

At Level 2, delivery should be considered, which includes reviewing the timings of the presentation, the environment in which the presentation is to be delivered and what resources you have available to run the presentation.

B1.6   Organise and combine information of different forms or from different sources for presentations

Information can be combined by combining text, images, tables with text, or by importing information produced by other software.

Another way of combining information is to insert a hyperlink. A hyperlink places a link on one word to electronically link to another part of the same document or create a link to another file.

Hyperlinks take the viewer of the document from one location to another; this can be either within the same document or to another file, in either the same or different software.

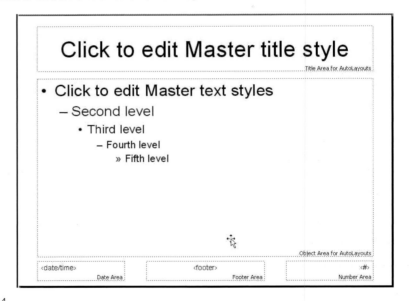

Figure 6.24

Using the hyperlink option you can choose from the following:

- Existing File or Web Page

- Place in This Document

- Create New Document

- E-mail Address.

Whichever file format you choose to link to, you will then need to choose the file location in a different file. If the link you make is to another presentation document, the link will only take you to the first slide of the presentation. You can, however, place a bookmark in the presentation to be linked to prior to creating the hyperlink. You can then choose the option of linking to a bookmark.

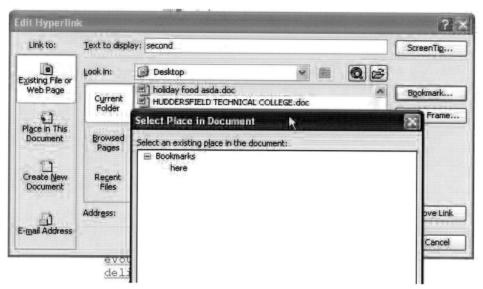

Figure 6.25

Watch the demonstration to see how this works.

6.15 Demonstration

Worked Example B1.5

1 Open the file **Sans.**
 On slide 4, there is a picture of a cloud. You are going to add a hyperlink to a website here.
2 Select **Insert → Hyperlink → Existing file or Web page**. Key in the following text in Address: **http://www.sfgate.com/weather/**.
3 Save your file as **Sanfranw.**
4 Test that the link works by previewing your presentation as a show. Click on the link → select **View → Slide Show**.

B1.7 Store and retrieve presentation files effectively, in line with local guidelines and conventions where available

When creating any types of files, make sure that you save them correctly.

Presentations can be:

- saved

- saved as

- opened

- closed

- named using short filenames with no spaces

- reduced in file size by saving them as a Microsoft PowerPoint® show

- saved as a stand-alone show

- saved as a web page.

We will look at these different options throughout this unit.

B2 Use presentation software tools to structure, edit and format slides

B2.1 Identify what slide structure and other presentation effects to use

In Level 1, we looked at design, colour and animation schemes and how slides are structured. To review these, look back to Level 1. Alternatively, templates within PowerPoint® can be used or adapted to meet the needs of the user.

B2.2 Select, change and use appropriate templates for slides

In Microsoft PowerPoint®, you can use and change templates – see pages 255–6 to see how to do this.

In Level 1, we looked at resizing, cropping and positioning objects and changing slide order. At Level 2, we will also look at adding captions and changing the orientation of slides.

Captions can be added to pictures added through the photo album. If you add a picture, click on **Insert** → **Picture** → **New Photo Album**. Choose a file and then choose captions to go under each picture.

The orientation of slides can be changed from the default setting of landscape to portrait orientation. This can be done through **File** → **Page Setup** and clicking on the portrait icon.

B2.3 Select and use appropriate techniques to edit slides and presentations

Styles and background

Using a Slide Master ensures a consistent display and is the most efficient way to store designs, including style sheets and backgrounds. In the Slide Master, you can set up the following:

- font styles/sizes
- images
- headers and footers
- background designs.

Fonts and styles of text

Select the text you wish to change. Using the text toolbar, select:

- font
- size
- enhancement – bold, italic, underline, shadow
- alignment – left, centre, right.

Once you have set up all the Master Slide elements, select the dialog box **Close Master View.** If this is not visible, click on the **Normal View** at the bottom left of your screen.

B2.4 Select and use appropriate techniques to format slides and presentations

Various options in PowerPoint® exist to allow you to change the format on a slide. For example different bullet styles can be used, line spacing can be increased or decreased, alignment can be changed, backgrounds and colour schemes and Master slides can be changed. PowerPoint® 2007 includes themes which can be added/changed to enhance a presentation and are similar to colour schemes in 2003.

B2.5 Select and use animation and transition effects appropriately to enhance presentation

You can add different presentation effects to a presentation. We have already looked at video, sounds and hyperlinks. In this section, we will look at animations, transitions and timings, and using effects appropriately to enhance slide sequences.

What are animations and transitions?

Animations: effects that make text and other screen items move, appear and disappear. They can, at the best of times, significantly enhance a presentation and focus the audience's attention on the point or points you'd like them to be focusing on. They can also distract if overdone.

Transition: a visual motion when one slide changes to the next during a presentation. By default, one slide simply replaces the previous one on screen, much the same way that a slide show of photographs changes from one to the next.

Timings: once you have set transitions, you can set timings for each slide; this then can make the presentation automated to run.

Loop: with timings, transitions and animations set, you can then add loops to your presentation. This will run the presentation continuously.

Watch the demonstration to see how this is done.

6.16 | *Demonstration*

> **Worked Example B2.5.1**

1 Open the file **CurrentSales2**.
   You are going to set up animations on the slides to enhance the presentation.
2 Choose **Slide Show → Animation Schemes**. Choose from **Subtle, Moderate, Exciting** and select **Play** to view how your animation will appear. You can then choose whether to **Apply to All Slides** or **Apply to this slide only**.
3 Choose other elements on your slides and select options for animation. Do not overdo these effects, as this becomes very busy for viewers and you may lose their attention or the point you are making.
4 Save as **Cons2**.
5 Continue working with **Cons2**.
6 You are going to set up transitions on the slides to further enhance the presentation.
   Click on **Slide Show → Slide Transition**. Choose a design, speed and sound. Choose how to advance your slides during the presentation. Select **Play** to view how your transitions will show. Choose whether to **Apply to All Slides**.
7 Set a timing **Automatically after: →** deselect **On mouse click**.
8 Save your show as **modsales**.

Now it's your turn to have a go.

Task B2.5.1

1 Open a new presentation.
  You are going to set up the Master Slide so that the text on each slide conforms to the house style of the company.
2 Select **View** → **Master Slide**. What you see is the template, not an actual slide.

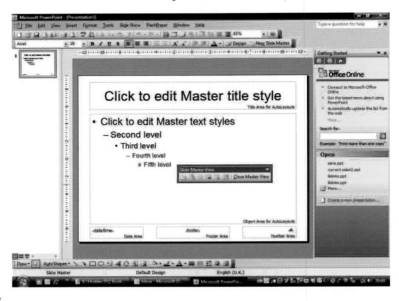

Figure 6.26

3 Here you click on the respective areas of the slide you wish to format and, using the **Format** drop-down menu, make changes to the font, alignment, colour, size, bullet type, and so on.
4 You can add your name in the footer area.
5 You can add images to this layout – be careful – they should only be small, as you will have text on your slide.
6 Once you are happy with the text styles, backgrounds, images, and so on, click on **Close Master View** (or **View** → **Normal view** if the Master View dialog box is not displayed).
7 Add a background colour.
8 Add four slides with content of your choice – the theme should be **a job agency**.
9 Add transitions and animations to the slide show – set the show to run automatically with timings and not on mouse click.
10 Set a loop, so the presentation can run continuously. Click on **Slide Show** → **Set up show** → select **Loop continuously until 'Esc'** → **OK**.
11 Run your presentation to test it works without user intervention.
12 Save as **jobagency**.

Consolidation

1 Open the file **Sans**.
2 Add a colour scheme through slide design.
3 Add transitions and animations to the slide show.
4 Add a sound clip.
5 Add a video clip.
6 Using Master Slide View, add an image to appear on each slide as well as your name.
7 Save as **Sans2**.

B3 Prepare slideshow for presentation

B3.1 Describe how to present slides to meet needs and communicate effectively

Microsoft PowerPoint® gives the user different options of how the slide show is presented. The options are both electronic and paper-based.

To view the slides, you can choose from different options:

- slides
- outline
- show.

To check the slide show works and presents as you wish, it is best viewing the show as it will be seen by the audience. Do this through the **View** → **Show** option.

Paper-based copies can be presented in different formats:

- slides
- handouts
- notes pages
- outline.

How you present your slide show will depend on what facilities you have at hand and whether it is to be an electronic presentation or a paper-based format. You should check that timings are not too slow or too fast, that the meaning is correct and that the presentation is appropriate for the audience.

Before delivering a presentation you should think about the audience to whom you will deliver it. For example, you might have to present some information in an interview: the interviewers will be familiar with the topic, but they might be assessing you on your Level 1 presentation skills. You should consider the level of knowledge the audience has, and whether you need to add or delete any information to suit them. You might also need to think about backgrounds and colours: can people at the back of the room read the presentation clearly? Make sure the transitions and animations do not detract from the presentation. Whether the presentation should be formal or informal in style depends on the organisational culture.

Before you finalise the presentation, view it to check the slide order: re-order the slides if necessary.

Once you have applied all timings and effects, these should be rehearsed to check that they meet the needs of the audience.

Templates

Microsoft PowerPoint® has many default templates available. These templates allow you to create a presentation without the need to set up master slides, colours, fonts, backgrounds, and so on.

> **Worked Examples B3.1**

1 Open the file **home2**.
2 Select **Format** → **Slide Design**.

3   Here you can choose from many slide designs that appear to the right of your screen in the dialog box.
4   Choose one style and watch what happens to your presentation. All the formatting you set up will have disappeared and the layout will now be changed to the template design you have chosen.
5   You can adjust the choices made by adding your own background colour and changing the fonts in the Master Slide View, just as you did earlier on your own design.
6   You do not have to accept all the template features.
7   Check that the content and meaning is correct and meets organisational requirements.
8   Save as **home4**.
9   Print your presentation as three slides per page.

Now it's your turn to have a go.

Task B3.1

1   Open the file **Sans2**.
2   Select a template layout.
3   Check everything on each slide is still visible and suitably laid out before you save the presentation.
4   Make any necessary changes.
5   Save as **Sans3**.
6   Print your presentation as two slides per page.

Consolidation

1   Open the file **Currentsales2**.
2   Select a template layout.
3   Check that everything on each slide is still visible and suitably laid out before you save the presentation.
4   Make any necessary changes.
5   Save as **Cons5**.
6   Print your presentation as six slides per page.

B3.2   Prepare slideshow for presentation

When presenting your slide show electronically, you have two options. One is as we have been practising throughout. The other option is to save the file as a slide show and not as a presentation. Use this when you are going to take your presentation to another machine or send it to view by email to another user, who may not have Microsoft PowerPoint® on their machine. You can also use this feature to ensure that no changes are made to your presentation by another user. You can rehearse timings to check the length of the presentation.

As with any presentation that is to be given by a speaker, it is useful to add some speaker notes to the slides. These notes do not print with the slides or show on the presentation; they are only available in a Notes printout version.

Watch the demonstration to see how this is done.

6.17 Demonstration

Worked Example B3.2

1 Open the file **Currentsales2**.
2 Rehearse timings. Click **Slide Show → Rehearse Timings** and time the length of the presentation.
3 If you want to increase or decrease the length of the presentation, change the timings at this point.
4 Select **File → Save As**. Keep the same filename. **Save as type: PowerPoint Show (*.pps)**.
5 Close your file and open the file **Currentsales2.pps**. Your presentation will go straight into running as a show. You do not have access to the setup of the file.

Now it's over to you.

Task B3.2.1

1 Open the file **Sans**.
2 Rehearse timings to check that the presentation runs for no longer than 45 seconds – make any changes to the timings.
3 Select **File → Save as** and keep the same filename. **Save as type: PowerPoint Show (*.pps)**.
4 Close your file and open the file **Snafranw3.pps**. Your presentation will run.

Watch the demonstration to see how speaker notes are added.

6.18 Demonstration

Worked Example B3.2.2

1 Open the file **Sans.ppt**, not the slide show.
You are going to add speaker's notes to Slide 3, titled: **Shop till you drop**.

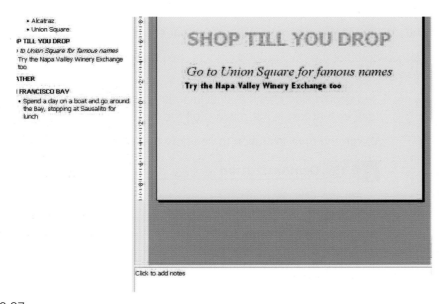

Figure 6.27

1   In the area at the bottom of your screen, you have the notes input area, which says 'click to add notes'.
2   In this area, key in the following notes for the speaker:
    Downtown San Francisco's best wine shop
    Napa Valley Winery Exchange features hard-to-find, small production California wine gems. They offer a delivery service and a discount rate for larger orders of 12 bottles or more.

1   Print the presentation as **Notes view**. Select **File** → **Print** → **Print what** → **Notes Pages** → **OK**.
2   You should have a miniature of the slide at the top of the page and any notes in the lower half of the page.
3   Save as **Sanfranw4**.

Now it's your turn to have a go.

Task B3.2.2

1   Open the file **CurrentSales2**.
2   Add speaker's notes to the slide with the Sales Team names, as follows.
    P Davies – Senior Sales Advisor
    J Brown – 1st year
    D Charlesworth – 1st year
    G Sands – Apprentice
    B Daniels – Senior Sales Advisor
    M Williams – 2nd year
    W Rogers – Apprentice
1   Print the presentation as speaker's notes.
2   Save as **sales4**.

B3.3   Check presentation meets needs, using IT tools and making corrections as necessary

As you are producing a presentation that is either going to be viewed on a large screen, website or in a theatre, with paper-based handouts for the audience, it is vital that you check that the presentation has no spelling or grammar errors.

You should also check that the background colours, text colours, images, and so on work and are not too glaring.

You should also check that all images and pictures are not overlaying text, or that text is not missing off the bottom of the slide.

Watch the demonstration to see how this is done.

6.18   *Demonstration*

Figure 6.28

Worked Example B3.3

1   Open the file **home2**.
2   Check that this presentation has no spelling errors.
3   Check that the background colour is suitable and change if necessary.
4   Check that the graphics are suitably placed.
5   Check animations and transitions.

6   Check orientation and layout.
7   Check that any links work as expected.
8   Save as **home2**.

Now it's your turn to have a go.

Task B3.3

1   Open the file **Sans**.
2   Check that this presentation has no spelling errors.
3   Check that the background colour is suitable and change if necessary.
4   Check animations and transitions.
5   Check orientation and layout.
6   Check that the graphics are suitably placed.
7   Check that any links work as expected.
8   Save as **Sans**.

B3.4   Identify and respond to any quality problems with presentations to ensure that presentations meet needs

Quality problems within a presentation will vary according to content and may cover:

■ Text formatting and styles – is all text consistent and formatted using the same style, size and enhancement?

■ Image size, position and orientation – are the images the right size or are they too large or too small? Are they positioned professionally on the slides? Is their orientation correct?

■ Effects: timing, brightness, contrast, sound levels, order of animations. Have you rehearsed the timings – are they too long or too short? Is the brightness and contrast suitable for your audience? Are the sound levels OK – are the animations too loud or not loud enough? Do you have speakers? Have the animations been applied correctly so that the text appears on screen at the correct time?

Ensure that you check all these factors before printing and finalising your presentation.

Mini Assignment

1   In this Mini Assignment, you will practise all the skills you have learned so far.
2   The Mini Assignment is based around the travel agency Escape Travel. Your manager has given you the following instructions and you are required to complete these, producing evidence.
3   You are employed as the clerical assistant for Escape Travel and produce a variety of documents to advertise their holidays.
4   You have been provided with a text file **escapetravel.txt**.
5   Create a new folder to store your work for this assignment and then produce evidence to meet the unit requirements.
6   You have been asked to create a presentation in line with the company house style:
7   Include a menu slide as slide 2. This slide will enable viewers to select which slide to view. Therefore, you will need to set up links from this slide to each of the other slides and from each slide back to the menu slide.
8   Open the file **staff.txt** and copy/paste the text onto the slides as indicated in this file.

9 Add some images and/or create some drawings/lines to add variety to the slides. The drawings/images should be relevant to the slide.

10 Insert the following table on the slide titled **Prices**:

COUNTRY	ACCOMMODATION	NIGHTS' STAY	NUMBER OF PEOPLE	COST EACH		
				LOW	MID	HIGH
Spain	Flat	7	2	120	175	210
Germany	Apartment	3	4	75	110	160
France	Hotel	5	2	100	130	175

The table should be:
Sans serif   16 point   Normal   Left-aligned

11 Add speaker's notes to the slide titled **Booking arrangements**.
The following are the terms and conditions of booking a holiday with Escape Travel – we hope you have a wonderful holiday.

12 Proofread your slide show, making any corrections or layout amendments where needed.

13 Add a movie clip.

14 Add a sound clip.

15 Add an organisation chart.

16 Add a flow chart.

17 Spell the check the document before producing for final copy.

18 Save the presentation as **conditions.**

19 Re-order the slides.

20 Add timings, animations and transitions.

21 Rehearse timings.

22 Add a pie chart.

23 Print as handouts, three slides per page.

24 Print speaker's notes for one slide only – slide 1.

25 Print an outline view.

26 Save the presentation as a show.

27 Save the presentation as a web page.

28 Close the presentation.

18 Save the presentation as **conditions.**

19 Re-order the slides.

20 Add timings, animations and transitions.

21 Rehearse timings.

22 Add a pie chart.

23 Print as handouts, three slides per page.

24 Print speaker's notes for one slide only – slide 1.

25 Print an outline view.

26 Save the presentation as a show.

27 Save the presentation as a web page.

28 Close the presentation.

Styles

Headings

Font	Size	Colour	Enhancement	Alignment
Sans serif	**24**	**Dark blue**	***Bold and italic***	**Centre**

Bullets

Font	Line Spacing	Size	Colour	Enhancement	Alignment
Serif	**1.5**	**12**	**Dark blue**	*Italic with ❯ as a bullet*	**Left**

Master Slide information

Background colour	**Pale blue**		
Include a slide number	**Include your name**	Image bottom right	**escape.jpg**
Transitions	**1 per slide used consistently**	Animations	**1 used consistently on each slide**
Timings	**30 seconds each slide**	Loop	**Yes**

7

Word Processing Software

This unit will develop knowledge and skills relating to the production of various simple word processed documents. You will develop the skills to produce a range of business documents, such as:

- letters
- envelopes
- memorandums
- simple reports
- faxes
- CVs
- agendas
- posters
- travel directions
- simple web pages.

By working through the **Overview, Worked Examples, Tasks** and the **Consolidations** in this chapter, you will demonstrate the skills required for Word Processing Software Level 1:

ELEMENT The competent person will…	PERFORMANCE CRITERIA To demonstrate this competence, they can…	KNOWLEDGE To demonstrate this competence they will also…
WP: A1 Enter, edit and combine text and other information accurately within word processing documents	A1.3 Use keyboard or other input methods to enter text or insert and other information A1.4 Combine information of different types or from different sources into a document A1.5 Enter information into existing tables, forms and templates A1.6 Use editing tools to amend document content A1.7 Store and retrieve document files effectively, in line with local guidelines and conventions where available	A1.1 Identify what types of information are needed in documents A1.2 Identify what templates are available and when to use them
WP: A2 Structure information within word processing documents	A2.1 Create and modify tables to organise tabular or numeric information A2.2 Apply heading styles to text	
WP: A3 Use word processing software tools to format and present documents	A3.2 Select and use appropriate techniques to format characters and paragraphs A3.3 Select and use appropriate layout to present and print documents A3.4 Check documents meet needs, using IT tools and making corrections as necessary	A3.1 Identify what formatting to use to enhance presentation of document

Step-by-step examples are provided as a demonstration of what to do. These demonstrations are based on Microsoft Word® 2003 and are produced for each **Worked Example** task.

Review the overview in each section and then watch the demonstration in the **Worked Example** before commencing any tasks.

If you are familiar with the topic covered, move onto the **Tasks** section of this chapter.

Consolidation exercises are provided throughout the chapter for extra practice.

The **Worked Examples** are based on producing documents for a local estate agency and the **Tasks** are based on a theme of creating documents for an electronic resources retail company.

In the **Consolidation** sections, you will produce a document for a publishing company.

For the **Mini Assignment,** you will be working on the theme of creating documents for Escape Travel, a holiday company.

A1 Enter, edit and combine text and other information accurately within word processing documents

A1.1 Identify what types of information are needed in documents

One of the most common uses for computers in business today is word processing. Different documents are produced in the course of the day, from general correspondence to reports, price lists, minutes, memos, newsletters and brochures – you name it, it has probably been done with a word processing application like Microsoft Word®.

The use of a word processor simply involves entering text on a computer. The text can be moved or copied before printing out. Word processors have many other facilities to aid writers, such as spelling and grammar checkers, and the ability to import pictures and graphs and format documents. Most word processors are WYSIWYG (What You See Is What You Get). The text onscreen looks how it will print.

The features that you need from a word processor will depend on what sort of documents you are producing. At Level 1, you will be producing simple word processed documents.

There are at least three ways to perform most operations in Microsoft software. This chapter will give instructions in one method – using the menus. Other methods are using the icons on the toolbars and shortcut keys on the keyboard. A full listing of shortcut keys is provided at the end of the chapter.

A1.2 Identify what templates are available and when to use them

A template is a document which has pre-set styles, formats and layouts so that when a new document is created, it is based on a template. You would not change any of the layout or format. An example of a template would be a letter.

The example in Figure 7.1 shows a template that has been created.

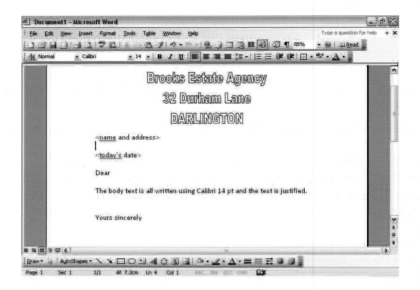

Figure 7.1

Watch the demonstration to see how a template can be used.

7.1   *Demonstration*

Worked Example 1.2

1 Open the **letter.dot** template.
2 Add text to the letter as shown below:

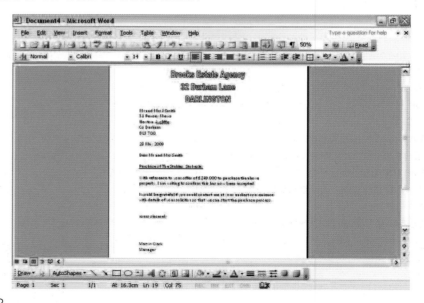

Figure 7.2

3 Save the letter as **smith.doc** in your local file area.
4 Close the file.

Now it's your turn to have a go.

Task A1.2

You are going to create a letter-headed page to be used for all letters sent out by the company.

1 Open the template **letter.dot**. This file has no details yet – you are going to add these.
2 Select **File → Open**. Choose the files of type **.dot → letter.dot**.
3 Add the following text and align it to the right on the page:
 Learning Explorers
 New Road
 Huddersfield
 HD1 5NN
 Tel: 01484 123456
 Fax: 01484 333333
4 Insert an appropriate Clip Art image to the left of this text. Ensure that the size of the graphic is small enough to fit alongside the text and large enough to be visible.
5 Save this document as **brookslet.dot**.
6 Close the file.

A.1.3 Use keyboard or other input method to enter text and other information

A1.4 Combine information of different types or from different sources into a document

The standard keyboard has functional keys to be used when keying in text. These are:

Enter – pressed when wishing to enter a line space between paragraphs or to make space on a page.
Shift (at each side of the keyboard) – pressed to give an initial capitals, e.g. Initial Capitals.
Caps Lock – pressed to give continuous capitals, e.g. CAPITALS.
Tab – pressed when wanting to put measured space between words.
Backspace – used when wishing to delete text already keyed in.
Delete – pressed to delete words forwards.
Insert – the standard setting is that characters typed will automatically insert – pressing the Insert key will change Insert to Overtype and **OVR** will be highlighted at the bottom of your screen on the status bar.
End – pressing this takes you to the end of a line of text or the end of the document.
Home – pressing this takes you to the beginning of a line of text or the start of the document.
Page Down – scrolls down a page at a time, depending on the length of your document.
Page Up – scrolls up a page at a time, depending on the length of your document.
Arrow keys ←↓↑→ move your cursor around your document.

Keyboard input point on screen

You have an input point known as a cursor – this is represented on the screen as an 'I' pointer.

Figure 7.3

Once you have opened a new document, you can begin typing straight away. Do not press enter at the end of each line of text as word wrap will take the text to the next line. The only time you press enter is when you wish to break up the text into paragraphs or make space between text and objects on the page.

Other input methods

Voice recognition software, a touch screen or a stylus can be used to enter information into a word processor.

Voice recognition software can be used instead of typing text straight into the computer – the software converts your spoken voice into text. It is more accurate than it used to be, although with a strong accent sometimes the interpreted words are not quite the same!

Touch screens allow you to enter information through the screen – this is becoming increasingly popular and it is rumoured the new Microsoft Windows® operating system includes this. This means that instead of using a keyboard or mouse, you can enter information by touching the monitor.

A stylus is traditionally used with PDAs so that you can touch the screen to enter data.

Watch the demonstration to see how this is done.

7.2   Demonstration

Worked Example A1.4

1   Open Microsoft Word® and the **letter.dot** file.
2   Enter the following data into the document:

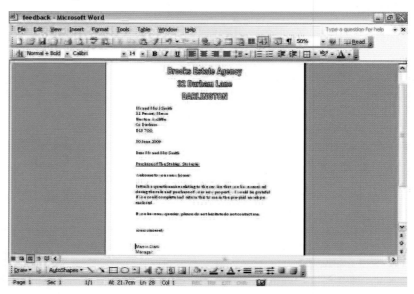

Figure 7.4

3   Save the file as **feedback.doc**.
4   Close the file.

A1.5   Enter information into existing tables, forms and templates

When you first open Microsoft Word®, you can enter text directly into the first document that is open. However, you can also enter text into tables, forms and templates.

Watch the demonstration to see how this is done.

7.3 Demonstration

Worked Example 1.5.1

1 Open Microsoft Word® and create a new document.
2 Add the following table. Click on **Table** → **Insert** → **Table**.
3 Select four columns and two rows.
4 Enter the data in Figure 7.5 – when you get to the end of each row, press the tab key and a new row will be added.

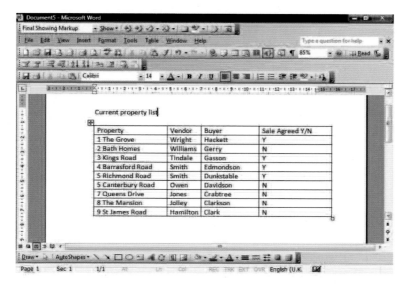

Figure 7.5

5 Save and close the file as **propertylist.doc**.

Now it's your turn to have a go.

Task 1.5.1

1 Create a new Microsoft Word® document.
2 Create the table as shown below:

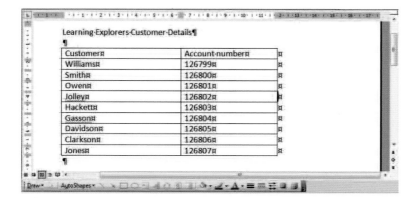

Figure 7.6

3 Save and close the file as **customers.doc**.

Another way for data to be entered can be via a form.

Watch the demonstration to see how to complete a form.

7.4 *Demonstration*

Worked Example 1.5.2

1 Open the file **form.doc**.
2 Key in the following information to complete the form.

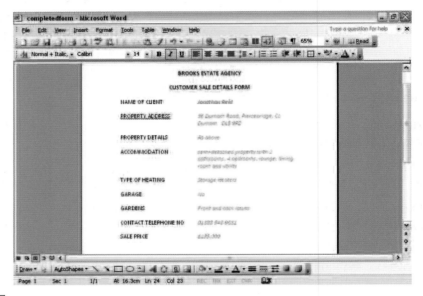

Figure 7.7

3 Save the file as **completedform.doc** and close the file.

Now it's over to you.

Task 1.5.2

---

1 Open the form **Learning Explorers Customer Order Form.doc**.
2 The following order has been taken over the telephone. Enter the following details into the form:

Miss J Harris, 2 Long Road, Paington, TW4 7EL has rung this morning and she wishes to order the L1PS DVD which has the product code LS1006. The DVD includes instruction and skill building activities for level 1 learners to help them problem solve. The cost of the product is £159.99 and as the order is over £150.00 there are no postage costs. The expected delivery date is seven days from today and there are no special requirements. Miss Harris has an account with us and therefore we have debited her account. The order was taken by JB.

3 Save and close the form as **harris.doc**.

A1.6 Use editing tools to amend document content

To edit text, you can highlight the text with your mouse or key combination keys, then use the DELETE key or the BACKSPACE key on the keyboard.

To highlight text with mouse: click, hold down the mouse button and drag the mouse pointer over the text. Then release the mouse button and the text is highlighted.

To highlight using the keyboard: with your cursor at the beginning of the text using the key combination **SHIFT** and right arrow – this will select a character at a time or you can use **CTRL** and right arrow to select a word at a time.

Once you have deleted the text, you can then key in the new text.

If the text has been highlighted, you do not need to hit the DELETE or BACKSPACE key, but key in the text and this action will automatically delete the highlighted text.

Text can also be edited by using cut/copy/paste/find and replace or drag and drop and in the next few exercises you will see how this is done.

A1.6.1 Cut text

Worked Example A1.6.1

---

1 Open the file **housing.doc**.
2 Highlight text in the last paragraph that starts 'New Developments like these … to may have found a solution.'
3 Select **Edit → Cut**.
   The highlighted area has now been deleted. This text can also be used with the **Paste** option to move the text from one location to another.
4 Leave the file open for the next activity.

A1.6.2 Copy text

Worked Example A1.6.2

---

1 Carry on from the previous activity and select the text 'The Land Use Plan'.
2 Select **Edit → Copy**.
   The highlighted area has been copied into the clipboard ready for you to paste into another area.

3   Keep the file open.

A1.6.3 Paste text

> **Worked Example A1.6.3**

1   Move the cursor to the very end of the document.
2   Select **Edit** → **Paste**.
    The text that has been cut or copied into the clipboard will now appear where your cursor is.
3   Keep the file open for the next activity.

A1.6.4 Drag and drop

> **Worked Example A1.6.4**

1   Highlight text 'Initial urban design and' to 'new environment' in the last paragraph.
2   Using the mouse, click and hold, then drag the text to the end of the very first paragraph.
3   Release your mouse button. The text will have moved to a new location.

A1.6.5 Find and Replace

> **Worked Example A1.6.5**

1   Select **Edit** → **Find**.
2   Find **Danetown**.
3   Select **Find Next** – your cursor will move to the next instance of the word you have keyed in.
4   Select **Edit** → **Replace**.
5   Key in the word you wish to be replaced (**Waterfront**). You can choose to Replace, Replace All or Find Next.
6   Replace will replace the first instance and you will need to press **Find Next** to move through the document. If you know that the word is repeated throughout the document and you wish to replace all instances, then use the **Replace All** option. **Note:** check out the **More** option in **Find and Replace** – this is where you can select **Whole words only** and other options.
7   Save and close as **WEA166.doc**.

A1.6.6 Insert a graphic

> **Worked Example A1.6.6**

1   Open the file **insert**.
2   Save the document as **images**.
3   At the top of the document, you are going to insert a graphic from the Clip Art section of Microsoft Word®.
4   Select **Insert** → **Picture** → **Clip Art**. Search for **people** and click on **Go**. Choose an image, click on the blue arrow down the right side of the image and select **Insert**.

A1.6.7 Resize a graphic

1   The graphic inserted may be too large for your page. You can easily resize it.
2   Choose to view your document at 50 per cent. Click on **View** → **Zoom** → **50%** → **OK**.

3 Click on the image. Handles (squares) will appear around the outside edge of the image – these appear as a line around with boxes in the centre top, sides and bottom of the image.

4 Select **Format** → **Picture** → **Size** → **Height = 5 cm** → **OK**.

A1.6.7 Position a graphic

You can position the graphic on your page, relative to the page or to text.

> **Worked Example A1.6.7**

1 Select **Format** → **Picture** → **Layout** → **Square** → **Horizontal Alignment** → **Centre**. Click on the **Advanced** tab at the bottom of the **Layout** tab → **Text Wrapping** tab → **Top and Bottom** → **OK** → **OK**.

2 Save document as **Task8**.

A1.6.8 Resize an image

> **Worked Example A1.6.8**

1 Insert the file **property.jpg**.
2 Enlarge the image by resizing it.
3 Crop the image so that the hedge has been removed.
4 Save and close the file as **house_amend.doc**.

Now it's your turn to have a go.

> **Consolidation**

1 Open the file **Task 1a**. You are going to modify a Memo that has been created as a draft.

2 Change 'Company Name Here' to read '**Learning Explorers**'.

3 Insert the following:

To: **All Managers**
From: **Nick Smith**
cc: **HR**
Date: **(insert the current date here)**

4 Change the time of the meeting to **11.30 am** and the venue is now the **Board Room**.

5 Insert a suitable picture to the right of the word Memo – resize it so that it takes up a small space.

6 Add the following text after the second paragraph ending '... we will be discussing':
We will provide a working lunch as we know there will be working parties set up to write up new standards to meet the requirements.

7 Save the file as **memo** and close the file.

Figure 7.8

A1.7 Store and retrieve document files effectively, in line with local guidelines and conventions where available

Once you have created a file, it should be saved using sensible filename conventions so that it will be easy to retrieve in the future.

There are various options available to you – you can save the file and give it a name, you can open and save an existing file with a different name or, you can search for a file and close a file.

See the demonstration to see how this is done.

7.5 Demonstration

> **Worked Example A1.7.1**

1 Open Windows Explorer® and then find the file **river.doc**.
2 Open the file.
3 Save it as **river.doc**.
4 Save as **river_amend.doc**.
5 Close the file.

A2 Structure information within word processing documents

A2.1 Create and modify tables to organise tabular or numeric information

In this section, we will use more advanced tools for creating and modifying tables to organise information.

> **Task A2.1.1**

1 Create a new document and insert a table of three columns and two rows.
2 Select **Table → Insert → Table → columns = 3 → rows = 2 → OK**.
3 You should now see an empty table appear in your document. To move around the table, click with your mouse or use the **Tab** key on the keyboard once you have your cursor in the table.
4 In the first cell of the table, type in the following:

January	February	March
20548	62310	90012

If you wish to continue adding information to the table, press the **TAB** key after you have entered the last number and a new row will be added.

5 Adjust the column widths. Place your mouse pointer between January and February on the line and drag this to the left to make the column smaller.
6 Reduce the size of each column so that it is just wide enough for the text to be displayed.
7 Add a new row above January, February and March. Highlight the top row of the table and click **Table → Insert → Row**. Enter the text **Monthly sales**.
8 Save the document as **sales.doc**.

A2.2 Select and use appropriate page layout to present and print documents

Documents can be produced and printed either in portrait or landscape. Figures 7.9 and 7.10 give examples of both.

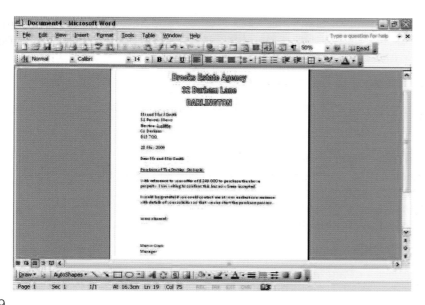

Figure 7.9

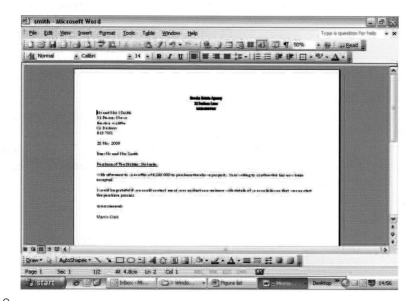

Figure 7.10

The white space around the text is known as the margins. This can be increased or reduced depending on the overall size and layout of your document. Changes to page layout are all made through **File → Page Setup**.

In addition, automatic fields can be added in either the header or footer space and this can be page numbers, dates or filenames.

Watch the demonstration to see how this is done.

7.6 Demonstration

Worked Example A2.2.1

1 Open the file **insert.doc**.
2 Save the document as **layout.doc**.

3   Change the layout to landscape. Click **File** → **Page Setup** → **Landscape**.
4   Select **File** → **Page Setup** → **Margins** → **3 cm** each margin (top, bottom, left, right) → **OK**.

Notice the difference to the document.

Now you are going to change the orientation of the document.

Check the paper size is set to **A4**.

1   Select **File** → **Paper** → **A4** → **OK**.
2   At the end of the document, key in your name and add today's date and time using the **Insert** menu for date and time.
3   Select **Insert** → **Date and Time** → choose a date format → **OK**.
4   Select **Insert** → **Date and Time** → choose a time format → **OK**.

Page numbering each page

1   Select **Insert** → **Page number** → choose position and alignment → **OK**.
2   Save the document as **margins**.

Now it's your turn to have a go.

Task A2.2.1

Create the following document:

1   Set the Margins: **All** → **2cm**.
2   Set the Page Orientation: **Portrait**.
    There should be **No** page numbering.
    Enter the **Date and Time** as a footer on the page.
    Text: Heading: **Arial, 24 point, bold, centre aligned, red**
    Learning Explorers
    New Road
    Huddersfield
    HD1 5NN
    Tel: 01484 123456
    Fax: 01484 333333

    Text: **Arial, 14 point, normal, left aligned, black, 1.5 line spacing**
    Add the following text:

<Today's date>

Mr John Butler
23 Highgate Lane
Highgate
Halifax
HX1 5PP

Dear Mr Butler

Skill Building Activities

*Many thanks for booking to attend the next **practical skills workshop**. We look forward to ensuring that all the plans we have put in place will satisfy your needs.*

The workshop begins at 10.30 am on day one and will finish at 4.30 pm. The workshop is a practical hands-on 'have a go' session using our online resources so that you can 'try before you buy'. You will receive a demonstration CD, which you can take away with you to evaluate the products further.

I enclose a copy of the map, which shows our location. It is quite easy to find and just a two-minute walk from the station.

If you decide to make a purchase on the day, we will give you a 5 per cent discount.

Many thanks for booking. I look forward to meeting you.

Yours sincerely

Learning Explorers

Encs

3   Save the document with the filename **TaskA222.doc** and close the document.

A3 Use word processing software tools to format and present documents

A3.1   Identify what formatting to use to enhance presentation of document

A3.2   Select and use appropriate techniques to format characters and paragraphs

Within Microsoft Word®, there are many different ways that a document can be formatted. All of the following are performed from the **Format → Font** menu:

Characters

Size	Change the size of text.
Font	Change the font style of the text e.g. This text has been produced using Verdana, 12. This text has been produced using Times New Roman, 12.
Colour	Change the colour of text.

The following are performed using either the icons on the toolbar at the top of your screen or by using key combinations:

Bold	Add **bold** to text – Ctrl+B or the **B** on the toolbar.
Italic	Add *italic* to text – Ctrl+I or the *I* on the toolbar.
Underline	Add <u>underline</u> to text – Ctrl+U or the <u>U</u> on the toolbar.

All of the following are performed from the **Format → Paragraph** menu:

Paragraphs

Alignment	Change the alignment of text or paragraphs.
Line spacing	Change the space between lines of text.

Lines

Spacing alignment	Sets spacing between lines of text or paragraphs.
Breaks	Inserts breaks between lines of text.

All of the following are performed from the **Format** menu:

Bullets	• Add a symbol before the text.
Numbering	1 Add a number before the text.
Borders	Add borders to text.
Shading	Add shading to text.
Tabs	Place a stop (tabulation) to align text and numbers.

Watch the following demonstration to see how this is done.

7.7   *Demonstration*

Worked Example A3.1.1

1   Open the file **housing.doc** and make the following amendments:
- Increase the size of the heading **Housing** to be 18pt and centre this across the page.
- Change the text **The Land Use Plan** to colour blue, Calibra, 14 and underline and change to italics.
- Change the text to 1.5 line spacing.
- Add a border around the page.
- Add bullets to the text after **New support facilities** so it looks like:
  - Primary school
  - Community facilities
  - Local convenience shop

2   Save the file as **characters.doc** and keep it open for the next activity.

A3.3   Select and use appropriate page layout to present and print documents

Before printing you should check that everything is shown accurately and professionally on the page.

A3.4   Check documents meet needs using IT tools and making corrections as necessary

Microsoft Word® will highlight spelling mistakes with red underlines and grammar errors with green underlines – these will not be printed out.

Spell check	Check highlighted word or whole document.
Grammar check	Check highlighted word or whole document.

When using a spell checker, make sure it is set to UK English. At the bottom of the screen it should say **English (UK)** – click here to check that the default setting is **English (UK)** and change it if necessary.

You should also check that the document is consistent and that the formatting options are appropriate. Check the page layout and margins to ensure that text is not split inappropriately across two pages, e.g. that you do not have the first line of a new paragraph at the bottom of page one, with the rest of the paragraph on page two. Use print preview to see how the document will look. To do this click **File** → **Print Preview**. Check that the font and size are consistent, page layout looks professional and that line and page breaks fall in appropriate places. Check that text is split appropriately across pages and that margins are appropriate.

You also have options for formatting when using the right mouse button. This option changes depending on what you are working on. When working on normal text, the options provide:

- Cut
- Copy
- Paste
- Font
- Paragraph
- Bullets and Numbering
- Hyperlink
- Look Up.

When working within a table, you get additional formatting options:

- Insert Table
- Delete Cells
- Split Cells
- Borders and Shading
- Text Direction
- Cell Alignment
- AutoFit
- Table Properties.

Watch the demonstration to see how this is done.

7.8 | *Demonstration*

Worked Example A3.4.1

1 Using **characters.doc,** insert a page break after the word **barrage.**
2 Place your cursor on the first word of the paragraph starting **For River Road to be successful.**
3 Select **Insert** → **Break** → **Page Break** → **OK.**
4 Save the document as **A341.doc**

Now it's your turn to have a go.

Task A3.4.1

1 Open the file **Micro.**
2 Save the document as **Task2.**
3 Select the whole document and change the font to **Arial.**
4 Select **Edit** → **All.**
5 Select **Format** → **Font.**
6 Make changes to the size and font and click **OK.**
7 Highlight the heading text at the top of the page.
8 Select **Format** → **Font.**
9 Change the size of the text from **12** to **24.**
10 Still in the **Font** dialog box, change the **Colour** from **Automatic** to **Red,** then add **Bold** and **Italic** and **Underline** to the text.
11 Click **OK** to close the dialog box. Your text will now be formatted with the new features you have added.
12 Save the document as **Micro1.doc.**

Align text

1 Highlight the first paragraph starting **Have you studied …**
2 Change the paragraph alignment to justified.

Select **Format** → **Paragraph** → **Alignment** → **Justified** → **OK.**

Add bullet symbol

1 Highlight the four lines of text with the – symbol in front, below the text **Study the …**
2 Select **Format** → **Bullet and Numbering** → select a bullet type → **OK.**

Numbered paragraphs

1 Highlight the nine lines of text below the heading **Points to look for …** from **Automatic defrost** to the end of the text … **Memory Programmes.**
2 Select **Format** → **Bullet and Numbering** → **Numbered** choose numbering **1, 2, 3** → **OK.**

Line spacing

1 Highlight the text from **SAFETY** to the final text ending **…domestic socket.**
2 Select **Format** → **Paragraph** → **Line Spacing** → **1.5 lines** → **OK.**
3 Save the document as **Task3.**

Borders and shading

1 Continue working on **Task3.**
2 Save the document as **Task4.**
3 Highlight the first paragraph of text starting **Have you...** and ending **...for everyone!**
4 Select **Format** → **Borders and Shading** → **Box** → select the tab **Shading** → **Grey 5%** → **OK.**

Tabulations

1 Highlight all the text you have created as a numbered list (nine lines) below the heading **Points to look...**
2 Select **Format** → **Tabs** → **Clear All.** In the **Tab stop position** box, type in **3** → **Set** → **OK.**

Indents

1   Highlight the next paragraph starting **More and more ...** and ending **... your alphabet**.
2   Select **Format** → **Paragraph** → **Indentation** → **Left = 1 cm** → **Right = 1 cm** → **OK**.

Lines

1   Highlight the nine numbered text lines previously formatted.
2   Select **Format** → **Paragraph** → **Spacing** → **Before = 6 pt** → **After = 6 pt** → **OK**.

Breaks

1   Press **Ctrl** → **Enter** to insert new page break

Watch the demonstration to see how to spell check a document.

🖱 7.9   *Demonstration*

> **Worked Example A3.4.2**

1   Open the file **spelling**.
2   Save the document as **Task342**.
3   There are some spelling mistakes in the document. Correct these by selecting **Tools** → **Spelling and Grammar**. Ignore any grammar mistakes at this time, only correct spelling mistakes.
4   Grammar checking is just the same as the spell checker function. Microsoft Word® checks each line of text to see whether there are any grammar errors and gives you a suggestion if it can. You can then accept or ignore this suggestion and move through the document updating the grammar and spelling.
5   Save the document as **Task342**.

Now it's your turn to have a go.

> **Task 3.4.2**

1   Open the document **Cons1**.
2   Change the page orientation to portrait.
3   Change the margins to **2.5 cm** left and right.
4   Change the margins to **2 cm** top and bottom.
5   Format the whole document to **Arial**, size **12**.
6   Change the format of the whole document to be justified.
7   Change the line spacing on the whole document to 1.5 lines.
8   Format the heading of the document **Types of Packages / Software** to:
  ■   Times New Roman
  ■   Size 24
  ■   Bold and italic
9   There are several paragraph headings that need to be formatted to display as:
  ■   Arial
  ■   Size 18
  ■   Bold
  ■   Set the paragraph spacing below to 6 point.
  The paragraph headings are:
  ■   Word Processing
  ■   Spreadsheets
  ■   Database
  ■   Desktop Publishing (DTP)

- Graphics
- Information Managers
- Integrated Packages
- Electronic Mail
- Multimedia
- Internet / World Wide Web (www)
- Intranet

10 At the end of each introduction to software, there are examples of software packages.
11 Format the list below **Examples include** to display as a bulleted list.
Examples include:
- Lotus Ami Pro®
- Lotus Word Pro®
- Microsoft Word®
- Corel WordPerfect®
12 At the end of the document, add your name and today's date. This text needs to be displayed with a border and shading added.
13 Check your entire document for spelling, making any necessary changes.
14 Check the layout of the document and insert page breaks where text is split from headings.
15 Insert page numbering at the bottom middle of each page.
16 Save the document as **Cons3**.
17 Perform a word count on the document and before closing, add the text:
Total number of words: xxx (Replace xxx with the number of words counted).
18 Save the document maintaining the filename **Cons3**. Close the file.

Consolidation

1 Open the file **Cons3**.
2 At the top of the document below the heading, insert a graphic from Clip Art that represents computers.

1 Format this image to fit **2 cm** height, keeping the image proportions.
2 Ensure that the text is set to appear below the image and that no text wraps around the image.
3 Save the file as **Cons3**.

Consolidation

1 Open the file **Cons3**.
2 At the end of the document before your name and word count, and after the text ... **current news and general company information,** add the following text:
Below is a summary of applications available for a variety of software.
3 After this text, create the table shown on page 311.
4 Save this document as **Cons4**.

Word Processing	Lotus Word Pro®	Microsoft Word®	Corel WordPerfect®
Spreadsheets	Lotus 1-2-3®	Microsoft Excel®	
Database	Lotus Approach®	Microsoft Access®	
Desktop Publishing (DTP)	Microsoft Publisher®	Corel Ventura®	Adobe PageMaker®
Graphics	Freelance	Microsoft PowerPoint®	Adobe Photoshop®
Information Managers	Lotus Notes®	Microsoft Outlook®	Novell GroupWise®
Integrated Packages	Works	Open Office	
Electronic Mail	cc:Mail	Microsoft Outlook®	Yahoo
Multimedia	Encarta	Educational software	
Internet (www)	Google	Yahoo	Microsoft Internet Explorer®

Mini Assignment

1 In this Mini Assignment, you will practise all the skills you have learned so far.
2 The Mini Assignment is based around the travel agency Escape Travel. Your manager has given you the following instructions and you are required to complete these, producing evidence for your portfolio.
3 You are employed as the clerical assistant for Escape Travel and produce a variety of documents to advertise the holidays.
4 You have been provided with a text file **conditions.rtf**.
5 Create a new folder to store your work for this assignment and then produce evidence to meet the unit requirements.
6 You have been asked to format the document in line with the company house style as follows:
7 Format the text below the **Cancellations** paragraph, beginning **42 days ...** and ending **... 100% of cost** to display as bullet text.
8 Add borders and shading to some parts of the text to make it stand out from the rest.
9 Insert the following table after the final paragraph:
The table should be:
Sans serif   16 point   Normal   Left aligned
Format the top row of the table to be bold with 5 per cent shading. Include the Low, Mid, High cells.

COUNTRY	ACCOMMODATION	NIGHTS STAY	NUMBER OF PEOPLE	COST EACH		
				LOW	MID	HIGH
Spain	Flat	7	2	120	175	210
Germany	Apartment	3	4	75	110	160
France	Hotel	5	2	100	130	175

10 Ensure that there are no widows and orphans, for example, headings without text or paragraphs of text split over columns or pages by less than one line. Insert page breaks where necessary.
11 Spell check the document before producing the final copy.
12 Save the document as **conditions.doc**.
13 Use Word Count and check that you have between 524 and 530 words. If you have only added the table above, you should have 524 words, but you may have added your name, date, page number, and so on. These will count in your word count.

Page format	Page number: Centre/bottom	Orientation: Portrait	Margins: 2 cm all	Date and time: inserted as Header

Styles

Headings

Font	Paragraph spacing	Line spacing	Size	Colour	Enhancement	Alignment
Sans serif	6 pt above and below	Double	24	Red	Bold and italic	Centre

Subheadings

Font	Paragraph spacing	Line spacing	Size	Colour	Enhancement	Alignment
Sans serif	6 pt above and below	Double	16	Black	Italic and underlined	Left

Body text

Font	Paragraph spacing	Line spacing	Size	Colour	Enhancement	Alignment
Sans serif	Normal	Single	12	Black	Normal	Justified

Bullets

Font	Paragraph spacing	Line spacing	Size	Colour	Enhancement	Alignment
Serif	Normal	1.5	12	Red	Italic with ❯ as a bullet	Left

14 Close the file.
15 Open a new document and create a letterhead template for EscapeTravel.
The address is:
Escape Travel Ltd
Broad Lane

Durham
DH1 3JJ
Tel: 0191 123456
Fax: 0191 333333
16 Insert a suitable Clip Art image.
17 Save and close the document as a template.

Shortcut keys in Microsoft Word®

Ctrl+A	Select all – everything on the page.
Ctrl+B	Make **Bold** highlighted selection.
Ctrl+C	Copy selected text.
Ctrl+E	Align selected text to the centre.
Ctrl+F	Open Find and Replace box.
Ctrl+I	Make *Italic* highlighted selection.
Ctrl+K	Insert link.
Ctrl+L	Align to the left of the screen.
Ctrl+M	Indent the paragraph.
Ctrl+P	Open the print window.
Ctrl+R	Align to the right of the screen.
Ctrl+U	<u>Underline</u> highlighted selection.
Ctrl+V	Paste.
Ctrl+X	Cut selected text.
Ctrl+Y	Redo the last action performed.
Ctrl+Z	Undo last action.
Ctrl+Shift+*	View or hide non-printing characters.
Ctrl+left arrow	Move one word to the left.
Ctrl+right arrow	Move one word to the right.
Ctrl+up arrow	Move to the beginning.
Ctrl+down arrow	Move to the end of the paragraph.

Ctrl+Del	Delete word to right of cursor.
Ctrl+Backspace	Delete word to left of cursor.
Ctrl+End	Move the cursor to the end of the document.
Ctrl+Home	Move the cursor to the beginning of the document.
Ctrl+1	Single line spacing.
Ctrl+2	Double line spacing.
Ctrl+5	1.5 line spacing.
Ctrl+Alt+1	Change text to heading 1.
Ctrl+Alt+2	Change text to heading 2.
Ctrl+Alt+3	Change text to heading 3.
Alt+Ctrl+F2	Open new document.
Ctrl+F2	Display print preview.
Shift+Insert	Paste.
Shift+F3	Highlighted text will change from upper to lower case or a capital letter at the beginning of every word. Keep repeating and it scrolls through these options.
Shift+F7	Run a thesaurus check on the word.
Alt+Shift+D	Insert the current date.
Alt+Shift+T	Insert the current time.
F1	Open Help.
F3	Run Autotext.
F4	Repeat the last action performed.
F5	Open Find and Replace.
F7	Spell and grammar check selected text and/or document.
F12	Save As.
Shift+F12	Save.
Ctrl+Shift+F12	Print the document.

The mouse can also be used to perform quick actions. Examples of mouse shortcuts are shown on page 315.

MOUSE SHORTCUTS	DESCRIPTION
Click, hold, and drag	Select text from where you click and hold, highlighting to the point you let go.
Double click	Within a word, select the complete word.
Triple click	In the margin, select the whole document.
Ctrl+mouse wheel	Zoom in and out of document.

Level 2

This unit will develop knowledge and skills relating to the production of a variety of professional looking word processed documents. You will develop the skills to produce a range of business documents, such as:

- mail-merged business letters
- invoices
- complex reports
- content for web pages.

By working through the **Overview, Worked Examples, Tasks** and the **Consolidations** in this chapter, you will demonstrate the skills required for Word Processing Software Level 2:

ELEMENT The competent person will …	PERFORMANCE CRITERIA To demonstrate this competence they can …	KNOWLEDGE To demonstrate this competence they will also …
WP:B1 Enter and combine text and other information accurately within word processing documents	B1.2 Use appropriate techniques to enter text and other information accurately and efficiently B1.3 Select and use appropriate templates for different purposes B1.5 Select and use a range of editing tools to amend document content B1.6 Combine or merge information within a document from a range of sources B1.7 Store and retrieve document and template files effectively, in line with local guidelines and conventions where available	B1.1 Identify what types of information are needed in documents B1.4 Identify when and how to combine and merge information from other software or other documents
WP:B2 Create and modify layout and structure for word processing documents	B2.3 Create and modify columns, tables and forms to organise information B2.4 Select and apply styles to text	B2.1 Identify the document requirements for structure and style B2.2 Identify what templates and styles are available and when to use them
WP:B3 Use word processing software tools to format and present documents effectively to meet requirements	B3.2 Select and use appropriate techniques to format characters and paragraphs B3.3 Select and use appropriate page and section layouts to present and print documents B3.4 Check documents meet needs, using IT tools and making corrections as necessary B3.5 Respond appropriately to quality problems with documents so that outcomes meet needs	B3.1 Identify how the document should be formatted to aid meaning B3.4 Describe any quality problems with documents

Step-by-step examples are provided as a demonstration of what to do. These demonstrations are based on Microsoft Word® 2003 and are produced for each **Worked Example** task.

Review the overview in each section and then watch the demonstration in the **Worked Example** before commencing any **Tasks**.

If you are familiar with the topic covered, move onto the **Tasks** section of this chapter.

Consolidation exercises are provided throughout the chapter for extra practice.

Throughout the **Worked Examples** and **Tasks** sections, you will be working on a theme of creating documents for a publishing company, producing documents requested by various organisations and people.

In the **Consolidation** sections, you will produce a document for the publishing company above.

For the **Mini Assignment**, you will be working on the theme of creating documents for Escape Travel, a holiday company.

B1 Enter and combine text and other information accurately within word processing documents

At Level 1, we looked at how text, numbers and images can be added into a word processor. At Level 2, hyperlinks, charts and objects can also be combined with text.

B1.1   Identify what types of information are needed in documents

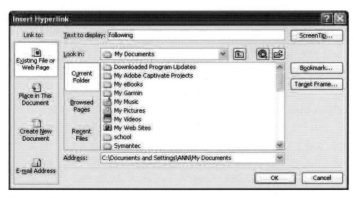

Figure 7.11

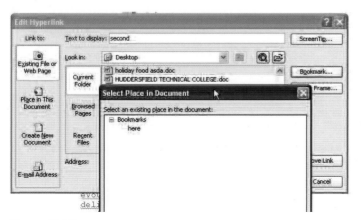

Figure 7.12

Before you start adding information to a document, you need to decide what type of information is needed and where it will be used.

Hyperlink

A hyperlink is where one word electronically links to another part of the same document or to another file.

The use of hyperlinks is to take the viewer of the document from one location to another; this can be either within the same document or to another file, in either the same or different software.

Using the hyperlink option, you can choose from the following:

- Existing File or Web Page

- Place in This Document

- Create New Document

- E-mail Address.

You will then need to choose the file location, if you are linking to a different file. If the link you make is to another word processed document, the link will only be to the top of the page of the document. However, you can place a bookmark in the document to be linked prior to creating the hyperlink and you can then choose the option of linking to the bookmark.

Insert a chart, item or image from a different software package and embed it in the word processed document

Another method of linking is when you have created, for example, a graph in Microsoft Excel® that you wish to embed within a word processed document. The keyword is 'embed'. This means that once the graph is embedded into the word processed document, you can double click on the graph and the spreadsheet program will open and you can amend the data.

If you simply copy and paste the graph, this will not form a link. You have to instruct the computer to create a link by using **Paste Special**.

Your graph is now embedded in your word processed report.

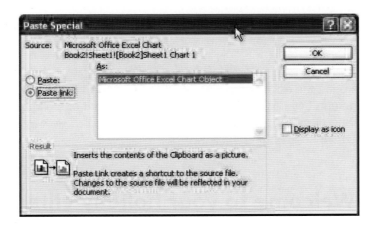

Figure 7.13

To make any changes, double click on the graph and Microsoft Excel® will open showing the graph and data, ready to change. Once you have updated the spreadsheet, save in the normal way. When you go back to the word processed report, right click and select **Update Link.** The data on the chart will update to include the new information you have changed in the spreadsheet.

Once all files are closed, when you next open the report containing the graph, you will get a dialog box asking whether you would like to update the link. Choose **yes**; this will update any data that has changed since you last opened the word processed document.

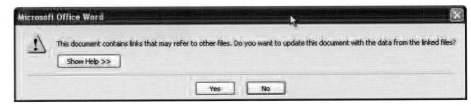

Figure 7.14

Overlaying an image with text

To do this, you insert the image, and then format it to display the image behind the text.

Within Microsoft Word®, insert the image file you wish to add text to. **Choose Insert →
Picture → From File.** Select the image location and name. Next, double click on the image to bring up the **Format Image** dialog box. Here you can change the layout of the image so that text can be placed in front of the image, by selecting the option **Behind Text.**

Figure 7.15

Handles appear around the edges of the image. You can move the image to a suitable place on your page and any text on the page will appear in front of the image. Alternatively, you can add text and place the image over the text. Other graphic elements include lines and borders, which are covered on pages 329–30.

Figure 7.16

B1.2 Use appropriate techniques to enter text and other information accurately and efficiently

The standard keyboard has functional keys to be used when keying in text. These are:

Enter – pressed when wishing to enter a line space between paragraphs or to make space on a page.
Shift (at each side of the keyboard) – pressed to give an initial capital, e.g. Initial Capital.

Caps Lock – pressed to give continuous capitals, e.g. CAPITALS.
Tab – pressed when wanting to put measured space between words.
Backspace – used when wishing to delete text already keyed in.
Delete – pressed to delete words forwards.
Insert – the standard setting is that characters typed will automatically insert – pressing the Insert key will change insert to overtype and **OVR** will be highlighted at the bottom of your screen on the status bar.
End – pressing this takes you to the end of a line of text or the end of the document.
Home – pressing this takes you to the beginning of a line of text or the start of the document.
Page Down – scrolls down a page at a time – depending on the length of your document.
Page Up – scrolls up a page at a time– depending on the length of your document.
Arrow keys ←↓↑→ move your cursor around your document.

Figure 7.17

Keyboard input point on screen

You have an input point known as a cursor – this is represented on the screen as an **I** bar.

Once you have opened a new document, you can begin typing straight away. Do not press enter at the end of each line of text as word wrap will take the text to the next line automatically. The only time you press enter is when you wish to break up the text into paragraphs or make space between text and objects on the page.

Other input methods

Voice recognition software, a touch screen or a stylus can be used to enter information into word processing software.

Voice recognition software can be used instead of typing text straight into the computer. The software converts your spoken voice into text – it is more accurate than it used to be, although with a strong accent sometimes the interpreted words are not quite the same!

Touch screens allow you to enter information through the screen – this is becoming increasingly popular and it is rumoured the new Microsoft Windows® Operating system includes this. This means that instead of a keyboard or mouse, you can enter information through the monitor.

A stylus is traditionally used with PDAs so that you can touch the screen with a pen to enter data.

Typing accurately and efficiently

When adding any text/data into a word processed document, you must ensure that you type it accurately. There are various touch-typing courses that you can access to help you develop typing skills. Once any documents are complete, you should proofread very carefully.

Proofreading

Proofreading techniques include spell checking, scanning (reading quickly) to check for problems with the layout of text and checking grammar and punctuation.

In Microsoft Word®, you can use the Spelling and Grammar Checker, which will pick up most of these types of errors, but if a word is misspelt but is a real word then it will not be found. This is the reason for scanning or proofreading your document. Some people can do this on screen; others need to see a printout.

Keyboard shortcuts

Other methods of entering data into a word processor can be by using the icons on the toolbars and shortcut keys on the keyboard. A full listing of shortcut keys is provided at the end of the chapter.

B1.3   Select and use appropriate templates for different purposes

Templates

Templates are documents created with standard content. When you open Microsoft Word®, you will find that the document that opens is a template. This has preset font styles, page layout and margins. In the example below (Figure 7.18), it shows the default settings when a new document is created.

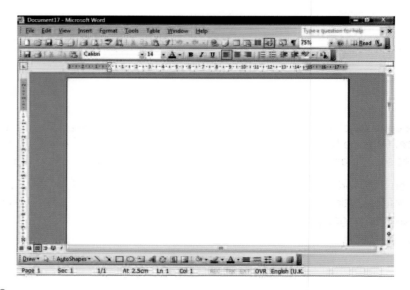

Figure 7.18

A letter will be produced on a letter-headed page; the font may be in a house style of the organisation.

Memos and fax messages may also have a set format.

All business documents can be created once and used many times, if saved in a template rather than a document format.

There are already many pre-saved templates that can be adapted and used. Templates are stored in a specific location on your PC.

Watch the demonstration to see how this is done.

7.10   *Demonstration*

> Worked Example B1.3

1   Open the template **Business Fax.**
    Select **File** → **New** → templates screen should open at the right of your computer

screen → select **On my computer** → select **Letters & Faxes** → **Business Fax** → click **OK**.

2   Modify this document by entering the following details:

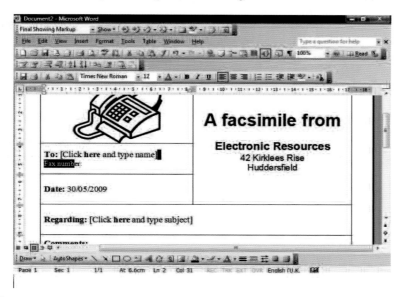

Figure 7.19

3   Save the document as a template. Select **File** → **Save As** → **Save as type: Document template**. Give the file the name **comemo** and save. This could be in the hard drive, templates section of the PC you are working on. Then click **Save** → select **File** → **Close**.

TIP: do not do any work on the document you have saved as a template other than change the default settings to your desired settings. To use the template once you have made and saved changes, open a new document using the template.

Now it's over to you.

Task B1.3

In this task, you will create your own memo.

1   Create a new document as shown below:
    To:
    From:
    Subject:
    Date:
    cc:
2   Save the template as **ememo**.
3   Open a new document using the template **ememo**.
4   Add the following:
    To: **All staff**
    From: **[add your name here]**
    Subject: **Reception area changes**
    Date: **[Today's date]**
    cc: **Managing Director**
    During the summer holiday we are changing the layout of the reception and would like any suggestions or ideas before the end of June. Please send all comments to me.

We cannot change the location of the toilets, but any other suggestions will be considered.

5   Save the file as **recpmemo**.

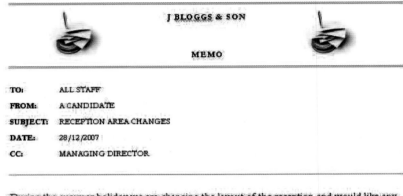

Figure 7.20

B1.4   Identify when and how to combine and merge information from other software or other documents

B1.5   Select and use a range of editing tools to amend document content

To edit text you can select, cut, copy, paste, undo, redo, drag and drop, find, replace, size, crop and position. If necessary, revise these in the Level 1 chapter – see pages 299–301.

B1.6   Combine or merge information within a document from a range of sources within a document

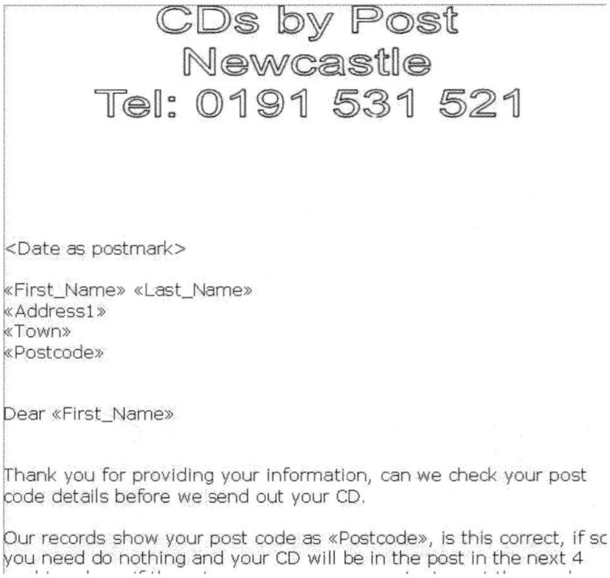

There are several ways that information can be merged or combined.

Mail merge

Mail merge is used to link a data file holding strings of information to a text document.

An example would be a data file containing names and addresses, added to a text document of a letter to send to each name and address in the data file.

The data file can be a document created in Microsoft Access®, Excel® or Word®. If it was created in Microsoft Word®, it would be best created in a table format with headings across the top of each data set. Each set of data would be known as a field, for example First Name, and an example is shown in Figure 7.21.

The text document would have insertion points placed where each set of data (field) was to be merged.

Figure 7.21

FIRST NAME	LAST NAME	ADDRESS 1	POSTCODE
Carl	Smith	123 Hope Street	HD1 5NN
Susanne	Juniper	38 New Road	HD5 0JJ
Marianne	Digby	1 High Street	LS12 8HJ
Jonathan	Ingleby	363 Forest Road	BD4 6PP

The aspect of creating a data file and a text file means that you can use the same data file for many text documents, adding to the data as necessary. This is time-saving when letters, envelopes, and so on need to be created and posted out. The names and addresses only need to be created once, and if this data is kept in a database of customers, the list can be extracted from the database without having to create a new list.

Watch the demonstration to see how this is done.

 **7.11 Demonstration**

> **Worked Example B1.6.1**

1 Open the file **merge letter**.
2 Display the mail merge toolbar – this is the easiest way of creating a mail merge: Select **View** → **Toolbars** → **Mail Merge**.
3 Next you need to open the **Data Source**.
4 Select the second icon on the toolbar. Open **Data Source**. Locate and select the file **Data**.
5 The sixth icon on the toolbar will allow you to insert Merge Fields. These are the data sets in the table of information in the file **Data**.
6 Place your cursor below the text [Date as postmark] leaving one clear line space. Select **Insert Merge Fields** and choose the following:
   First Name Last Name
   Address1
   Town
   Postcode

Figure 7.22

Figure 7.23

1 Place your cursor next to **Dear**, leaving one clear character space. Select **Insert Merge Fields** → choose **First Name**.
2 Place your cursor next to **code as** in the second paragraph, leave one character space and insert the field name **Postcode**.
3 Check your merge by viewing the records or by viewing the code. To view the code or records, select the **View Merged Data** button. This is a toggle – it switches between code and text by clicking.

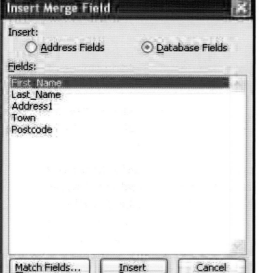

Figure 7.24

Figure 7.25

4   Once you are happy with your document, select the fourth icon from the right –
    Merge to New Document.
5   Microsoft Word® will now complete the process of mail merging your data file and
    text file and produce individual documents for each row of data in your data file.
6   Save the merged file as **Letmerge,** and close all open files. You will be prompted to
    save the original mail merge file – keep the same filename.

Task B1.6.1

1   Open a new document – you are going to
    create a new mail merge document, using the
    same data file you used in the above Task.
2   Key in the following:

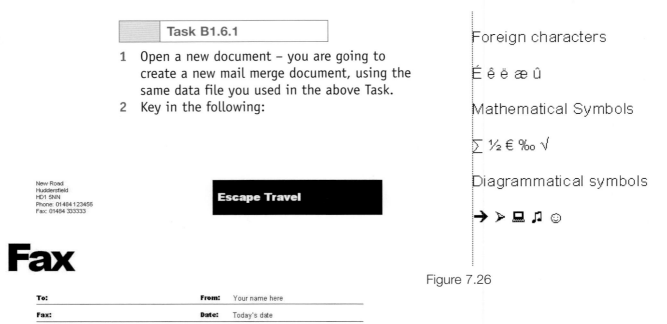

Foreign characters

É ê ë æ û

Mathematical Symbols

∑ ½ € ‰ √

Diagrammatical symbols

➜ ➢ ▣ ♫ ☺

Figure 7.26

New Road
Huddersfield
HD1 5NN
Phone: 01484 123456
Fax: 01484 333333

Escape Travel

Fax

To: _____   From: Your name here

Fax: _____   Date: Today's date

Re: Product update meeting

We will be holding a product review meeting on Friday this week – please ensure you are free to attend
as we will be showing the latest deals to be launched by John Airways.

Figure 7.27

1   Link the data file **data.doc** to the new text file and perform a mailmerge. Save the
    merged document as **merge2**.

Worked Example B1.6.2

1   Open the Microsoft Excel® file **Sales**.
2   Here you can see a graph, which you will be embedding into your word processed
    report.
3   Open the Word file **Current Sales**.
4   Place your cursor after the second paragraph ending **The data is as shown below**.
5   Select **Edit → Paste Special →** select **Paste Link**.
6   Select the source **Excel Chart Object → OK**.
7   Save the updated file as **Current Sales1**.

B1.7 Store and retrieve document and template files effectively, in line with local guidelines and conventions where available

Once you have created files, you need to save these in a suitable file format and in a location where you can find them again easily.

Files can be saved in different file types, versions, folders and can be imported/exported to be used in different software packages.

File types

Files saved in Microsoft Word® end with either the extension **doc** or **docx** or (if a template) **dot.**

Files can be saved in different formats, e.g. html, rtf, txt.

If you wish to send a file to someone but are unsure of the system they have, it can be worthwhile saving your file in a generic file type prior to sending. The generic file types are:

- **html** – a hypertext mark-up language (web page)
- **rtf** – rich text format.

Both of the above file types can be read by any system and the files will also keep their formatting, any inserted tables, and so on.

Other formats are available such as **txt** but this file type does not keep any formatting, inserted tables or images.

Version control

When you create and update documents, instead of overwriting and saving the amendments you may decide to save the file as a different version, for example, when updating this text I would save the file as v2 (version 2) so that I could go back to the original file later if I needed to.

Folders

A folder allows you to effectively file documents and files in a logical place. It makes sense to save all the files for a project in the same folder. An example of folder structure is shown in Figure 7.28.

Figure 7.28

Import/Export

Sometimes you might decide to import or export text to use it in different software packages. For example, you may produce some text and decide to use it in a word processing package. The file could be saved as a .txt file and the imported into a desk-top processing package rather than being retyped.

Consolidation

1 Open the file **Cons2**.
2 This is standard text. You must first format the text as follows:
  Font style
  Font sizes
  Orientation
  Line spacing
3 This document is to be used as a mail merge document, to be sent to customers on a company's database.
4 You need to insert merge fields before performing a merge.
  The data file is called **customers**.
5 Add the names and addresses at the top of the letter and lay out the document with a letter head of your choice.
  Insert today's date.
  Insert your name as a reference.
6 Merge the file. Select only to merge the data for customers who live in Leeds (four in total).
  - Using the third icon on the Mail Merge toolbar, follow the instructions by clicking on the **Town** heading to sort the list by order of town.
  - Select the option **Clear All**. This deselects all the data entries.
  - Select only the data entries that have **Leeds** as the Town by placing a tick in the box alongside the entry. Click **OK**.
  - Using the **View Merge** button, check that only entries for Leeds will display.
  - Perform the merge.
7 Save the merged file as **L2consmerge**.
  Other data that can be combined include graphs and charts.
  Watch the demonstration to see how graphs and charts can be combined in a word document.

7.12 *Demonstration*

B2 Create and modify layout and structures for word processing documents

Once the text has been entered it can be altered so that it fits effectively on the page.

B2.1 Identify the document requirements for structure and style

B2.2 Identify what templates and styles are available and when to use them

Organisations usually use a house style or document layout for all their documents. For example, they may decide that all letters to be created use the same font style and size, layout and house style, which may include the company logo so that customers become familiar and recognise this. This also allows the organisation to produce professional looking documents, with everyone in the organisation using the same templates. An example of a template is shown in Figure 7.29.

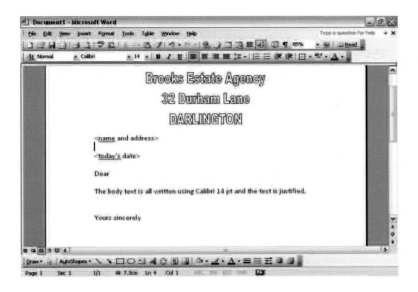

Figure 7.29

This shows the company name and address and font styles to be used throughout the document. It shows the staff member who is going to use the template what information is to be imported, when and where.

House styles

Different companies have set styles that each document created must adhere to. This usually includes the font style and size, the paper size, a standard letter heading, memo layout, fax layout and envelope display.

Templates are usually created to be used for any of the above documents and these must be used by all members of staff within the company when sending out any work. Any new documents usually have to get approval before being used. This does not only apply to large organisations but to smaller ones also. One of the main reasons for keeping to this format is to ensure that all documents being used in the company are professional looking.

House styles can also be defined for a variety of other formatting techniques within documents.

There are several formatting techniques that can be used to display text in a document to a professional standard.

Styles

Styles can be created and applied (tagged) to each line of text. The use of styles in a document can be time-saving when changes are made.

If styles are created and then at a later stage it is decided to modify one style, only that particular style needs to be changed and any text that has been assigned to that style will automatically update to the new formatting.

B2.3 Create and modify columns, tables and forms to organise information

Documents can be formatted as columns, tables or forms.

Columns

As with tabulations, columns can be defined to have a consistent display at the start of each column of text.

Columns can also be formed using tables.

Tables do not need to display the outside or inside borders.

Watch the demonstration to see how this is done.

7.13   *Demonstration*

Worked Example B2.3.1

1 Create a new folder and name this **SectionB**.
2 Open the document **virus.doc**.
3 You are now going to set this document into two columns.
4 Select the whole document, apart from the heading.
5 Select **Format** → **Columns** → select **Two** → **OK**.
6 Your document should now be in two columns. Check the page layout – you may need to insert some page breaks or column breaks to make the text flow correctly.
7 You are now going to set headers and footers on each page as this is a multi-page document.
   Select **View** → **Header and Footer**. A new toolbar opens. Hover your mouse across the toolbar:
   ■ Insert AutoText – gives you options to insert automatic text where your cursor is placed.
   ■ Insert Page Number – inserts the page number where your cursor is placed.
   ■ Insert date – inserts the current date.
   ■ Insert time – inserts the current time.
   ■ Select Author, Page #, Date from the **Insert AutoText** drop-down list.
   ■ This information will appear in the header of the document.
8 Save the file as **virus3**.
9 Save the file in an html format. Select **File** → **Save As**. In **Save as type**, select **Web page** and use the same filename **virus3** in the Section B folder, and close.
10 From My Computer or Windows Explorer, open the file **virus3.html**. Notice that the file does not open in Microsoft Word®.

Now it's your turn to have a go.

Task B2.3.1

1 Open the file **housing.doc**.
2 Format this so that it is all shown as two columns.
3 Add a header showing your name and add a footer showing the page number.
4 Save the document as **house1.doc** in the Section B folder.
5 Save the file in an html format in the Section B folder.
6 Close the file.

Tables

Tables can be used to arrange text and numbers in columns. A table is made up of rows and columns of boxes, called cells, which can be filled with text and graphics.

Text wraps within each cell of a table, so you can easily add or delete text. You can format the contents of a cell the same way as for paragraphs. If you select multiple cells and format, the formatting applies to all selected cells.

Tables can be formatted to produce different kinds of layout by splitting cells, merging cells, shading cells, and so on.

Alignment of text can be changed within tables.

Watch the demonstration to see how this is done.

Figure 7.30

7.14 Demonstration

> Worked Example B2.3.2

1 Create a new document.
2 There are two ways to create a table. The quickest is:
  ■ Select the Table icon on the Toolbar (Figure 7.31).
  A grid appears. By clicking inside cell one on the grid and holding down the mouse button, then dragging the mouse across, you can expand the table to the size you require. When you release the mouse button, the table grid will appear on your document.
  ■ Alternatively, select **Table → Insert → Table → 3 columns → 10 rows → OK**.
3 There are two ways to adjust the width of a table:
  ■ On the ruler line, you will notice new grids showing the sections of the table. By clicking on and dragging the grids, you can reduce or expand the column width.

Figure 7.31

Figure 7.32

  ■ Alternatively, highlight the whole table or the area you wish to change. Select **Table → Table Properties**. Here you can change the appearance of the table cells or columns.

TIP: be careful when formatting tables. You can change just one cell by mistake, rather than the whole table – always remember your **Undo** button on your toolbar if all goes wrong.

4 Add borders and shading to the table. Select **Format → Borders and Shading → add as you wish → OK**.
3 Save this file as **table1**.

Now it's your turn to have a go.

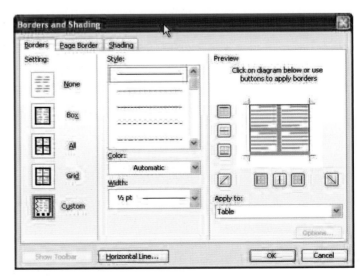

Figure 7.33

Task B2.3.2

1 Open the file **storage** and make the necessary amendments to create the layout in Figure 7.34.
2 Make the following changes to the layout of the table:

   Merge cells
   Highlight the respective cells to be merged, by selecting → **Table** → **Merge Cells**.

   Split cells
   Click inside the cell to be split → **Table** → **Split Cells**. Choose number to be split into.

   1 **Rotate text in a cell**
      Select **Format** → **Text direction** → choose the direction → **OK**.

Figure 7.34

Add shading and borders
1 Highlight the whole table. Then select **Format** → **Borders and Shading** → choose your options → **OK**.
2 Save the document as **storage1**.

Sorting text

Another layout option is the use of **sort** when producing a list of items. This can help the reader scan the text.

Sort can be performed both numerically (on numbers only) or alphanumerically (on text and numbers).

Highlight the list → select **Table** → **Sort**. The choices you get depend on the type of list you have selected to sort.

For example, in the list on the next page, sorting on number will change the order of the display – you can choose in ascending or descending order.

NON SORTED AVERAGE PRICE	SORTED AVERAGE PRICE
15,000	7000
20,000	7500
15,000	12,000
7000	15,000
12,000	15,000
7500	20,000

Sometimes you might want to convert a table to text.

Watch the demonstration to see how this is done.

7.15 Demonstration

> **Worked Example B2.3.2**

1 Open the file **chart.doc**.
2 Highlight the table and click **Table** → **Convert** → **Text to table** → **Tabs**.
3 Add a line space after **Embed a Chart or Image**.
4 Save the file as **chart1.doc** in the Section B folder.

Now it's your turn to have a go.

> **Task B2.3.2**

1 Open the file **tablesofcolours.doc**.
2 Highlight the table and convert this to text using tab setting.
3 Save and close the file as **colours.doc** in the Section B folder.

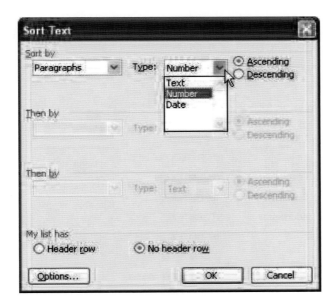

Figure 7.35

Forms

At Level 2, you are required to complete a form and insert/modify form fields.

Forms have many elements ranging from simple text input to drop-down selection lists.

The standard elements on the forms toolbar are:

Figure 7.36

Text	Allows the user to insert text
Check box	Inserts a ☑ when selected
Drop-down	Allows the user to select from a variety of options

Example of a form:

Registration Details

Title: Mr

First name:

Surname:

Address:

Post code:

Phone number:

Room type: Single

Payment type: Credit Card

Number of nights:

1 night   ☐

7 nights   ☐   Special offer

14 nights   ☐   Special offer

Other   ☐   We will contact you

Figure 7.37

The setup of this form is as follows:

Title:	{FORMTEXT}
First name:	{FORMTEXT}
Surname:	{FORMTEXT}
Address:	{FORMTEXT}
	{FORMTEXT}
	{FORMTEXT}
Post code:	{FORMTEXT}
Phone number:	{FORMTEXT}
Room type:	{FORMATDROPDOWN}
Payment type:	{FORMATDROPDOWN}
Number of nights	
1 night	{FORMCHECKBOX}
7 nights	{FORMCHECKBOX} Special offer
14 nights	{FORMCHECKBOX} Special offer
Other	{FORMCHECKBOX} We will contact you

Figure 7.38

Watch the demonstration to see how this is done.

7.16   Demonstration

Worked Example B2.3.3

1 Create the following registration form:

Title	(Drop-down)
First Name	(Text box)
Last Name	(Text box)
Address – leave three lines here	(Text box)
Post Code	(Text box)
Telephone number	(Text box)
Room type – double, single, family	(Drop-down)
Payment type – debit card, credit card, cash	(Drop-down)
Number of nights	(radio buttons 3, 5, 7, 10, 14)

2 Add your name as a header or footer.
3 Save your document as **E1**.
4 Close your document.

Now it's your turn to have a go.

Task B2.3.3

1 Open Microsoft Word®.
2 Create the following registration form showing:

Title	(Drop-down)
First Name	(Text box)
Last Name	(Text box)
Address – leave 3 lines here	(Text box)
Post Code	(Text box)
Telephone number	(Text box)
Joining date	(Text box)
Membership evidence produced – utility bill, driving licence, bank statement	(radio)

2 Add your name as a header or footer.
3 Save your document as **E2**.
4 Close your document.

B2.4 Select and apply styles to text

Now that you have learned what a house style is, you will see how you can create your own styles, which can be used in a document.

Watch the demonstration to see how this is done.

7.17 *Demonstration*

Worked Example B2.4

1 Open the file **virus**.
2 This is standard text. You are going to create three styles and then assign these styles to different parts of the document.

3   Select **Format** → **Styles and Formatting**. A menu appears to the right of your screen. Select **New Style**. A style dialog box appears.

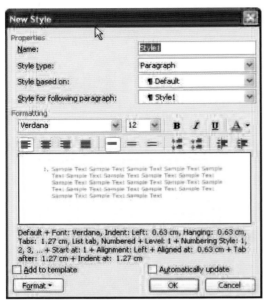

Figure 7.39

1   You can set the top four boxes and set the text style, alignment, enhancement and paragraph spacing from the initial dialog box using the Formatting area.
2   Change the first top box to the name of your first style:
    Bodytext
3   Change the Formatting area to read:
    Tahoma   12
    Colour   black
    Justified   1.5 line spacing
    Increase the paragraph spacing.
1   Repeat this for two further styles:
    Subheading
    Change the Formatting area to read:
    Comic Sans   16
    Colour   black
    Left
    Increase the paragraph spacing.
    Heading
    Change the Formatting area to read:
    Comic Sans   24
    Colour   black
    Centre

1   Select the whole document by choosing **Edit** → **Select All**.
2   Assign the **bodytext** style to the whole document.
3   Deselect the document, assign the **heading** style to the top heading **Computer Viruses.**
4   Work your way through the document and assign each subheading the **subheading** style.
5   Check your document for spelling.
6   Check your document for widows and orphans and place page breaks where needed. Select **Insert** → **Break** → **Page Break** → **OK**.
7   Save the file as **virus2**.
    Another way to change the layout of a document is to change the page layout. Page layout can be changed by altering the paper size and type, orientation, margins, by adding page breaks, numbering, headers/footers and date and time. You can revise these by viewing the Level 1 chapter, pages 302–6.
    You can also insert section breaks and adjust the page setup for printing.

Break types

■ Page break – inserts a break after the cursor and places the rest of the document on a new page.

■ Column break – inserts a break after the cursor and flows the rest of the text onto the next column or page.

■ Text wrapping break – wraps the text around images and objects in the document.

■ Section breaks – used to divide the document into sections, then different formatting of each section can take place. For example, you could format a section as a single column for the introduction of a report, and then format the following section as two columns for the report's body text.

To place a break, select **Insert** → **Break** → choose the type of break.

Section break types can be set as:

- Next page – inserts a section break to the next page.

- Continuous – places a section break but keeps the flow continuous.

- Even page and odd pages – inserts a section break and starts the new section on the next odd-numbered or even-numbered page.

Page setup for printing

Once you have changed the formatting options of the document, you should use print preview to check how the page will be shown when it is printed out. When you look at print preview, you can check that the text is displayed how you want it to be printed out. You can change the margins and other print options from here.

Consolidation

1 Open the document **housing.doc** and create the following styles:
   Heading: Sans Serif, 14, bold, underscore, centre
   Subheading: Serif, 12, underscore, left
   Bodytext: Sans serif, 11, justified, 1.5 line spacing
2 Apply these styles to the document.
3 At the end of the document, create a registration form using the following details:
   Title   (Drop-down)
   First Name   (Text box)
   Last Name   (Text box)
   Address – leave three lines here   (Text box)
   Post Code   (Text box)
   Telephone number   (Text box)
   Registration Date   (Text box)
   Property type: apartment, terraced, semi, detached   (radio)
4 Change the text throughout the document to display as two columns.
5 Add the following table before the text about the river development.

PROPERTY TYPE	BEDROOMS	APPROXIMATE PRICE
Apartment	1	£249,000
Terraced	2–3	£229,000
Semi	3–5	up to £400,000
Detached	4–6	up to £500,000

6 Format the table appropriately and add borders and shading.
7 Add a section break before the page with the form and create a new section for this page.
8 Add your name as a header and date created/page numbers as a footer. Only show the footer on the form page.

9 Carry out a spell check and check print preview for layout.

10 Print one copy of the document.

11 Save and close the file using the filename **houseform.doc** in the SectionB folder.

B3 Use word processing software tools to format and present documents effectively to meet requirements

B3.1 Identify how the document should be formatted to aid meaning

B3.2 Select and use appropriate techniques to format characters and paragraphs

In Microsoft Word®, there are many different formatting options. In Level 1 we looked at size, font style, colour, bold, underline and italic and you can revise these by looking at page 305.

At Level 2, you can also use superscript, subscript, special characters and symbols.

Superscript/subscript

Superscript is a character above the line and subscript is a character below the line. An example is shown below:

Superscript: 22nd December
Subscript: H_2O

You can add these characters by using shortcut keys.

Superscript can be added by selecting **Ctrl, Shift and +.**

Subscript can be added by selected **Ctrl + Shift.**

Insert symbols/foreign characters

You can insert foreign letters or symbols within a document. These can be characters with accents such as the letter é in café or the letter ô in côté.

Symbols are also available that cannot be created on the keyboard. These can be mathematical symbols or diagrammatical symbols, e.g. $\sum$ or →, etc.

This is achieved at the point you wish to insert the character:

Select **Insert** → **Symbol** → **Normal Text**. Choose the correct letter or symbol.

Watch the demonstration to see how this is done.

7.18 *Demonstration*

Worked Example B3.2.1

1 Create a new document and key in the following:
   Special characters can be inserted using the Insert drop-down menu and these can be:
   Foreign characters
   É ê ë æ û
   Mathematical symbols
   $\sum$ ½ $\in$ ‰ $\sqrt{}$

2   Save and close the file as **symbols.**

Now it's your turn to have a go.

Task B3.2.1

---

1   Create a new document and insert the following:
    →) ▭
    22ⁿᵈ December 2010 is a great day to drink lots of H₂0.
3   Save and close the file as **symbols2** in the Section B folder.

B3.3   Select and use appropriate page and section layouts to present and print documents

In Level 1, we looked at alignment, bullets, numbering, line spacing, borders and shading. At Level 2, we will look at widows/orphans, tabs and indents.

Widows or orphans

Checking for widows or orphans is important and must be done prior to final production of the document. A widow is a very short line – usually one word, or the end of a hyphenated word – at the end of a paragraph or column. A widow is considered poor typography because it leaves too much white space between paragraphs or at the bottom of a page. This interrupts the reader's eye and diminishes readability.

Like a widow, an orphan is a single word, part of a word or very short line, except it appears at the beginning of a column or a page. This results in poor horizontal alignment at the top of the column or page. The term 'orphan' is not as commonly used as 'widow', but the concept is the same.

The easiest remedy is to place either page or column breaks before the problem. This will depend on how the document is laid out.

> In typesetting, widow refers to the final line of a paragraph that falls at the top of the following page of text, separated from the remainder of the paragraph on the previous page. The term can also be used to refer simply to an uncomfortably short (e.g. a single word or two very short words) final line of a paragraph.
>
> A related term, orphan, refers to the first line of a pargraph appearing on its own and the remaining portion of the paragraph appearing on the following page; in other words the first line of the paragraph has been "left behind" by the remaining portion of text.
>
> Note that a widow can also fall at the bottom of the page, in the sense that the page ends on a very short line at the end of a paragraph.
>
> One easy way to remember the difference between an orphan and a widow is to remember that orphans "have no past, but a future", while widows "have a past but no future" just as an orphan or widow in life.

Tabs

If you have set tabulations and wish to clear them before setting any new ones, click on **Format → Tabs → Clear All → OK.**

Watch the demonstration below to see how tabs are set.

Figure 7.40

🖱 **7.19** | *Demonstration*

Worked Example B3.2.2

---

1   Create a new document and look at the default tabulations that are set every 1.27 cm.
2   To set tabulations, click in the box **Tab Stop Position** and type in a measurement, then click on **OK.**
3   To set more than one tabulation, follow step two but click on **Set** rather than **OK** and only click on **OK** when you have finished setting all your tabulations,
4   If you require leader dots, click on the appropriate number/style, for example 1 None 2 ... 3 —- 4 __. The option called a **leader** will place a line of dots between your current tabulation and the preceding tabulation or text – leading the reader's eye from the text to the next point.

5   If you want to set the alignment of the tabulation, click on the appropriate alignment, for example, left, centre, right, decimal.
    There are four kinds of tabulation that can be set in Microsoft Word®. They are:

TYPE	RESULT AT TAB STOP
Left	Left Justified Tab
Right	Right Justified Tab
Decimal	Decimal Alignment Tab 9.99
Centred	Centred Text Tab

Now it's your turn to have a go.

Task B3.2.2

1   Open a new document. You are now going to set this document into four columns using tabulation settings.
    Click on **Format** → **Tabs** → **Clear All**.
    The settings for this exercise are:
    Right   7.5 dot leaders **set**
    Centre   9.5 **set**
    Decimal   13 **set**
    Click on **OK**.
    The ruler bar should now appear like this:

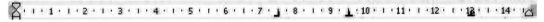

Figure 7.41

To get to a tabulation position while you are typing, press the TAB key. Key in the following:

Yorkshire TV	21.11.92	1000	21.00
BBC London	30.11.92	0730	45.50
Granada Studio	09.12.92	1230	8.50
Emley Moor Mast	20.12.92	1445	2.50

2   Save the file as **visit**.

Indents

Indents can be used to indent the text from the margin and can be used instead of using tabs so that instead of just one line being indented whole paragraphs can be intended.

Watch the demonstration to see how this is done.

7.20   *Demonstration*

> ### Worked Example B3.2.3
>
> 1 Open the file **indents.doc**.
> 2 Highlight the text in the first paragraph.
> 3 Click on **Format** → **Paragraph**. Change the left indentation to 2 cm.
> 4 The text should automatically be indented by 2 cm.
> 5 Close and save the file as **indent2.doc**.

Now it's your turn to have a go.

> ### Task B3.2.3
>
> 1 Open the file **Current Sales.doc**.
> 2 Select the second paragraph and indent this from both the left and right margins by 3 cm.
> 3 Close and save the files as **sales.doc**.

B3.5 Check documents meet needs, using IT tools and making corrections as necessary

Once your documents are complete you need to check:

- spelling/grammar using spell/grammar checkers

- consistent use of fonts/styles

- hyphenation

- language and dictionary settings

- page layout

- margins

- line and page breaks

- accuracy, consistency and clarity.

B3.4 Describe any quality problems with documents

B3.6 Respond appropriately to quality problems with documents so that outcomes meet needs

Once the documents are complete, you will need to respond to problems with documents. Problems can include text styles, structure or inappropriate layout, images that have been positioned incorrectly or numbers that have not been formatted correctly.

You also have options for formatting when using the right mouse button. This option changes depending on what you are working on. When on normal text on a page the options provide:

- Cut

- Copy

- Paste

- Font

- Paragraph

- Bullets and Numbering

- Hyperlink

- Look Up.

When working within a table you get additional formatting options:

- Insert Table

- Delete Cells

- Split Cells

- Borders and Shading

- Text Direction

- Cell Alignment

- AutoFit

- Table Properties.

Consolidation

1 Open the document **aromatherapy1.doc**.
2 Review the document and check the format for:
   - widows/orphans
   - consistent format
   - spelling/grammar
   - tabulation/indents
   - hypenation
   - language and dictionary settings.
3 Make the required changes and save and close the document as **aromptherapy2.doc**.

Mini Assignment

1 In this Mini Assignment, you will practise all the skills you have learned so far.
2 The Mini Assignment is based around the travel agency, Escape Travel. Your manager has given you the following instructions and you are required to complete these steps.
3 You are employed as the clerical assistant for Escape Travel and produce a variety of documents to advertise the holidays.
4 You have been provided with a text file **conditions.rtf**.
5 Create a new folder to store your work for this assignment and then produce evidence to meet the unit requirements.
6 You have been asked to store a template using the following page setups:

7 Save the template as **escape**.
8 Using this template, you have been asked to create styles for each of the following text styles – this is the company house style:

9 Insert the file **conditions.rtf** into your open document with the styles.
10 Assign each style to relevant text within the document.

11 Set the text between the headings **Booking Arrangements** and **Prices** to display as two columns – do not include the headings.

12 Format the text below the **Cancellations** paragraph, beginning – **42 days...** and ending **...100% of cost** to display as bullet text.

13 Insert the following table after the final paragraph:

COUNTRY	ACCOMMODATION	NIGHTS STAY	NUMBER OF PEOPLE	COST EACH		
				LOW	MID	HIGH
Spain	Flat	7	2	120	175	210
Germany	Apartment	3	4	75	110	160
France	Hotel	5	2	100	130	175

Add some interest to this table by using directional text, alignment and shading.

14 Ensure that there are no widows and orphans. Insert page breaks where necessary.

15 Spell check the document before producing for final copy.

16 Save the document as **conditions.html**.

17 Close the file.

18 Close all open files.

19 Check that your **conditions** document opens in a web browser.

20 Check that your template is available for future use as a template and not as a document.

PAGE FORMAT	PAGE NUMBER: CENTRE/BOTTOM	ORIENTATION: PORTRAIT	MARGINS: 2 CM ALL
Image	Insert an image at the top right as a header – the image should be travel-related and reduced in size to fit within the header space.		

Styles

Headings

Font	*Paragraph spacing*	*Line spacing*	*Size*	*Colour*	*Enhancement*	*Alignment*
Serif	6 pt above and below	Double	18	Blue	Bold	Left

Subheadings

Font	*Paragraph spacing*	*Line spacing*	*Size*	*Colour*	*Enhancement*	*Alignment*
Sans serif	6 pt above and below	Double	14	Black	Italic	Left

Body text

Font	Paragraph spacing	Line spacing	Size	Colour	Enhancement	Alignment
Sans serif	Normal	1.5	10	Black	Normal	Left

Bullets

Font	Paragraph spacing	Line spacing	Size	Colour	Enhancement	Alignment
Serif	Normal	1.5	10	Red	Italic with ✱ as a bullet	Left

Shortcut keys in Microsoft Word®

Ctrl+A	Select all – everything on the page.
Ctrl+B	Make **Bold** highlighted selection.
Ctrl+C	Copy selected text.
Ctrl+E	Align selected text to the centre.
Ctrl+F	Open Find and Replace box.
Ctrl+I	Make *Italic* highlighted selection.
Ctrl+K	Insert link.
Ctrl+L	Align to the left of the screen.
Ctrl+M	Indent the paragraph.
Ctrl+P	Open the print window.
Ctrl+R	Align to the right of the screen.
Ctrl+U	<u>Underline</u> highlighted selection.
Ctrl+V	Paste.
Ctrl+X	Cut selected text.
Ctrl+Y	Redo the last action performed.
Ctrl+Z	Undo last action.
Ctrl+Shift+*	View or hide non-printing characters.

Ctrl+left arrow	Move one word to the left.
Ctrl+right arrow	Move one word to the right.
Ctrl+up arrow	Move to the beginning.
Ctrl+down arrow	Move to the end of the paragraph.
Ctrl+Del	Delete word to right of cursor.
Ctrl+Backspace	Delete word to left of cursor.
Ctrl+End	Moves the cursor to the end of the document.
Ctrl+Home	Moves the cursor to the beginning of the document.
Ctrl+1	Single line spacing.
Ctrl+2	Double line spacing.
Ctrl+5	1.5 line spacing.
Ctrl+Alt+1	Change text to heading 1.
Ctrl+Alt+2	Change text to heading 2.
Ctrl+Alt+3	Change text to heading 3.
Alt+Ctrl+F2	Open new document.
Ctrl+F2	Display print preview.
Shift+Insert	Paste.
Shift+F3	Highlighted text will change from upper to lower case or a capital letter at the beginning of every word. Keep repeating and it scrolls through these options.
Shift+F7	Runs a thesaurus check on the word.
Alt+Shift+D	Insert the current date.
Alt+Shift+T	Insert the current time.
F1	Open Help.
F3	Run Autotext.
F4	Repeat the last action performed.
F5	Open the Find and Replace.
F7	Spell and grammar check selected text and/or document.

F12	Save As.
Shift+F12	Save.
Ctrl+Shift+F12	Print the document.

The mouse can also be used to perform quick actions. Examples of mouse shortcuts are:

MOUSE SHORTCUTS	DESCRIPTION
Click, hold, and drag	Selects text from where you click and hold/highlighting to the point you drag and let go.
Double click	Within a word, selects the complete word.
Triple click	In the margin, selects the whole document.
Ctrl+Mouse wheel	Zooms in and out of document.

IT Communication Fundamentals

This unit will develop knowledge and skills relating to finding and evaluating information and sending and receiving emails using IT-based communication systems, such as:

- finding the details for a journey
- gathering information about competing products or services
- using email to arrange the time and place of a meeting and agree agenda
- using IT-based collaboration to support collaborative development and refinement of a document.

By working through the **Overview, Worked Examples, Tasks** and the **Consolidations** in this chapter, you will demonstrate the skills required for IT Communication Fundamentals:

ELEMENT The competent person will…	PERFORMANCE CRITERIA To demonstrate this competence *they can…*	KNOWLEDGE To demonstrate this competence they will also…
ICF: A1 Use a variety of sources of information to meet needs	A1.1 Use appropriate sources of IT-based and other forms of information to meet needs A1.3 Recognise copyright constraints on the use of information	A1.2 Identify different features of information
ICF: A2 Access, search for, select and use internet-based information and assess its fitness for purpose	A2.1 Access, navigate and search internet sources of information purposefully and effectively A2.2 Use appropriate search techniques to locate and select relevant information	A2.3 Outline how information meets requirements and is fit for purpose
ICF: A3 Select and use IT to communicate and exchange information safely and effectively	A3.1 Create, access, read and respond appropriately to email and other IT-based communication A3.2 Use IT tools to maintain an address book and schedule activities	

Step-by-step examples are provided as a demonstration of what to do. These demonstrations are based on Microsoft Internet Explorer® and Microsoft Outlook® and are produced for each **Worked Example** task.

Review the overview in each section and then watch the demonstration in the **Worked Example** before commencing any tasks.

Once you are familiar with the topic covered, move onto the **Tasks** section of this chapter.

Consolidation exercises are provided throughout the chapter for extra practice.

Throughout the **Worked Examples,** you will find out information relating to planning a trip to an adventure park and in the **Tasks,** you will find information relating to music downloads.

In the **Consolidation** sections, you will find information relating to mobile phones and tariffs.

For the **Mini Assignment,** you will plan a holiday.

A1 Use a variety of sources of information to meet needs

When you need to find information for a specific purpose, there are many sources of information available to you, including the internet. However, it is important to make sure that whatever information you use, it is reliable and does not breach copyright regulations.

A1.1   Use appropriate sources of IT-based and other forms of information to meet needs

When searching for any type of information, make sure that you select and use the most appropriate sources. For example, you could use newspapers, books, CDs, podcasts, the internet, intranets, web logs, web-based reference sites or even text messages. Once you have been given a topic, for example, planning a trip to an adventure park, you need to ensure that whatever information sources you choose, they are the most appropriate.

If you were thinking about planning a trip to an adventure park, what sources of information do you think would be the most appropriate?

Your first choice might be the internet or any reference materials relating to the adventure park. Alternatively, you might decide to borrow a book from the library or even ring the adventure park for details.

A1.2   Identify different features of information

Once you have chosen your information source, you need to identify the different features. If you have been asked to carry out research into planning a trip to an adventure park, you might need to think about what factual information you need, for example, opening times, costings and details about the park. Do you need to identify any images or pictures you could use in the information about the park? Could you ask anyone that has been to the park for their opinion?

One recent trend in keeping up to date with information is by subscribing to RSS feeds. These keep you up to date with information you have subscribed to. First, you need to subscribe to an RSS feed on a website. You need an RSS reader to check feeds and read the latest articles that have been added and then decide what information you want to receive. For example, you might want to carry out a search for BBC weather feeds, select one and then subscribe to it.

A1.3   Recognise copyright constraints on the use of information

Any information posted to the internet and published is subject to UK copyright law. This means that the author is protected in the same way as material printed or available on CD.

Some websites will include a statement about whether or not any of the material is available to be used in schools. Sometimes, you may need to contact the author and seek permission to use the information.

A2 Access, search for, select and use internet-based information and assess its fitness for purpose

Once you have decided on the information you need to find, you then need to efficiently and effectively carry out the search. In this section, we will concentrate on accessing, searching for and selecting information from the internet.

A2.1 Access, navigate and search internet sources of information purposefully and effectively

When you open an internet browser, there are various tools available which allow you to navigate web pages.

On opening Internet Explorer®, you will be met with a screen similar to that shown in Figure 8.1.

Figure 8.1

Watch the demonstration.

8.1 Demonstration

Worked Example A2.1.1

1 Click on the **Start** button in Microsoft Windows®.
2 Click the Microsoft Internet Explorer® icon.
3 On the home page find the back button.
4 Find the forward button.
5 Find the refresh button.
6 Find the home button.
7 In the search bar, type in 'adventure park' and view the search results.

Figure 8.2

Task A2.1.1

1   Click on the **Start** button in Microsoft Windows®.
2   Click the Internet Explorer® icon.
3   On the home page, find the back button.
4   Find the forward button.
5   Find the refresh button.
6   Find the home button.
7   In the search bar, type in 'music downloads' and view the search results.

A2.1.2 Browser tools

The address bar in Internet Explorer® shows the web address of the page accessed. For example, the web address of google is **www.google.co.uk** – this is shown in the address bar (see Figure 8.3).

Figure 8.3

Google is one of many search engines available on the internet. A search engine is used to search for information hosted on the internet. It will look at the search words that have been keyed in and display what it thinks are the best matches.

A URL is a Uniform Resource Locator – **www.google.co.uk** is an example of a URL. This can be typed directly into the address bar.

The first part of the URL identifies the protocol to use , for example, **www** (World Wide Web).

The second part specifies the domain name – for example, **google**.

The final part of the URL shows the country, for example, **co.uk**.

Domain names can be purchased so web addresses can be hosted at specific addresses, for example, iTQ 2009. This is a domain name purchased by the author of this book.

Once you carry out a search in google, you can then follow the links to the pages you want to access. For example, if you wanted to search for mobile phones, you could key this information directly into a search engine and follow the links to one of the websites to see the different features of a mobile phone.

Watch the demonstration.

🖱 **8.2** **Demonstration**

Worked Example A2.1.2

1   Open your internet browser and in the search engine type in "**adventure theme park**".
2   Click on one of the links returned by the search engine and follow it to see information of various adventure theme parks.
3   Close your browser.

Now it's over to you.

> ### Task A2.1.2
>
> 1 Open your internet browser and in the search browser type in **"mobile phone tariffs"**.
> 2 Click on one of the links and follow it to see what some of the stores are advertising as the latest mobile phones.
> 3 Close your browser.

Favourites

Internet Explorer® can store useful web pages in a favourite's folder. This folder 'bookmarks' the web page (URL) and stores it in a folder, which makes it easy to retrieve. To store web addresses in the Favourites folder, click on the **Favorites** button → **Add to Favorites.**

Within the Favourites folder, you can create sub-folders so that you can store similar web pages together. To arrange favourites into folders you need to: click **New Folder** to create a new folder. Then click **Add** to save in the favourites list.

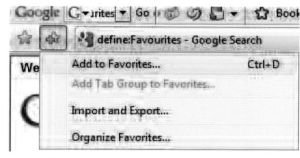

Figure 8.4

Bookmarks

Bookmark is another name for favourites and is used by different internet browser packages. A bookmark does exactly the same as favourites and stores web page locations (URLs) so they can be quickly retrieved.

Watch the demonstration to see how this is done.

 **8.3** *Demonstration*

> ### Worked Example A2.1.3
>
> 1 Open your internet browser and carry out a Google search for **"adventure theme park UK"**.
> 2 Select one of the results displayed.
> 3 Save this link in your favourites folder.
> 4 Close the internet browser.

Now it's your turn to have a go.

Figure 8.5

> ### Task A2.1.3
>
> 1 Open your internet browser and carry out a Google search for **"cheapest mobile phone tariff"**.
> 2 Select one of the results displayed.
> 3 Save this link in your favourites folder.
> 4 Close the internet browser.

A2.2 Use appropriate search techniques to locate and select relevant information

When you input words into a search engine, you can get thousands of pages displaying the search results – some of which are not really related to what you are looking for. There are a number of different search engines that make finding information easier by using search spiders. Another way to make searches more effective is to use keywords. Keywords are words or phrases that you key into a search engine to look for information contained in a website. The search engine spiders look at the keywords and display the sites that they think relate the best to the information requested.

To make searches more effective, you can use special characters and punctuation, which are shown in the table below.

Space	A space means 'and' in Google and if you type in **South America** it will be interpreted as South 'and' America. If you key this into Google, you will get approximately 173,000,000 results
–	The minus sign means to exclude words – e.g. **South America – weather** – this brings up 54,300,000 in Google.
"	Quotation marks around text interpret as a phrase, e.g. **South America – weather 'atlas'** = brings the search to 1,690,000
OR	OR searches for pages with either of the words in, e.g. **South America OR Africa – weather 'atlas'** – brings up 4,3000,000
[	less than
]	more than

In Google there is an option at the bottom of the page to 'Search within results'.

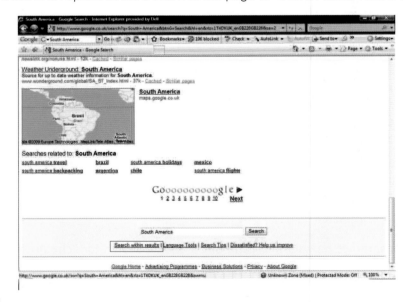

Figure 8.6

This allows you to narrow down the search results again, and only look within the results you have been presented with. For example:

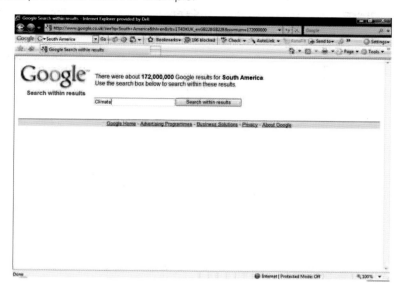

Figure 8.7

Results are shown:

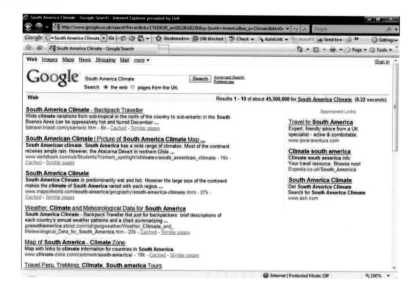

Figure 8.8

Searches can include relational operators, like > greater than or < less than. For example, you could type into Google "Interest Rate <3%" and about 78,600,000 results will be displayed.

Some search engines allow you to ask questions, for example, ask.com and askjeeves.com. If you load ask.com, you could ask 'What is it?' and ask.com will display the results:

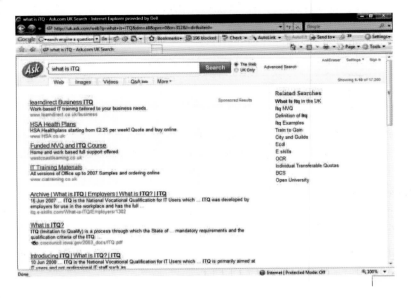

Figure 8.9

Watch the demonstration.

8.4   Demonstration

Worked Example A2.2.1

1   Open Internet Explorer® and navigate to **google.co.uk**.
2   Search for "**adventure park**" and click **Search within results** and type in "**theme**".
3   Now type in the search bar "**>10**" and search.
4   Navigate to **ask.com** and type in "**what is an adventure theme park?**". Access one of the pages and bookmark it.
5   Carry out another search and compare the information you have found.
6   Produce a one-page Microsoft Word® document that includes text and images relating to the adventure theme park you have found.
7   Save the document and keep it for later in the task.
8   Close the browser.

Over to you.

Task A2.2.1

1   Open Internet Explorer® and navigate to **google.co.uk**.
2   Search for "**mobile phones**" and click **Search within results** and type in "**3G**".
3   Now type in the search bar "**>£100**" and search.
4   Navigate to **ask.com** and type in "**what is 3G?**". Access one of the pages to find out what 3G is.
5   Paste the information and images into a Microsoft Word® document and save this file for later.
6   Close the browser.

A2.3 Outline how the information meets requirements and is fit for purpose

When searching for information on the internet, displayed results may not be reliable or accurate. There is a vast amount of information available. Information can be posted anonymously and you should evaluate any information you find before using it. Review the URL to find out whether it is a personal page or perhaps an educational/commercial website. You should also consider who 'published' the page? How up-to-date is the information? Many web pages show the date published. It is important to note whether the date on the website is old. The information could be out of date or the author may have since abandoned the site.

Some websites allow anyone to update web pages and this does not make them reliable, for example, wikis. Sometimes by 'googling' a sentence from a website, you can see whether or not it has been taken from elsewhere.

Once you have carried out your search, you need to decide if the information you have received is sufficient, current, reliable and accurate and how it meets your requirements – sometimes you may need additional searches.

Watch the demonstration to see how to check information found on the internet.

8.5 Demonstration

> **Worked Example A2.3**

1 Open Internet Explorer® and visit **www.bbc.co.uk**.
2 On the home page, you will see the date and time – this shows when the website was last updated.
3 Close the internet.

Now it's your turn to have a go.

> **Task A2.3**

1 Open Internet Explorer® and visit **http://www.w3.org/WAI/References/Browsing**.
2 This website shows that it is out of date and not maintained. Therefore, you would be strongly advised not to use this information.
3 **Visit http://www.york.gov.uk/news/newsarchive/2005/december/160982.** This page gives you the opening times of various facilities in York during 2005 – again, it is out of date. Make sure to check that websites are being updated – this information is usually shown. On this website, it shows the last updated date as 2007.
4 Bookmark the pages.

> **Consolidation**

Your line manager has asked you to find information relating to the latest hand-held game releases. You will need to find some information from the internet, produce a flyer and email this information to them when complete.

1 Carry out a search on the internet into latest hand-held game releases.

2   Visit at least one of the sites you have found and decide how suitable the information is.
3   Bookmark this site and then visit another site to compare the information.
4   Bookmark your second site.
5   Create a one-page document that includes suitable text and graphics relating to games and save this as **games.doc**.

A3 Select and use IT to communicate and exchange information

A3.1 Create, access, read and respond appropriately to email and other IT-based communication

In Chapter 3 Using Email Level 1 you can find detailed instructions and examples of using email. In this section, you will practise what you have learned so far.

Worked Example A3.1

1   Compose a new message to your line manager so that you can send information relating to your research on the adventure theme park day trip on. His email address is **editor@itq2009.com**.
2   Add your own email address in the cc field.
3   Add the subject **Adventure Day Trip**.
4   Using the research you have carried out and the flyer you have produced, attach this to the email you are to send to your line manager.
5   Type in the following text using suitable font, size and colour and netiquette guidelines.
    I have been carrying out research on the internet and have produced the attached flyer – please have a look at it and let me know which trip you think is the best. Any questions, please do not hesitate to contact me.
6   Add a suitable close.
7   Send the message.
8   Create a new email folder and name this **trip**.
9   Move a copy of the message you have received into the 'trip' folder.
10 Delete any unwanted messages, including SPAM messages.
11 Add your line manager's email address to your address book.
12 Save and close all open files.

Instant messaging allows you to have a conversation just like on the telephone but over the internet. Information is sent in real time so that one user types the message and the other person can read it as soon as it is sent. AOL, Yahoo and Google Talk are all examples of instant messaging.

Discussion forums

A discussion forum is where users with the same interest can exchange ideas, post questions or offer answers/help on relevant subjects over the internet. There are many discussion forums available and they are sometimes useful if you are looking for answers to questions.

Web conferencing

Web conferencing allows users to contribute to a meeting via the internet. A web camera or other special equipment can be used to transmit the data so that users can see each other 'virtually' and take part in the meeting without travelling. This is useful if you have people in different areas of the country or world and need to save on travel costs. However, it would mean all staff need the required equipment.

Web-based reference sites

There are many web-based reference sites that you can subscribe to and pay for access to the information or, in some cases, use freely – some of the free ones, for example, wikis, can be edited by anyone and therefore you should check how accurate the information is before using it.

A3.2 Use IT tools to maintain an address book and schedule activities

Section B1.5 in the Level 1 email chapter of this book shows how to create and maintain an address book. Review this section before trying the task below.

Task A3.2

1 Create the following new contact details:
   Full Name: Emma Ashton
   Job Title: Line Manager
   Business: 01237 1234568
   Business: 21 St Michaels Way
   Bishops Way
   Cambridge
   CB1 5PP
   Email: linemanager@itq2009.com
   Display as: Emma – Manager
2 Create a distribution list and name it **Trips**.
   Add the following email addresses to the list:
   Full Name: Paul Harris
   Job Title: Assessor
   Business: 01237 12346267
   Business: 21 St Michaels Way
   Bishops Way
   Cambridge
   CB1 5PP
   Email: paul@itq2009.com
   Display as: Emma – Manager
   Full Name: Stephen Morris
   Job Title: Deputy Manager
   Business: 01237 1234568
   Business: 21 St Michaels Way
   Bishops Way
   Cambridge
   CB1 5PP
   Email: Stephen@itq2009.com
   Display as: Stephen

Full Name: Karen Vickery
Job Title: Quality Manager
Business: 01237 1234568
Business: 21 St Michaels Way
              Bishops Way
              Cambridge
              CB1 5PP
Email: Karen@itq2009.com
Display as: Karen

1   Compose an email to **trip group**.
2   Use the subject heading: **Annual trip**.
3   Add message text:
    *I am pleased to let you know that we have now decided that our annual trip will be
    held on the 12 July and I attach the information you require.*
    Regards
    <Your name>
4   Send the message.

A3.2.2 Schedule activities: task, list, calendar, send and respond to meeting invites

In Microsoft Outlook®, in addition to using email you can use the calendar, tasks and invite attendees to meetings.

If you click on 'Calendar', you will be able to see your calendar – you can view the calendar by day, week or month and quickly see any upcoming appointments. You can also set reminders so that you are reminded of upcoming appointments.

Figure 8.10 shows the typical layout of the Outlook calendar.

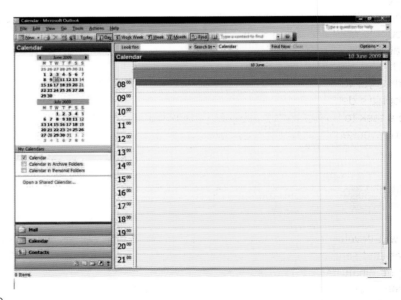

Figure 8.10

Watch the demonstration to see how to create appointments.

6.8   Demonstration

Worked Example A3.2.2

1 Open Microsoft Outlook® and click on **Calendar**.
2 Create the following appointments:

Monday	9.30 am	Team meeting
Wednesday	10.30 am	Appraisal
Friday	1.00 pm	Team lunch

3 Set each appointment with a reminder of 15 minutes before the start.
4 Add a task for Friday morning at 10.00 am to check that the menus have been completed so that they can be faxed to the restaurant before the lunch meeting.

Task A3.2.2

1 Open Microsoft Outlook and click on **Calendar**.
2 Create the following appointments:

Tuesday	9.45 am	CPD review	30 minutes
Wednesday	2.30 pm	Product review	30 minutes
Friday	1.00 pm	Claire's leaving lunch	1 hour

3 Set each appointment with a reminder of 15 minutes before the start.
4 Add a task for Friday morning at 10.00 am to check that the menus have been completed so that they can be faxed to the restaurant before the lunch meeting.

Mini Assignment

Your line manager has asked you to carry out research into a holiday abroad.

1 Carry out a search on the internet to find two suitable locations for a weekend break – the holiday should be Friday to Monday and a European destination is preferred.
2 Bookmark suitable sites.
3 Work out the cost of the hotel and transport.
4 Using all the information you have found, produce a one-sided flyer recommending one of the locations.
5 Email the flyer to your friend Sophie – **sophie@itq2009.com**.
6 Add Sophie's details to your address book.
7 Create a task to check to see whether Sophie has responded in seven days' time.
8 Book the weekend break into your calendar.

Level 2

This unit will develop the knowledge and skills relating to finding and reviewing information and sending and receiving messages using IT-based systems, such as:

■ setting up email folders
■ using the internet to research a new product and select a reliable supplier.

By working through the **Overview, Worked Examples, Tasks** and the **Consolidations** in this chapter, you will demonstrate the skills required for IT communication fundamentals:

ELEMENT The competent person will …	**PERFORMANCE CRITERIA** To demonstrate this competence they can …	**KNOWLEDGE** To demonstrate this competence they will also …
ICF: B1 Select and use a variety of sources of information to meet needs	B1.1 Select and use appropriate sources of IT-based and other forms of information which match requirements B1.3 Recognise copyright and other constraints on the use of information	B1.2 Describe different features of information.
ICF: B2 Access, search for, select and use internet-based information and evaluate its fitness for purpose	B2.1 Access, navigate and search internet sources of information purposefully and effectively B2.2 Use appropriate search techniques to locate relevant information B2.3 Use discrimination to select information that matches requirements and is fit for purpose	B2.4 Evaluate information to make sure it matches requirements and is fit for purpose
ICF: B3 Select and use IT to communicate and exchange information safely, responsibly and effectively	B3.1 Create, access, read and respond appropriately to email and other IT-based communication, including attachments, and adapt style to suit audience B3.2 Use IT tools to maintain an address book and schedule activities B3.3 Manage storage of IT-based communications B3.5 Respond appropriately to common IT-based communication problems	B3.4 Describe how to respond to common IT-based communication problems.

Step-by-step examples are provided as a demonstration of what to do. These demonstrations are based on Microsoft Internet Explorer® and Microsoft Outlook® and are produced for each **Worked Example** task.

Review the overview in each section and then watch the demonstration in the **Worked Example** before commencing any tasks.

Once you are familiar with the topic covered, move onto the **Tasks** section of the chapter.

Consolidation exercises are provided throughout the chapter for extra practice.

Throughout the **Worked Examples** and **Tasks** sections, you will be searching and providing information to your line manager to find a gardener and DIY person for Durham House, a local historic house.

For the **Mini Assignment,** you will research and collate information relating to a history project.

B1 Select and use a variety of sources of information to meet needs

B1.1 Select and use a variety of sources of information to meet requirements

B1.2 Describe different features of information

In the Level 1 chapter you reviewed the different sources of information that can be used to find information. Revisit page 346–9 to review this information.

B1.3 Recognise copyright and other constraints on the use of information

At Level 1, you looked at copyright, acknowledgement of sources and avoiding plagiarism. At Level 2, you also need to consider data protection. The Data Protection Act protects individual's personal information from misuse, for example, organisations have to keep names, addresses, financial, medical and criminal record data secure and cannot release these without the owners' permission. This includes information stored on a computer or in paper records.

B2 Access, search for, select and use internet-based information and evaluate its fitness for purpose

B2.1 Access, navigate and search internet sources of information purposefully and effectively

In Level 1, you looked at how to search for information effectively. Review pages 349–52 to see how this works. Have a go at the example below to recap on how to search for information.

Worked Example B2.1

You are currently carrying out some voluntary work at Durham House and you have been asked to search the internet for details of a local gardener who can help maintain the gardens. The gardener will need to visit and maintain the gardens every two weeks over the summer but once a month during the winter months.

1 Carry out a search on the internet and find at least three local gardeners who could be employed at Durham House.
2 Bookmark the information and save it for later.

Now it's your turn to have a go.

Task B2.1

1 Carry out a search on the internet and find at least three local DIY people who could be employed at Durham House.
2 Bookmark the information and save it for later.

B2.2 Use appropriate search techniques to locate and select relevant information

In addition to the information you looked at in Level 1, at Level 2 you need to be able to use the following search techniques:

- multiple search criteria

- logical operators

- wildcards

- database query techniques.

Multiple search criteria are where you include more than one criterion in the search, for example you might decide to search for Durham 'OR' Leeds.

Logical operators include AND, OR and NOT.

The table below shows the logical operators that can be used in Microsoft Access®.

NOT	WHERE NOT (Author = Jones)
	This will search for all records where the author is 'not' Jones.
AND	WHERE Author = Jones AND Date = 1999
	This will search for all records where the author is 'Jones' AND had a book published in '1999'.
OR	WHERE Author = Jones OR Date = 1999
	This will search for all records where the author is 'Jones' OR had a book published in '1999'.

Example range operators to be used in queries

The table below shows the range operators that can be used in Microsoft Access®:

OPERATORS	DESCRIPTION
]	greater than
[	less than
]=	greater than or equal to
[=	less than or equal to
[]	not equal to

Wildcard or like queries

The asterisk (*), percent sign (%), question mark (?), underscore (_), number sign (#), exclamation mark (!), hyphen (-), and brackets ([ ]) are wildcard characters. These can be used in queries and expressions to include all records, filenames, or other items that begin with specific characters or match a certain pattern. These can also be used when searching the internet.

Watch the demonstration to see how this works.

8.7 | Demonstration

Worked Example A2.2.1

1 Open Internet Explorer® and carry out a search for **"gardeners in Durham (UK)"** and see what results are shown.
2 Navigate to Google and click on **Advanced Search**. Carry out an advanced search for **"Gardeners NOT Durham"**.

Figure 8.11

3 Carry out a search for **"garden maintenance 'Durham or Newcastle'"**.
4 Bookmark the results.

Task A2.2.1

1 Open Internet Explorer® and carry out a search for **"gardener and Durham"** and see what results are shown.
2 Navigate to Google and click on **Advanced Search**. Carry out an advanced search for **"DIY and NOT Durham"**.
3 Carry out a search for **"house maintenance 'Durham or Newcastle'"**.
4 Bookmark the results.

B2.3 Use discrimination to select information that matches requirements and is fit for purpose

Once you have found enough information, you need to decide whether or not it is sufficient to meet purposes. You will have to review what you were asked to find and then decide how useful the information is. Any information you do use should be read and synthesised and reproduced using your own words.

B3 Select and use IT to communicate and exchange information safely, responsibly and effectively

B3.1   Create, access, read and respond appropriately to e-mail and other IT-based communication, including attachments, and adapt style to suit audience

In Level 1, we looked at how to communicate effectively using Microsoft Outlook®. Review pages 354–7 to revise this topic if you need to. Then, have a go at the examples below.

Worked Example B3.1

Now that you have found information on a local gardener in Durham, you need to email the information to your colleagues.

1 Open Microsoft Outlook®.
2 Create the email signature:
   (add your name)
   Think of the environment – do you really need to print this email?
3 Create a new folder in Personal Folders and name this **Goods**.
4 Compose the following message to **catherine@itq2009.com** with the heading **Gardener** (remember to send yourself a copy of the message).
   Great News! I have been looking into finding someone locally to maintain the gardens over the summer months. You know how busy it gets here so hope you all agree.
   (insert the details you have found from the internet search).
5 Add the hyperlink **www.itq2009.com/durhamhouse**
6 Take a screen print of the bookmarks folder and paste this into a Word document.
7 Attach the Word document to your email.
8 Send the message.
9 Once you have received a copy of the message, save a copy of the file attachment to your file area.
10 Save and close all messages and Microsoft Outlook®.

Task B3.1

Create and email RE:staffing

1 Open Microsoft Outlook®
2 Create the email signature:
   (add your name)
   Think of the environment – do you really need to print this email?
3 Create a new folder in Personal Folders and name this **Staff**.
4 Compose the following message to **susan@itq200.com** with the heading **Staffing** (remember to send yourself a copy of the message).
   The holiday season is upon us and we wonder if you could increase your hours over a six-week period. Can you contact me please?
5 Add the hyperlink **www.itq2009.com/durhamhouse**.
6 Take a screen print of the bookmarks folder and paste this into a Word document.

7 Attach the Word document to your email.

8 Send the message.

9 Once you have received a copy of the message, save a copy of the file attachment to your file area.

10 Save and close all messages and Microsoft Outlook®.

B3.2 Use IT tools to maintain an address book and schedule activities

At Level 1 we looked at how to set up and maintain an address book and use a calendar. Review pages 355–7 to revise this topic if you need to, then have a go at the examples below.

Worked Example B3.2

1 Open Microsoft Outlook® and create the following distribution list.

2 Add the following contacts to the address book:

Full Name:	Sandra Ainsley
Job Title:	Supervisor
Business:	01237 1234569
Business:	Durham House
	St Cuthbert's Way
	Sunderland
	SR1 6PW
Email:	supervisor@itq2009.com
Display as:	Sandra
Full Name:	Noel Payne
Job Title:	Curator
Business:	01237 1234570
Business:	Durham House
	St Cuthbert's Way
	Sunderland
	SR1 6PW
Email:	Noel@itq2009.com
Display as:	Noel
Full Name:	Lynn Tomlin
Job Title:	Assistant
Business:	01237 123456971
Business:	Durham House
	St Cuthbert's Way
	Sunderland
	SR1 6PW
Email:	sales@itq2009.com
Display as:	Lynn

3 Create a distribution list and call it **Maintenance** and add Sandra, Noel and Lynn to the list.

4 Send the maintenance list a message to say:
Thank you for the recent information, I confirm that a gardener has now been appointed.

5 Send the message.

6 Schedule the following appointments:

DAY	START TIME	DURATION	DESCRIPTION	REPEATING	ALARM
Monday	10.30	30 mins	Curator update	Weekly	Yes
Tuesday	11.00	1 hour	Cleaning supplier	No	No
Friday	13.00	2 hour	Team lunch	No	No

7   Save and close Microsoft Outlook®.

Task B3.2

1   Open Microsoft Outlook® and create the following distribution list.
2   Add the following contacts to the address book:

Full Name: Peter Chaplin
Job Title: Supervisor
Business: 01237 1234569
Business: Durham House
             St Cuthbert's Way
             Sunderland
             SR1 6PW
Email: supervisor@itq2009.com
Display as: Peter

Full Name: John Dobie
Job Title: Curator
Business: 01237 1234570
Business: Durham House
             St Cuthbert's Way
             Sunderland
             SR1 6PW
Email: John@itq2009.com
Display as: John

Full Name: Janey Hewitson
Job Title: Assistant
Business: 01237 123456971
Business: Durham House
             St Cuthbert's Way
             Sunderland
             SR1 6PW
Email: sales@itq2009.com
Display as: Janey

3   Create a distribution list and call it **DIY** and add Peter, John and Janey to the list.
4   Send a message to the DIY distribution list with the following message:
To book a joiner or carpenter in the summer months, please complete form A123 and email to me so that the appropriate arrangements can be made.
Thank you.
5   Send the message.
6   Schedule the following appointments:

DAY	START TIME	DURATION	DESCRIPTION	REPEATING	ALARM
Tuesday	11.00	60 mins	Draw up guidelines for gardener	No	Yes
Wednesday	11.00	1 hour	Deliver school tour	No	No
Friday	08.30	30 mins	Team meeting	Yes	No

7   Save and close Microsoft Outlook®.

B3.3   Manage storage of IT-based communications

In the Level 1 email chapter, we looked at how to create folders and store messages. In Level 2, we looked at how to compress, archive and retrieve messages. Have a go at the task below.

Worked Example B3.3.1

1   Create a new folder in Personal Folders and name this **Sales**.
2   Compose the following message to the distribution list **Gardener** with the heading **Shopping** (remember to send yourself a copy of the message).
Great News! We now have in stock mugs, scarves and glasses that show the new logo for Durham House. We hope these will be very popular.
Please display these prominently for purchase.
Thank you.
3   Add the hyperlink **www.itq2009.com/shopping**.
4   Add the zipped folder **gardener.zip**.
5   Send the message.
6   Once you have received a copy of the message, save a copy of the file attachment to your file area.
7   The received message should have automatically moved with the rule.
8   Save and close all messages and Microsoft Outlook®.

Task B3.3.1

1   Create a new folder in Personal Folders and name this **DIY**.
2   Compose the following message to the distribution list **DIY** with the heading **Joiner** (remember to send yourself a copy of the message).
Great News! We have appointed a local guy who will come in once a week to do maintenance and DIY-type jobs!
He is very reasonable and we have agreed a one-month trial – his name is Paul.
I will introduce you next week when he arrives.
Thank you.
3   Add the hyperlink **www.itq2009.com/shopping**.
4   Add the zipped folder **diy.zip**.
5   Send the message.
6   Once you have received a copy of the message, save a copy of the file attachment to your file area.
7   Save and close all messages in Microsoft Outlook®.

B3.4 Describe how to respond to common IT-based communication problems

B3.5 Respond appropriately to common IT-based communication problems

In the email chapter we looked at how to deal with file attachments, emails from unknown users, emails containing inappropriate content, SPAM or chain mail, viruses, spyware and key loggers.

Mini Assignment

You are working as the administrative assistant for the local history society and they have asked you to use Microsoft Outlook® to organise your working week and to keep contact details. You will use email to send and receive messages.

1 The history society has appointed two new staff – enter these in your contact list

Full name	Emma Totten
Job title	Assistant
Work telephone	0112 5974532
Email	emma@itq2009.co.uk

Full name	Christopher Khan
Job title	Caretaker
Work telephone	0112 5974535
Email	Christopher@itq2009.co.uk

2 Create an email distribution list and name this **history**. Add the two contacts above to the distribution list.
3 Save and close the distribution list.
4 Create a folder to store messages and name this **society**.
5 Send a message to **laura@itq2009.com** with the title **Programme of Events**. Add Laura's email address to the list of contacts with the job title – manager. Add the zipped folder **history**. Send a copy of the email to yourself.
   Hi Laura
   I attach the completed copy of the annual programme, which is now ready for distribution.
   Please can you check this and let me know if it meets your requirements?
   Many thanks
   (your name)
6 Send the message.

7   Create a new mail message to the **society** distribution list and send to the list members the file **history.doc,** which needs to be extracted from the **history**.zip folder that you have now received via email.

8   Copy the message to **Stephanie@itq2009.co.uk** and yourself.

All

I am pleased to confirm the programme for the autumn has now been approved and I attach a copy.

Let me know if you have any comments to make.

(your name)

9   Schedule the following meetings:

DAY	START TIME	DURATION	DESCRIPTION	REPEATING	ALARM
Thursday	14.00	1 hour	Coaching session with Emma	No	Yes
Thursday	09.30	30 mins	Weekly review	Yes, every week	Yes
Friday	13.30	3 hours	Open afternoon	No	No

Index

A

absolute *versus* relative references 224
address books 355–56
   contacts 88–90, 91, 119–21
   distribution lists 91–92, 121–22
addresses, web 348
   see also URL (uniform resource locator)
ADSL (asymmetric digital subscriber line) 31, 54
adware 47, 71
animations 283–84
anti-virus software
   email 85, 118–19
   internet 46–47, 48, 70, 73
area charts 240, 242–43
attachments, email 48, 73, 79–80, 85, 113, 114, 118–19
automated routines 6–11
automatic signatures 107–8, 109
avatars 50, 72

B

bar charts 196, 214, 215
bcc (blind carbon copy) 86, 119
blogs 44, 66, 67
bookmarks 41, 60, 64, 349
breaks, page 309, 334–35
broadband 31, 53, 55
browser settings 35–37, 56–59
buddy icons 50, 72

C

cable connections (internet) 54, 55
cache, delete 60
calculations 229, 230, 233
calendars 45–46, 69, 356–57, 364, 365
cc (carbon copy) 86
chain mails 98, 119, 129
Chart Wizard 213–15
charts and graphs
   presentation software 273–75, 276, 279
   spreadsheets
      area charts 240, 242–43
      bar charts 196, 214, 215
      Chart Wizard 213–15
      column/bar charts 240, 241, 242
      continuous *versus* discrete data 245
      doughnut charts 240, 244
      format 239–45
      graphs 197
      histograms 195, 240
      line graphs 214, 215–16, 240, 241–42
      number formats 195
      pie charts 196, 213–14, 215, 240, 241
      radar charts 240, 244
      stock charts 240, 243–44
      surface charts 240, 244
      text 197
      XY (scatter) charts 240, 243
word processing software 317
check digit 163
circular references 247
clip art 253–55
column/bar charts 240, 241, 242
combo boxes 180, 181
communication fundamentals
   browser tools 348–49
   copyright 346–47, 359
   information
      features 346, 359
      reliability 353–54, 361
      sources 346–47, 359
   Level 1 specification 345
   Level 2 specification 357–67
   mini assignments 357, 366–67
   see also email; internet, using
Computer Misuse Act 1990 20
connection methods (internet)
   benefits and drawbacks 54–55
   broadband 31, 53, 55
   cable connections 54, 55
   connection problems 55
   dial-up 31, 53, 55
   DSL (digital subscriber line) 54
   equipment, for access 31
   3G 54, 55
   internet, history of 31
   intranets 54
   LAN (local area network) 32, 53
   modems 32, 54
   networks 31, 53
   routers 32, 54
   VPN (virtual private network) 32, 53
   WAP (wireless application protocol) 54
   wireless connections 32, 54
contacts *see* address books
cookies 37, 56
copyright 20–21, 346–47, 359
   email 94
   internet 50, 64, 74
   presentations 252
Copyright, Designs and Patents Act 1988 20–21

CSV (comma-separated values) 228–29
currency format (databases) 161
cyber bullying 47, 72–73

D
data integrity (databases)
　accidental/malicious alteration 162
　accuracy 162
　consistency 162
　primary key 162
　validation 162–64
Data Protection Act 20–21, 359
data security 20–21
database software
　accuracy 147
　consistency 147
　data check 147–48
　data entry 166, 169–71
　data integrity 162–65, 179
　data types 172–73
　databases
　　components 133–38, 157–60
　　create 139–40
　　definition 133
　datafile, import 171
　design stage 158, 161
　error messages 145–46
　fields
　　characteristics 158, 161, 172–73, 174
　　size 161, 172–73
　　structure 140–41
　　types 165–66
　formatting 147, 183
　help function 145, 146
　input masks 163–64, 166, 167
　Level 1 specification 132
　Level 2 specification 157
　mini assignments 155–56, 192
　records 158
　search and replace 143–44
　spell check 147
　tables 133–34, 136
　　create 139–41, 165–66
　　linked 186
　updated fields 142
　validation rules 145, 166, 167–69
　see also queries; reports
date/time (databases) 161
dial-up connections (internet) 31, 53, 55
digital rights 74
discussion forums 46, 69–70, 354
distribution lists 91–92, 121–22, 363
domain names 34, 348
doughnut charts 240, 244
drop-down lists 180, 181

DSL (digital subscriber line) 31, 54

E
email
　address books 355–56
　　contacts 88–90, 91, 119–21
　　distribution lists 91–92, 121–22, 363
　anti-virus software 85, 118–19
　archive 95, 96, 126–29
　attachments 48, 73, 79–80, 85, 113, 114,
　　118–19
　automated responses 124–26
　automatic signatures 107–8, 109
　background images 108–9
　bcc (blind carbon copy) 86, 119
　cc (carbon copy) 86
　chain mails 98, 119, 129
　colour scheme 108–9
　copy others in 95, 114
　copyright 94
　draft emails, save 107
　email accounts 33, 80, 95, 124
　email netiquette 94, 123
　Exchange Server 117–18, 124
　flag, add 116–17
　folders 94, 95, 96, 126, 127, 128–29, 365
　formatting
　　bullets and numbering 103–4
　　default settings, change 77–78, 100–102
　　HTML (hypertext mark-up language) 106–7
　　line spacing 77–78
　　plain text 105–6, 107
　　rich text format (rtf) 105
　　text alignment 102
　forward messages 85, 115
　hacking 129–30
　history, reply with 114
　housekeeping 127–28
　hyperlinks 110–11
　Inbox folder 82
　internet service provider (ISP) 82
　junk mail 97–98, 126, 129
　language, appropriate 119
　Level 1 specification 76
　Level 2 specification 99
　message size 97, 129
　　compress 113
　　determine 112–13
　mini assignments 98, 130–31
　movies 110–11
　offline working 108–9
　organisational standards 94, 112, 123
　out-of-office reply 95, 124
　page setup 108
　personal information safety 86, 119

phishing 98, 129–30
Preview Pane 118
priority, set 111
receipt, determine 116
reply *versus* reply to all 82, 86–88, 114, 115
rules 124–25
safety 48, 86–88, 119
security 124
send messages 114
sound 110–11
spam 97–98, 129
spell check 77–78, 105
subject line 80–81, 86
text, appropriate 86
voting buttons 117–18
equal opportunities 253
Exchange Server 117–18, 124

F
favourites 41, 59–60, 349
fields
    automatic, word processing 303–4
    databases
    characteristics 158, 161, 172–73, 174
    size 161, 172–73
    structure 140–41
    types 165–66
filter data 148, 152–53, 230–31
financial deception 48, 73
firewalls 32, 48, 49, 71
footers *see* headers/footers
forms
    databases 134, 137, 159, 180–83, 183–84
    word processing software 298–99, 331–33
formulas, in spreadsheets 205–8, 247
FTP (file transfer protocol) 66
functions, spreadsheet 207–8, 233–35

G
grammar check 306
graphs *see* charts and graphs
grooming 47, 73

H
hacking 21, 47, 71, 129–30
handouts 266, 267, 285
headers/footers
    spreadsheet software 217, 218, 246
word processing software 303–4
health and safety law 50, 74
histograms 195, 240
history
    email 114
    internet 41, 59
hoaxers 47, 71

house style 4, 5, 21, 326–27
HTML (hypertext mark-up language) 106–7
HTTP (hypertext transfer protocol) 66
hyperlinks
    email 110–11
    presentation software 272, 280–81
    word processing software 316–17

I
indents 309, 338–39
information
    disclosure 49, 72
    features 346, 359
    reliability 39–40, 353–54, 361
    sources 346–47, 359
input masks 163–64, 166, 167
instant messaging 44, 66, 67, 354
internet, using
    address bar, browser 34, 348
    AutoComplete 56, 58–59
    blogs 44, 66, 67
    bookmarks 41, 60, 64, 349
    browser help 37
    browser settings 35–37, 56–59
    cache, delete 60
    calendars 45–46, 69, 356–57, 364, 365
    content, filter 49, 72
    cookies 37, 56
    cyber bullying 47, 72–73
    disclosure of information 49, 72
    discussion forums 46, 69–70, 354
    domain names 34, 348
    download information 42–43
    false identities 47, 73
    favourites 41, 59–60, 349
    financial deception 48, 73
    firewalls 32, 48, 49, 71
    grooming 47, 73
    hacking 47, 71
    history list 41, 59
    hoaxers 47, 71
    home page 56
    inappropriate behaviour 47, 49, 72, 73
    information reliability 39–40
    instant messaging 44, 66, 67, 354
    interactive sites 46, 49, 70
    internet netiquette 46, 49, 70
    internet service providers (ISP) 33
    laws 50, 64, 73–74, 359
    Level 1 specification 30
    Level 2 specification 52
    log useful sites 41
    malicious programs 70–71
    message attachments 48, 73
    mini assignments 51, 74–75

monitoring software 47
name alternatives 50, 72
offline working 59
online sources, personal access 72
password security 48, 50, 72
personal information security 50, 72
personal profiles 48–49
photo sharing 45, 69
PIN numbers 48
podcasts 44, 66, 67
pop-up windows, blocking 35–36, 57, 58
privacy levels 57
privacy tab 37
protocols 67, 348
proxy servers 72
publish information 46, 66
ratings/reviews 46
recommendations 46, 69
references 41–42, 60–66
rogue diallers 47, 71
RSS feeds 69, 346
safety 46–50, 49, 70–74, 71
screen size 57, 58
security 48–49, 56–57, 73
shareware 47, 71
spam 46, 70
spyware 47, 71
submit information 46, 69–70
temporary internet files 57, 59, 60
tools and techniques 66–67
URL (uniform resource locator) 34, 40, 348
version trackers 57
viruses 46–47, 48, 70, 73
web addresses 348
web-based reference sites 355
web conferencing 355
web page
    email 45, 68
    format 57
web page link, email 44–45, 68
see also connection methods
internet protocols 34
internet service provider (ISP) 82
intranets 33, 54

J
junk mail 97–98, 126, 129

L
LAN (local area network) 32, 53
laws
    copyright 20–21, 50, 64, 74, 252, 346–47,
       359
    Data Protection Act 359
    digital rights 74

downloading materials 50
health and safety 50, 74
organisational guidelines 50, 73
line graphs 214, 215–16, 240, 241–42

M
mail merge labels 27, 322–24
media clips 276
mobile phones, internet connection 54, 55
modems 31, 32, 54
movies 110–11

N
navigation menu 276, 277–78
netiquette
    email 94, 123
    internet 46, 49, 70
networks 31, 53
notes pages 285

O
operators
    logical 360
    mathematical 205–8
    queries 149
    relational 39–40, 62, 351
organisational guidelines 50, 73
    email 94, 112, 123
    house style 4, 5, 21, 326–27
    presentations 261–62
out-of-office reply 95, 124

P
password security 21
    email accounts 33, 80, 95, 124
    internet 48, 50, 72
personal information management (PIM)
       programs 77, 100
personal profiles 48–49
phishing 20, 98, 129–30
photo sharing 45, 69
pie charts 196, 213–14, 215, 240, 241
PIN numbers 48
plagiarism 253
plain text 105–6, 107, 325
podcasts 44, 66, 67
pop-up windows, blocking 35–36, 57, 58
presentation software
    accuracy 270
    alignment 270
    alternate pathways 272
    animations 283–84
    backgrounds 272
    bibliography 252
    charts 273–75, 276, 279

clip art, add 253–55
constraints, identify 280
content 252
copyright 252
delivery 280
enter information 251
equal opportunities 253
files, store and retrieve 256–57, 281
graphics 269, 272
hide/show 272
hyperlinks 272, 280–81
images 276
import information 250
information types 272
layout 270
local guidelines 253
loop 283–84
media clips 276
mini assignments 270–71, 289–91
multimedia elements 272
navigation menu 276, 277–78
object rotation 269
orientation 269
paper-based presentations 266
plagiarism 253
quality 289
sound 276, 278
sources, acknowledgement of 252
spell check 269, 288
text, insert 251–52
user interactions 272
video 276, 278
see also slides
primary key 162
productivity, improving
  automated routines 6–11
  changes 21
  improvements 23, 24
  laws 20–21
  Level 1 specification 1
  Level 2 specification 15
  methods 2–3, 16–17
  mini assignments 1–14, 28–29
  outcomes 2, 16, 19–20, 23
  purpose 2, 16, 19–20
  requirements 2–5
  resources 2–3, 16–17
  skills 2–3, 16–17
  style definition 24–25
  systems/software selection 4–5, 19
  Table of Contents 26
  task execution 3–4, 17–19, 24–27
  templates 25–26
  testing 27–28
  tools/techniques selection 11–13, 21–22

protocols, internet 348
proxy servers 72

Q
queries (databases) 134–35, 136
  complex 185
  filter data 148, 152–53
  multiple criteria 148, 149
  multiple queries 185, 186–87
  operators 149, 185
  run 159–60
  simple 185
  single criteria 148
  sort data 148, 151
  tables, linked 186
  wildcard characters 43 149–50, 185–86

R
radar charts 240, 244
range check 163
replicate
  data 200
  formulas 207
reply *versus* reply to all (email) 82, 86–88, 114, 115
reports (databases) 135, 137, 160, 190–91
  customise 154, 188–89
  format 189–90
  menus 153–54, 188–89
  reports Wizard 153
  shortcuts 153–54, 188–89
  sort in 189
  templates 154, 188
rich text format (rtf) 105, 325
rogue diallers 47, 71
routers 32, 54
RSS feeds 69, 346

S
scatter charts 240, 243
search techniques, internet
  ask questions 62, 351, 352
  keywords 38, 350
  logical operators 360
  multiple search criteria 360
  relational operators 39–40, 62, 351
  search engines 34, 38, 57, 348
  search spiders 38, 60, 349–50
  search within results 38–39, 61–62, 350–51
  special characters/punctuation 38, 60–61, 350
  wildcards 360–61
shareware 47, 71
shortcuts
  macros 6, 8–9, 26

mouse shortcuts 7–78, 315, 344
reports 153–54, 188–89
templates 9–10
Word® 6–7, 313–14, 342–44
signatures, automatic 107–8, 109
slides (presentation software)
edit 262–63
format 263–65, 283
handouts 266, 267, 285
layouts 250–52
notes pages 285
organisational guidelines 261–62
outline 285
paper-based copies 285
print 266, 267
slide order 266, 267–68, 270
speaker notes 266, 286, 287–88
templates 258–60, 282, 285–86
timings 266, 267–68, 283–84, 285, 287
Title Slide 250, 251
transitions 272, 283–84
viewing options 265–66, 285
sort data
queries 148, 151
reports 189
spreadsheets 230
tables 330
spam 46, 70, 97–98, 129
speaker notes 266, 286, 287–88
spell check 77–78, 105, 147, 269, 288, 306,
307, 319
spreadsheet software
alignment 235
borders and shading 236
calculations 229, 230, 233
cells 222
comments 237
edit contents 198–200
format 210–11
columns 200, 202, 210–12, 236
files, store and retrieve 203, 228
filter, rows and columns 230–31
find and replace 200–201
formulas 205–8, 247
functions 207–8, 233–35
arithmetic and statistical 233
conditional and logical 233
financial 233
lookup 234
help, using 247
hide and freeze 236–37
Level 1 specification 193
Level 2 specification 221
margins
date and time 246

orientation 246
page breaks 246
page numbers 246
mathematical operators 205–8
mini assignments 220, 248
number formats 223, 235
page layout
Date Icon 218
headers/footers 217, 218, 246
legend 245
orientation 216, 246
paper size 217, 246
Print Preview 217
references
absolute and relative 224
circular 247
replicate
data 200
formulas 207
rows 200, 202, 210–12, 222–23, 236
sort and display order 230
spreadsheet
create 225–27
definition of 194, 222
design 225
text 224
user help
cell comments 237
conditional formatting 238
input message 238
validation 237–38
workbook, protect 238
workbooks 223, 238
worksheets, link 223, 227–28
wrap text 236
see also charts and graphs, spreadsheets
spyware 47, 71
stock charts 240, 243–44
stylus input 296, 319
surface charts 240, 244

T
tables
databases 133–34, 136
create 139–41, 165–79, 166
linked 186
word processing 302
convert to text 331
enter text 297–98
format 328–31
sort text 330
templates
documents 25–26, 293–95, 320–22
house style 326–27
productivity 25–26

reports 17–18, 154, 188
  shortcuts 9–10
  slides 258–60, 282, 285–86
temporary internet files 57, 59, 60
testing 27–28
3G internet connection 54, 55
timings, slides 266, 267–68, 283–84, 285, 287
touch screens 296, 319
transitions 272, 283–84
type check 163

U
URL (uniform resource locator) 34, 40, 348

V
validation
  databases 145, 162–64, 166, 167–69
  spreadsheets 237–38
version control 57, 325
video clips 276, 278
viruses 20
  email 85, 118–19
  internet 46–47, 48, 70, 73
voice recognition software 296, 319
VOIP (Voice Over Internet Protocol) 67
voting buttons, email 117–18
VPN (virtual private network) 32, 53

W
WAP (wireless application protocol) 54
web addresses 348
web-based reference sites 355
web conferencing 355
web page
  email 45, 68
  format 57
web page link, email 44–45, 68
wikis 46, 69
wildcard characters 43 149–50, 185–86
wireless connections (internet) 32, 54
word processing software
  alignment 305, 308
  borders and shading 306, 308
  break types 309
    column break 334
    page break 334
    section breaks 334–35
    text wrapping break 334
  bullets 308
  characters, format
    font 305
    subscript/superscript 336
    symbols/foreign characters 336–37
  columns, format 328
  file types

generic 325
    html 325
    rtf 325
    txt 325
    Word files 325
    Word templates 325
  files, store and retrieve 301–2
  folders 325
  forms 298–99, 331–33
  grammar check 306
  graph, insert 317
  graphic
    insert 300
    position 301
    resize 300–301
  headers/footers 303–4
  house style templates 326–27
  image
    overlay with text 317–18
    resize 301
  import/export 326
  indents 309, 338–39
  Level 1 specification 292
  Level 2 specification 315
  line spacing 305, 308
  lines 306, 309
  mail merge 322–24
  margins 303
  mini assignments 311–13, 340–42
  mouse shortcuts 315, 344
  numbering 308
  page layout 306
  page setup, for printing 335
  paragraphs, format 305
  portrait and landscape 302–3, 304
  quality 339–40
  shortcut keys 313–14, 320, 342–44
  spell check 306, 307, 319
  styles, applying 327, 333–35
  tables 302
    convert to text 331
    format 328–31
    sorting text 330
    text, enter 297–98
  tabs 306, 308, 337–38
  templates 25–26, 293–95, 320–22, 325
  text, enter
    accuracy 319
    copy text 299
    cursor 295, 319
    cut text 299
    delete text 299
    drag and drop 300
    find and replace 300
    highlight text 299

hyperlinks 316–17
keyboard functional keys 295–96, 316–19
paste text 300
proofreading 319–20
stylus input 296, 319
touch screens 296, 319
voice recognition software 296, 319
version control 325

widows or orphans 337
workbooks 223, 238
worksheets 223, 227–28
worms 47, 70

X
XY (scatter) charts 240, 243